Related titles from ESRI Press

Arc Hydro: GIS for Water Resources
ISBN 978-1-58948-034-6

Undersea with GIS
ISBN 978-1-58948-016-2

Marine Geography: GIS for the Oceans and Seas
ISBN 978-1-58948-045-2

GIS for Water Management in Europe
ISBN 978-1-58948-076-6

Hydrologic and Hydraulic Modeling Support
with Geographic Information Systems
ISBN 978-1-879102-80-4

Conservation Geography: Case Studies in GIS,
Computer Mapping, and Activism
ISBN 978-1-58948-024-7

Managing Natural Resources with GIS
ISBN 978-1-879102-53-8

Salton Sea Atlas
ISBN 978-1-58948-043-8

ESRI Press publishes books about the science, application, and technology of GIS. Ask for these titles at your local bookstore or order by calling 1-800-447-9778. You can also read book descriptions, read reviews, and shop online at www.esri.com/esripress. Outside the United States, contact your local ESRI distributor.

Arc Marine

GIS for a Blue Planet

Dawn J. Wright
Michael J. Blongewicz
Patrick N. Halpin
Joe Breman
Foreword by Jane Lubchenco

ESRI Press
REDLANDS, CALIFORNIA

ESRI Press, 380 New York Street, Redlands, California 92373-8100

Copyright © 2007 ESRI

All rights reserved. First edition 2007
10 09 08 07   1 2 3 4 5 6 7 8 9 10

Printed in the United States of America

Library of Congress Cataloging-in-Publication Data
Arc marine : GIS for a blue planet / Dawn J. Wright ... [et al.] ; foreword by Jane Lubchenco.—1st ed.
    p. cm.
   Includes bibliographical references.
   ISBN 978-1-58948-017-9 (pbk. : alk. paper)
   1. Oceanography—Geographic information systems. I. Wright, Dawn J., 1961–
GC38.5.A73 2008
551.460285—dc22   2007000708

Ask for ESRI Press titles at your local bookstore or order by calling 1-800-447-9778. You can also shop online at www.esri.com/esripress. Outside the United States, contact your local ESRI distributor.

ESRI Press titles are distributed to the trade by the following:

In North America:
Ingram Publisher Services
Toll-free telephone: (800) 648-3104
Toll-free fax: (800) 838-1149
E-mail: customerservice@ingrampublisherservices.com

In the United Kingdom, Europe, and the Middle East:
Transatlantic Publishers Group Ltd.
Telephone: 44 20 7373 2515
Fax: 44 20 7244 1018
E-mail: richard@tpgltd.co.uk

Cover and interior design by Savitri Brant

Contents

Foreword

The oceans are so vast and bountiful that for most of human history they have been thought of as infinitely resilient and inexhaustible. The mantra "Dilution is the solution to pollution" characterized attitudes toward oceans as convenient places for waste disposal. The mere idea that oceans could be overfished or disrupted was inconceivable. Fast-forward to the present. Evidence of disrupted ocean ecosystems abounds: A quarter of the world's most important fisheries are vastly depleted; 90 percent of the large fishes have disappeared due to overfishing; hundreds of "dead zones" (areas with oxygen levels too low to support most marine life) have appeared in the last few decades due to nutrient pollution from agriculture, livestock operations, and sewage; harmful algal blooms are increasing due to this nutrient pollution and the introduction of nonnative species, for example, via ballast water; sea level is rising, oceans are warming, and storm intensity is increasing because of climate change; and the oceans are becoming more acidic as they absorb about half of the carbon dioxide being released from the burning of fossil fuels and clearing of forests. In a very short period of time, the bounty of oceans has been depleted and ocean ecosystems have become seriously disrupted.

Because this depletion has serious social and economic consequences, there is increasing interest in devising solutions to recover the bounty and resilience of ocean ecosystems. In the United States, the Pew Oceans Commission and the U.S. Commission on Ocean Policy have made comprehensive recommendations on solutions. The Joint Oceans Commission Initiative and others are taking up the challenge of implementing these recommendations. Many states and other nations are evaluating their own policies and practices.

Emerging evidence indicates that some solutions are both feasible and effective—for example, modifying fishing gear to reduce habitat destruction and inadvertent impacts on nontarget species; establishing networks of fully protected "no take" marine reserves to protect habitat and allow fishes and invertebrates to recover, mature, and produce immense numbers of young; reducing land-based sources of pollution; protecting critical coastal wetlands from development; reducing introduction of nonnative species; aligning the economics of fishing with conservation interests; improving ocean governance; and more.

However, the diversity of drivers causing ocean changes and the different scales of ocean processes present challenges in understanding and evaluating problems and solutions. Civil society, managers, policy makers, business and industry, and scientists need better tools to visualize, examine, manipulate, and evaluate data and information. Scientific data and information play critical roles, but they must be organized and presented in ways that are understandable, relevant, useable, and credible. For the oceans, GIS has been a powerful tool because it integrates many kinds of data (for example, marine geology with marine biology, chemistry, ocean currents, etc.) in order to see the larger picture. It can turn the numbers that data represents into interpretations that help people understand what is happening and what different solutions would accomplish. This book is about applying GIS to the ocean, more efficiently and effectively than before, by using the latest available approaches in this exciting, evolving technology.

The power of GIS lies in its flexibility for both scientists and nonscientists. The organized structuring and layering of data allows accurate representations of information that can be tailored to the needs and interests of users by location, spatial extent, and type of information desired. Oceanic and coastal features, including natural and built structures, can be visualized and manipulated. For scientists, a data model such as Arc Marine is invaluable in enabling better management and sharing of data with other scientists, policy makers, and the public.

The publication of *Arc Marine: GIS for a Blue Planet* comes at a critical time. Oceans, and indeed the entire planet, are changing at faster rates, over broader scales, and in fundamentally new ways. As documented in the Millennium Ecosystem Assessment, these environmental changes have immediate consequences to human well-being. Hence, there is great urgency in addressing these problems and making a transition to sustainability. Scientific information is vital in helping society understand what is happening and the likely consequences of possible solutions. This is especially true for the oceans that to most people are normally represented simply as large blue areas on a map. New tools such as those described in this book provide unified approaches to and frameworks for processing, mapping, and sharing critical information about the oceans. These tools will inform and guide impending decisions and determine whether we can indeed recover the lost bounty and resilience of oceans.

Jane Lubchenco
Oregon State University Distinguished Professor of Zoology and Wayne and Gladys Valley Professor of Marine Biology; Member, Pew Oceans Commission and Joint Ocean Commission Initiative (http://www.jointoceancommission.org/); Convening Lead Author, Millennium Ecosystem Assessment (http://www.MAweb.org)

Preface

During the past several years, ESRI, with significant user-community input, has been building application-specific data models for ArcGIS software in many industries and scientific disciplines. Notable for the marine GIS community is the marine data model initiative, also called Arc Marine. Other industry data models have common touch points to Arc Marine, such as Arc Hydro, Groundwater, Climate and Weather, Petroleum, and the S-57 for Electronic Navigational Charts. In tandem with these efforts, the marine GIS community has grown significantly during the past few years. "Marine GIS community" is defined as users who apply GIS to the coasts, estuaries, marginal seas, and deep ocean. The community includes academic, government, and military oceanographers; coastal resource managers and consultants; marine technologists; nautical archaeologists; marine conservationists; marine and coastal geographers; fisheries managers and scientists; ocean explorers/mariners; and others.

This book reports the initial results of a successful effort to create and define a data model for this community, one that supports better management of complex spatial analyses within a variety of marine applications. Included are descriptions of database projects that focus on mapping the ocean floor, fisheries management in the water column, marine animal tracking in the water column and on the sea surface, nearshore and shoreline change, temporal analysis of water temperature, and the integration of numerical models. Our goal has been to create a database design that facilitates the collection of dynamic and multidimensional data from the oceans, seas, and coasts, and to provide a more logical way to represent these in the object-oriented world of the geodatabase.

The development of common, interoperable GIS tools based on such a framework can be immensely valuable: tools for data input, distributing or serving data, improved performance in data processing and analysis, and creating new information from the data. Designed with the data model in mind, these tools combined create useful ways to work with marine sensor data and human observations.

The data model improves our ability to manage and exchange large marine datasets using a framework that can be shared and implemented across many platforms and applications. The standards and best practices that have emerged from the case studies, lessons learned, and tutorials combine to form a diverse set of resources for the marine GIS practitioner to draw from.

As you use this book as a reference or laboratory manual, please refer to and download the many resources, including the core Arc Marine data model, at the accompanying mirror Web sites: http://dusk.geo.orst.edu/djl/arcgis/ and the Marine link at http://support.esri.com/datamodels. These sites include the Arc Marine design templates, the Arc Marine reference poster, a tutorial on using Arc Marine, sample datasets, background documents, Microsoft PowerPoint files, and links to Arc Marine tools.

Dawn J. Wright, Oregon State University
Michael Blongewicz, DHI Water & Environment
Patrick N. Halpin, Duke University
Joe Breman, ESRI

Acknowledgments

We gratefully acknowledge many people for providing comments and input on the early stages of Arc Marine, thereby ensuring its intellectual integrity and "connection to reality." These include members of the initial data model working group: Steve Grisé and Simon Evans of ESRI, Eric Treml of Duke University's Nicholas School of the Environment and Earth Sciences, and Jason Marshall of the NOAA Coastal Services Center; as well as Kevin Curtin, early coauthor of the UNETRANS (Transportation) data model; and Nancy von Meyer, lead author of the Land Parcel data model. We also were greatly assisted by members of an informal, yet much broader review team, those who attended several workshops at ESRI headquarters in Redlands, California, to help define and critique early drafts of the model:

Jan Benson, NOAA Alaska Fisheries Science Center, Washington

Rowena Carlson, Space and Naval Warfare Systems Center, California

Lu Crenshaw, General Dynamics, Global Maritime Boundaries Database Group, Virginia

Peter Etnoyer, Aquanautix Consulting, California

Tanya Haddad, Oregon Ocean–Coastal Management Program

Travis Hamrick, University of Redlands, California

Phil Henderson, PhotoScience Geospatial Solutions, Inc., Florida

Sue Heinz, NASA/JPL Physical Oceanography Distributed Active Archive Center, California

Eric Horowitz, University of Redlands, California

Pat Iampietro, California State University–Monterey Bay

Chris Jenkins, Institute of Arctic & Alpine Research (INSTAAR), University of Colorado at Boulder

Miles Logsdon, University of Washington School of Oceanography

Nazila Merati, NOAA Pacific Marine Environmental Lab, Washington

Ian Muster, The Redlands Institute, University of Redlands, California

Mi Ra Park, Pacific States Marine Fisheries Commission

Lorin Pruett, General Dynamics, Global Maritime Boundaries Database Group, Virginia

Rob Schick, NOAA Southwest Fisheries Science Center, California

Deidre Sullivan, Monterey Peninsula College, Marine Advanced Technology Education Center, California

Tiffany Vance, NOAA Alaska Fisheries Science Center, Washington

John Wood, Harte Research Institute for Gulf of Mexico Studies, Texas A&M University–Corpus Christi

The authors benefited from the participation of the following review team members by e-mail:

James Anderson, Naval Facilities Engineering Command (NAVFAC), Washington, D.C.

Jeff Ardron, Living Oceans Society, British Columbia, Canada (now with the German Federal Agency for Nature Conservation)

Andra Bobbitt, NOAA Pacific Marine Environmental Lab, Oregon

John Cartwright, NOAA National Geophysical Data Center, Colorado

Paul Eastwood, Fisheries GIS Unit, Canterbury Christ Church University College, United Kingdom

Alan Forghani, National Mapping Division, Geoscience Australia

Chris Friel, PhotoScience Geospatial Solutions, Inc., Florida

Ted Habermann, NOAA National Geophysical Data Center, Colorado

Rollo Home, Halcrow Group Ltd., United Kingdom

Tony Lavoi and David Stein, NOAA Coastal Services Center, South Carolina

Craig Kelly, Naval Oceanographic Office (NAVOCEANO), Mississippi

Robby Wilson, NOAA Office of Coast Survey, Maryland

Thanks to the following reviewers of chapter 8:

Jennifer Boehnert, National Center for Atmospheric Research (NCAR)

Gil Strassberg, Department of Civil Engineering, University of Texas

Steve Grisé, ESRI

Morakot Pilouk, ESRI

Steve Kopp, ESRI

Olga Wilhelmi, National Center for Atmospheric Research (NCAR)

A special reviewer to whom we owe exceeding great thanks is Jürgen Schulz-Ohlberg of the Bundesamt für Seeschifffahrt und Hydrographie (BSH, Federal Maritime and Hydrographic Agency), Germany. He made great contributions not only to the Mesh portion of the model, for which he prepared a case study, but to Time Series and Measurements, InstantaneousPoints, LocationSeriesPoints, and TimeDurationLines. Throughout the entire process, we have appreciated his insight, frankness, and advocacy, and that of his colleagues.

The authors would like to thank Debra Palka, James Gilbert, Catherine McClellan, and Brendan J. Godley for use of their datasets in this book.

In addition, we greatly appreciate the excellent work of Paulo Serpa (California Department of Fish and Game and the Pacific States Marine Fisheries Commission) on the final, Web-based Arc Marine tutorial and the general advocacy; and the assistance of Jim Ciarrocca, Jeanne Foust, Jason Willison, Aileen Buckley, Katsura Matsuda, and Ann Johnson, all at ESRI. We received great support and encouragement from our case study team: those who prepared specific applications of Arc Marine using their own datasets to test its viability and usability. They are acknowledged in full within chapters 3–7. We are most grateful to Professor Jane Lubchenco, who wrote the foreword.

Finally, the authors would like to thank the team at ESRI Press. Mark Henry patiently edited the text and guided it through production. Savitri Brant designed the book and its striking cover. Michael Law reviewed the cartography. Thanks also to Tiffany Wilkerson for her thorough copyedit, David Boyles for his editorial oversight, Michael Hyatt for his wisdom during production, Jay Loteria for his assistance with graphics, and Judy Hawkins for her enthusiastic support. Colleen Langley and Jennifer Galloway offered invaluable advice. Kathleen Morgan, Carmen Fye, Kelley Heider, and Lesley Downie provided administrative support, and Cliff Crabbe oversaw production. Valerie Perry prepared the index. The authors are especially grateful to ESRI President Jack Dangermond for his vision and support for a healthy marine environment.

chapter one

Introduction

Just as fish adapted to the terrestrial environment by evolving into amphibians, so GIS must adapt to the marine and coastal environment by evolution and adaptation.

M. F. Goodchild (2000)

Our ability to measure change in oceans and along coasts is increasing, not only because of improved measuring devices and scientific techniques, but also because new GIS technology is helping us better understand the marine environment. The domain has progressed from applications that merely collect and display data to complex simulation, modeling, and the development of new coastal and marine research methods and concepts. Marine GIS has evolved into an established application domain adapting a technology originally designed for land-based applications. However, a two-dimensional (2D) framework has never perfectly matched the ocean environment, where processes are dynamic and multidimensional in nature. Fortunately, technology has continually improved as increased commercial, academic, and political interest in coastal regions, oceans, and marginal seas have spurred fundamental improvements in the toolbox of GIS and extended the methodological framework for marine applications. Other challenges remain, such as how to best handle the temporal and dynamic properties of shoreline and coastal processes, how to deal with the inherent fuzziness of boundaries in the ocean, and the great need for spatial data structures that vary their relative positions and values over time. For a complete and chronological discussion of these various research challenges, see Li and Saxena (1993), Bartlett (1993a and b), Lockwood and Li (1995), Wright and Goodchild (1997), Wright and Bartlett (2000 and references therein), Valavanis (2002), Breman (2002), Green and King (2003), and Wright and Halpin (2005). The development of an effective conceptual and logical data model for marine objects and phenomena provides context and direction to meet these challenges.

As we move rapidly into the information era, in which decisions are based on available data and new information is created from existing data, the body of marine knowledge has surged forward at a rate that challenges our computer capacity to store, process, and share it (e.g., Ocean Information Technology Infrastructure Steering Committee 2002; Mayer et al. 2004; National Science Board 2005). Natural phenomena such as hurricanes and tsunamis illustrate the importance of a focused effort to manage and share information, while the slower processes of erosion and climate change also influence our environment in ways that demand our attention. A data model helps us categorize and give structure to the many different ways to store and analyze marine data. The benefits and added value come in the form of geospatially enabling the data to create maps and three-dimensional (3D) scenes of the marine environment that assist in representing the information in ways that are invaluable to decision making.

A data model for marine applications is complex because of the many, varied uses of the data (as discussed in detail in chapter 2). Modern marine datasets are generated by a wide array of instruments and platforms, all with differing formats, resolutions, and sets of attributes (figure 1.1). Users must deal with a variety of data sources and a myriad of data "structures" (e.g., tables of chemical concentration versus raster images of sea surface temperature versus gridded bathymetry versus four-dimensional [4D] data). A comprehensive

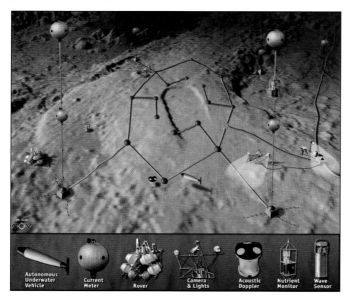

Figure 1.1   The North-East Pacific Timeseries Undersea Networked Experiments (NEPTUNE) ocean observatory envisions a hypothetical network of oceanographic instruments and vehicles to be deployed on Axial Volcano in the northeast Pacific Ocean. It is based on the existing NOAA New Millennium Observatory (NeMO) on Axial. This image also shows the many and varied sources of data that may be available from one major study site for marine GIS maps and analyses.

Graphic published by permission from NEPTUNE Program and University of Washington Center for Environmental Visualization.

data model is needed to support the much wider range of marine objects. This is essential for advanced management, cartographic, and analytical tasks. The ArcGIS marine data model, hereafter referred to as Arc Marine, endeavors to identify and organize these objects.

Just as language and the use of common symbols help us communicate and share our ideas, a data model with commonly accepted terminology and semantics (or ontology) helps us exchange information. We have spent a considerable amount of time and energy serving as translators or "semantic mediators" for a community that holds many of the same interests in gathering, understanding, and sharing information about the world's oceans and seas. Users can apply the resulting data model in many marine applications. It can serve as a starting point for the novice or as a resource for the expert in marine GIS and its implementation.

For the sake of clarity, "marine" (as in marine community, marine applications, and marine GIS) throughout this book refers to deep oceans and coasts. In the past, a distinction was made between ocean and coastal GIS because they developed fairly independently of each other (Wright 2000; Bartlett 2000). In this way, traditional oceanography departments in North America often grouped biological, chemical, physical, and geological studies of the ocean as "oceanography science programs" while creating a separate category for coastal studies, particularly if the emphasis was on coastal resource management. In general, ocean applications of GIS have traditionally been more in the realm of basic science, whereas coastal applications, due in part to the intensity of human activities, have encompassed basic and applied science and policy and management. But this is fast changing. Both subdomains collect similar datasets and have common interests and needs in terms of GIS implementation. In other words, the datasets are the same, regardless of how they are used (for basic or applied science, conservation, education, applied commercial use, etc.). As such, an essential data model should be applicable to all. Therefore, Arc Marine is for people applying GIS to the coasts, estuaries, marginal seas, and the deep ocean: academic, government, and military oceanographers; coastal resource managers and consultants; marine technologists; nautical archaeologists; marine conservationists; marine and coastal geographers; fisheries managers and scientists; ocean explorers/mariners; and so on.

Why Arc Marine?

As noted by Bartlett (2000) and Li (2000), rigorous modeling of data before attempting to implement a GIS database is one of the most important lessons to be learned from collective experience in the application domain of marine GIS. Data models lie at the heart of GIS, determining the ways in which real-world phenomena may best be represented in digital form. With regard to ESRI products, many marine and coastal practitioners and organizations have invested in the coverage or shapefile data structure (under the rubric of a "georelational data model"). Although this has largely been successful, there have been important shortcomings, such as the inability to distinguish between a feature that merely marks a location from one that may actively collect some form of data. In recent years, ESRI has introduced a new object-oriented data model called the geodatabase, in

3

which GIS features are "smarter," that is, they can be endowed with "behaviors" and more complex relationships. "Behavior" here primarily means providing the basic data input and data quality safeguards to ensure clean, consistent data. A geodatabase allows people to build validation rules, apply real-world behavior to features, and combine or link them to tables using relationship classes. For instance, a point representing a seafloor marker can be readily distinguished from a point that actually does something, such as a transponder that sends an acoustic pulse back to the surface. A line representing a coast can be attributed with time-varying sequences or intervals to enable it with behavior that more closely represents a dynamic shoreline. These capabilities are especially useful for large enterprise databases of geographic information (i.e., a GIS integrated in multiple departments or sections within an organization, institute, observing system, large project, etc.). For an overview of ArcGIS object and geodatabase concepts, see Zeiler (1999) or Arctur and Zeiler (2004).

One key benefit of the ArcGIS data model is its ability to help users take advantage of the most advanced manipulation and analysis capabilities of the GIS, particularly the capacity of the geodatabase to respond to events and processes acting on it (just as the marine environment itself is acted on by events and processes). For users, Arc Marine provides a basic template to implement a marine GIS project. This facilitates the process of extracting, transforming, and loading data (ETL), in addition to data input, formatting, geoprocessing, and analysis. For developers, it provides a framework for writing program code and maintaining applications. While ArcGIS data models do not create formal data standards, they do promote existing ones. This helps managers simplify data integration at various jurisdictional levels (i.e., local, state/provincial, national, global). Using a common data model (and the accompanying data structure) helps users merge disparate data sources, particularly as the exchange of Internet information becomes paramount. Data sharing and growth cycles accelerate if many people and organizations rely on the same model as their foundation.

Arc Marine aims to provide more accurate representations of the location and spatial extent of marine features and to help users conduct more complex spatial analyses of this data. The model also guides users in new approaches that effectively integrate marine data in space and time. The specific goals of the model include the following:

- Creating a common structure—a geodatabase template—for assembling, managing, and publishing marine data in ArcGIS. For example, the model is specified in an industry-standard modeling notation called the Unified Modeling Language (UML). Because UML code is easily converted to an ArcGIS geodatabase (or to data structures in other GIS packages), users can immediately begin populating the geodatabase rather than designing it from scratch.
- Producing, sharing, and exchanging data with a similar format and structure design.
- Providing unified approaches that encourage development teams to extend and improve ArcGIS for marine applications.

- Extending the power of marine GIS analyses by providing a framework for incorporating behaviors in data and dealing more effectively with scale dependencies.
- Providing a mechanism to implement data content standards such as the Federal Geographic Data Committee's Hydrography Data Content Standard for Inland and Coastal Waterways, critical for the Coastal National Spatial Data Infrastructure.
- Helping many users learn and understand the geodatabase in ArcGIS.

Intended audience and scope of Arc Marine

Arc Marine focuses on the deep ocean and the coast (and attempts to represent the essential elements for a broad range of marine and coastal data types and processes) but cannot include a comprehensive catalog of objects meeting the needs of all user groups and applications, data structures, and standard processes. However, the model is a starting point on which to build and leverage the experiences of a broader range of practitioners—a range much broader than the specialties of the authors.

Many marine GIS users have substantial experience with a smaller set of marine models and with existing data and metadata standards. Therefore, it is important to understand existing relationships to related efforts such as Arc Hydro (Maidment 2002) and other ArcGIS data models at http://support.esri.com/datamodels such as Climate and Weather, Groundwater, Biodiversity/Conservation, S-57 for Electronic Navigational Charts, and even Parcels (for coastal land development). As noted by Steve Grisé (pers. comm. 2001), designing a data model is like designing a new minivan: once it's designed and built, you still don't know how families will actually use it (there will be so many variations depending on the family). So once a data model is designed and initially implemented, the many ways it can be implemented become clearer, and it is refined accordingly.

Outline of book and accompanying resources

Chapter 1 discusses the need for a marine data model and lays out the objectives and scope of Arc Marine. Chapter 2 introduces the critical concept of Common Marine Data Types and summarizes the main thematic layers of Arc Marine. Chapters 3 through 7 describe the main components of the core data model: feature and object classes for various kinds of marine surveys, location series and time duration lines and areas, time series and measurements, nearshore and coastal/shoreline analysis, and model meshes. These chapters present the feature classes, attributes, relationships, and object tables used for these components, illustrating them with case studies contributed by several organizations. These case studies use a variety of datasets to show how users might adapt and implement the model within their desired application area. Some organizations, particularly smaller groups and those without marine GIS experience, may have trouble understanding the best way to implement the data model. The goal of Arc Marine, as discussed earlier, is to make it easier for people to implement successful, enterprise-level GIS projects so their organizations can enjoy the benefits of GIS. Chapter 8 discusses grid-based and multidimensional GIS (including 2D time series and network Common Data Form, also known as netCDF), and similarities and possible linkages to other models such as the Groundwater and Atmospheric data models. And finally, chapter 9 looks forward with a discussion of the importance of common tools arising from or serving data models, issues of interoperability, and the relationship of data models to generic Web services. Also discussed is the relationship to project-specific Internet map servers such as OBIS-SEAMAP (Ocean Biogeographic Information System-Spatial Ecological Analysis of Megavertebrate Populations), and the emergence of capabilities for streaming data from these sites directly into the Arc Marine structure.

This book serves as the primary reference for describing and explaining the data model (including feature-class glossaries), demonstrating its use in ArcGIS, and providing examples of marine applications that use the model and pointers to other reference material. The book should not stand alone, however, and is best used in conjunction with several additional resources available on the book's accompanying Web sites:

- A specification of Arc Marine in UML or XMI (XML Interchange) that marine application development teams can use as a starting point to structure marine data. These are detailed machine-readable schema of the design, providing specifications of data types, relationships, and other details. Users can create an actual ArcGIS geodatabase from these views of the database design. An additional design document that summarizes objects found in the database is the Common Marine Data Types diagram. The specific data needs of a given user may require modifications of, or extensions to, the basic data model.

- A detailed poster that presents the logical design of the data model. Project teams, managers, and technical leads can use this to review the data model as a starting point for finding similarities and common data types and to better understand the use of relationship classes and other elements of the database.

- A step-by-step guide on the practical use of the model, complete with a tutorial dataset. This should also be useful in university classrooms and professional workshops.

- Several Arc Marine schemas and geodatabases from the case studies that can be used to demonstrate the efficacy of the marine data model for several different applications. Public domain marine data comprises the datasets and may be freely used to support specific projects.

The data model has been tested, and organizations have implemented their datasets using the design, resulting in many common best practices and patterns. As one pattern, the model most often serves as a starting point. Users then modify the model to fit the needs of individuals and organizations. The model is designed to work this way, and specific tools make this process an easy revision. In working with marine data, it is important to harness the dynamic qualities of the data. Users can create and derive new information from tools for processing and analysis. Using a commonly shared data model design helps facilitate the transfer of the information stored in the model. It also provides a common frame of reference for design decisions and a foundation for further data interpretation.

The importance of an effective data model design is paramount in an era when our response to natural phenomena such as tsunamis, hurricanes, and global warming may be a matter of life and death. Together, drawing from the case studies in this book and other successful projects, we can realize the true potential of this community-driven, collaborative data model design, created to serve the discipline of marine GIS.

References

Arctur, D., and M. Zeiler. 2004. *Designing geodatabases: Case studies in GIS data modeling.* Redlands, Calif.: ESRI Press.

Bartlett, D. 1993a. Space, time, chaos, and coastal GIS. *Proceedings of the 16th International Cartographic Conference,* Cologne, Germany.

———. 1993b. Coastal zone applications of GIS: Overview. In *Explorations in geographic information systems technology volume 3: Applications in coastal zone research and management,* ed. K. St. Martin. Worcester, Mass.: Clark Labs for Cartographic Technology and Analysis.

———. 2000. Working on the frontiers of science: Applying GIS to the coastal zone. In *Marine and coastal geographical information systems,* ed. D. J. Wright and D. J. Bartlett, 11–24. London: Taylor & Francis.

Breman, J., ed. 2002. *Marine geography: GIS for the oceans and seas.* Redlands, Calif.: ESRI Press.

Goodchild, M. F. 2000. Foreword. In *Marine and coastal geographical information systems,* ed. D. J. Wright and D. J. Bartlett, xv. London: Taylor & Francis.

Green, D. R., and S. D. King, eds. 2003. *Coastal and marine geo-information systems: Applying the technology to the environment.* Berlin: Kluwer/Springer Science.

Li, R. 2000. Data models for marine and coastal geographic information systems. In *Marine and coastal geographical information systems,* ed. D. J. Wright and D. J. Bartlett, 25–36. London: Taylor & Francis.

Li, R., and N. K. Saxena. 1993. Development of an integrated marine geographic information system. *Marine Geodesy* 16:293–307.

Lockwood, M., and R. Li. 1995. Marine geographic information systems: What sets them apart? *Marine Geodesy* 18(3): 157–59.

Maidment, D. R., ed. 2002. *Arc Hydro: GIS for water resources.* Redlands, Calif.: ESRI Press.

Mayer, L., K. Barbor, P. Boudreau, T. Chance, C. Fletcher, H. Greening, R. Li, C. Mason, K. Metcalf, S. Snow-Cotter, and D. Wright. 2004. *A geospatial framework for the coastal zone: National needs for coastal mapping and charting.* Washington, D.C.: National Academies Press.

National Science Board. 2005. *Long-lived digital data collections: Enabling research and education in the 21st century.* Washington, D.C.: National Science Foundation.

Ocean Information Technology Infrastructure Steering Committee. 2002. *An information technology infrastructure plan to advance ocean sciences.* Washington, D.C.: National Science Foundation, http://www.geo-prose.com/projects/oiti_rpt_1.html.

Valavanis, V. D. 2002. *Geographic information systems in oceanography and fisheries.* London: Taylor & Francis.

Wright, D. J. 2000. Down to the sea in ships: The emergence of marine GIS. In *Marine and coastal geographical information systems,* ed. D. J. Wright and D. J. Bartlett, 1–10. London: Taylor & Francis.

Wright, D. J., and D. J. Bartlett, eds. 2000. *Marine and coastal geographical information systems.* London: Taylor & Francis.

Wright, D. J., and M. F. Goodchild. 1997. Data from the deep: Implications for the GIS community. *International Journal of Geographical Information Science* 11(6): 523–28.

Wright, D. J., and P. N. Halpin. 2005. Spatial reasoning for Terra Incognita: Progress and grand challenges of marine GIS. In *Place matters: Geospatial tools for marine science, conservation and management in the Pacific Northwest,* ed. D. J. Wright and A. J. Scholz, 273–87. Corvallis, Ore.: Oregon State University Press.

Zeiler, M. 1999. *Modeling our world: The ESRI guide to geodatabase design.* Redlands, Calif.: ESRI Press.

Common Marine Data Types

The Common Marine Data Types concept is a general framework for envisioning the core feature classes required to represent coastal and marine data. Because coastal and marine applications must often represent spatially and temporally dynamic processes in a three-dimensional volume, the data types attempt to extend standard geospatial features to include more explicit relationships between spatial, temporal, and depth (volume) referencing. This framework is intentionally designed to be generic and inclusive. With a few exceptions, the Common Marine Data Types define the broadest possible categories of marine features, not specific features for specific marine applications. Adding broad extensions to standard point, line, area, and surface feature classes allows for more precise representation of time and place. The two main purposes of the Common Marine Data Types concept and diagram are to help define and better understand the core features of the Arc Marine data model and to communicate these core design issues to the marine GIS user community.

Arc Marine Data Model

	Shorelines
Layer	**Shorelines**
Map Use	Interface between land and water, shoreline change analyses for erosion/accretion, hazards, planning
Data Source	Derived from coastal survey maps, nautical charts, aerial photos, lidar
Representation	Linear features
Spatial Relationships	Can be animated/modeled based on map units to represent tidal variance
Map Scale and Accuracy	Typical map scales range from 1:5,000 to 1:20,000; locational accuracy typically 10 m
Symbology and Annotation	Line symbology drawn with varying weights annotated with VDatum; national cartographic standards often used

	Tracks and Cruises
Layer	**Tracks and Cruises**
Map Use	Shiptracks during a cruise, tracks of vehicles towed from a ship or deployed from a ship untethered, autonomous
Data Source	Shipboard or vehicle GPS logs storing time, date, and position
Representation	Linear features
Spatial Relationships	Tracks have a direction with time stamps along route, particularly keep sampling stations
Map Scale and Accuracy	Typical map scales range from 1:24,000 to 1:50,000; locational accuracy ~10 m
Symbology and Annotation	Line symbology drawn with varying weights and patterns, annotated with date/time and ship/vehicle

	Time Duration Features
Layer	**Time Duration Features**
Map Use	Fisheries or algal bloom trawls, marine protected area boundaries, habitats, drifter tracks, oil spills
Data Source	Derived from survey maps/charts, legal definitions, clipping/masking; various measuring devices
Representation	Linear and polygonal features
Spatial Relationships	Size, shape, area and direction change over time; may be animated
Map Scale and Accuracy	Typical map scale is 1:24,000; locational accuracy ~10 m
Symbology and Annotation	Line and polygon symbology with varying weights, patterns and fills

	TimeSeries Locations
Layer	**TimeSeries Locations**
Map Use	Variations in time of variables measured at fixed observations stations at sea and onshore
Data Source	Fixed or moored measuring devices such as hydrophones, acoustic doppler current profilers (ADCP), ocean bottom seismometers (OBS), tide gauges
Representation	Point features
Spatial Relationships	Points can be related to center of a grid cell or associated to a time series or numerical model
Map Scale and Accuracy	Typical map scales range from 1:10,000 to 1:24,000; locational accuracy ~10 m
Symbology and Annotation	Point marker symbology with associated instrument attributes

	Instantaneous Measured Points
Layer	**Instantaneous Measured Points**
Map Use	Variations in space of variables measured at a given moment in time through the water column
Data Source	Instrument casts such as conductivity-temp-depth (CTD), expandable bathythermograph (XBT), sound velocity profile (SVP), fish density, etc.
Representation	Point features, vertical profiles
Spatial Relationships	Points can have varying depths associated to a single location, as well as multiple measurements
Map Scale and Accuracy	Typical map scales range from 1:10,000 to 1:24,000; locational accuracy ~10-50 m
Symbology and Annotation	Point marker and linear symbology annotated with associated instrument attributes

	Location Series Observations
Layer	**Location Series Observations**
Map Use	Tracking a series of recorded instances of a given species with varying time intervals
Data Source	Telemetry recorders and transmitters, animal/bird sightings, ship-mounted ADCP
Representation	Multipoint features, often with line symbols to establish animal track
Spatial Relationships	Multipoints can have varying depths associated to multiple locations, grouped into a series based on ID
Map Scale and Accuracy	Typical map scales range from 1:10,000 to 1:24,000; locational accuracy ~10-50 m
Symbology and Annotation	Point and line symbology annotated with species type

	Survey Transects
Layer	**Survey Transects**
Map Use	Geomorphic, sediment transport, or hydrodynamic analyses along profiles or cross sections, subsurface profiling
Data Source	Derived from bathymetry, scientific mesh, one-dimensional hydrological models; measured by sub bottom profilers
Representation	Interpolated, linear profile view of a surface or subsurface
Spatial Relationships	Cross sections perpendicular to shoreline or flowline; profiles at varying azimuths to align with surface control point or baseline
Map Scale and Accuracy	Typical map scale is 1:24,000; locational accuracy ~10 m
Symbology and Annotation	Line symbology for surface; often for subsurface tone, contrast and balance of grayscale according to data values

	Scientific Mesh
Layer	**Scientific Mesh**
Map Use	Mapping output of finite element models, hydrodynamic and hydrologic models, sea surface temperatures
Data Source	Numerical models and satellite datasets
Representation	Regularly or irregularly spaced point features, scalars or vectors; raster, TIN model
Spatial Relationships	Attribute values can be used to create interpolated surfaces of magnitude with point values representing direction
Map Scale and Accuracy	Map scale varies and locational accuracy can range from 1 m to 1 km depending on data
Symbology and Annotation	Rendered with graduated point symbols to reflect magnitude, rotated to represent direction; may be animate

	Mesh Volumes
Layer	**Mesh Volumes**
Map Use	Pelagic or open water environment
Data Source	Derived features from scientific meshes, point data from stationary, fixed, suspended, or floating devices
Representation	Extended cube or hexagonal pillars stacked to represent volumetric areas
Spatial Relationships	Volumes can be related to mesh points between varying depths, or from bathymetry to sea surface
Map Scale and Accuracy	Map scale varies and locational accuracy depends on data type and resulting volume calculation
Symbology and Annotation	May be polygonal with varying 3D base heights; applied transparency

	Bathymetry and Backscatter
Layer	**Bathymetry and Backscatter**
Map Use	Terrain analysis, benthic habitat classification, morpho-tectonic interpretation, cartographic background
Data Source	Interpolation of irregularly or regularly spaced single or multibeam soundings, lidar
Representation	Raster with depth or backscatter intensity, TIN surface model
Spatial Relationships	Coincident with point from which it was derived, or interpolated; if raster, each cell has a depth; if TIN, each face joins to form surface
Map Scale and Accuracy	Typical map scales and locational accuracies for shallow regions are 1:2,400/1 m, or 1:20,000-1:50,000/100 m for deep ocean
Symbology and Annotation	Usually shown with graduated colors; may be overlain with contours

The Thematic Layers

Introduction

The representation of the geography, behavior, and relationships of coastal and marine features is an especially challenging task for traditional geographic information systems. The dynamic nature of ocean and coastal systems and the three-dimensional nature of water volumes require a fundamental rethinking of the often static and planar representation of spatial features used in terrestrial applications. Coastal and marine features require a broad extension of our general view of geographic data types to accommodate more complex marine applications. We must extend the standard point, line, and polygon (area) representation of geographic features to meet the volumetric and temporally dynamic nature of marine environments.

The need to extend the fundamental structure of common geographic data types influenced the core design of the Arc Marine data model from the onset. A generic data model was needed to meet the core challenges of designing a more temporally dynamic and volumetric representation of marine features. The core idea was to develop "common data types" as core building blocks for the development of specific features classes for coastal and marine applications. These common data types needed to be broad and comprehensive to represent the wide range of features that marine analysts and managers would encounter when developing projects.

Developing these core data types was part of the initial phase in what is usually a three-stage process in data model design, increasing in abstraction as one goes from human-orientation to implementation in a computer (Laurini and Thompson 1992; Zeiler 1999; and Arctur and Zeiler 2004). The conceptual phase involves the challenges of defining the overall scope and content of the model and identifying the common, essential features modeled in most GIS projects within an application domain. Next is the creation of an analysis diagram with the identification of major thematic groups and an initial set of object classes within these groups. The Common Marine Data Types diagram was developed as an extension of the analysis diagram in that the groups included a number of classes to indicate specific data layers. The diagram focuses on the initial acquisition of ocean and coastal data. Thus, it is concerned with the accurate sensing and collection of measurements from the marine environment and the transformation of these measurements from raw to processed for GIS implementation. Therefore, the Common Marine Data Types diagram provides a high-level overview of the themes and products available for a specific marine GIS project.

Next, an initial model is built in Unified Modeling Language (UML) and a schema is generated in the ArcCatalog application. The UML diagrams and schema are at the "logical" stage in the data modeling process. The UML is exported to an Extensible Markup Language Interchange (XMI) template or *.mdb repository. Fortunately, the marine community will not have to deal directly with UML (unless it wants to!). Instead, with UML in hand, users may take advantage of an existing collection of CASE (computer-aided software engineering) tools in ArcGIS in order to generate their own schema (the final, "physical" stage). For example, in ArcCatalog, the Schema Wizard can be used to translate the XMI template or *.mdb repository into an empty geodatabase. This in turn allows users to populate that geodatabase with their own data for use in a specific GIS project, with the necessary feature classes, attributes, and relationships from the data model intact.

The Arc Marine development team took another approach after quickly finding that no one marine data model could define the seemingly unlimited number of possible features that researchers and managers use in coastal and marine applications. The team shifted its focus to developing an inclusive and explicitly generic definition of the core data types that generally described the spatial and temporal features of coastal and marine data. This exercise allowed us to step back and envision the broadest categories of marine data. Where marine datasets were not sufficiently represented by standard geographic features (points, lines, or areas) we developed new terms to describe new classes such as "location series points" or "time duration areas." We intended this approach to articulate new representations of common marine features that could be shown through combinations of spatial features and time series tables in the data model architecture.

While the Common Marine Data Types concept allows for the development of core functional features, this representation is too generic to convey the detailed definitions and nomenclature for specific marine applications. We could not hope to develop a unified model that would use the specific terms and definitions of the ocean exploration, fisheries management, marine conservation, shipping, navigation, and other marine user communities simultaneously. Instead, we wanted users to generically apply common data types presented in Arc Marine as the core model shared across these more specific user communities. These marine user communities can then modify the generic features into specific classes to fit the naming conventions and specific applications of a variety of marine applications, analyses, and industries. For example, a fisheries management user community may develop a modified fisheries submodel that contains feature names that fit its needs more specifically (figure 2.1). The fundamental issue is that if a wide range of marine geospatial practitioners adopt the common Arc Marine core model, then they can develop analytical tools and applications to function across these core features classes that also benefit the larger marine user community.

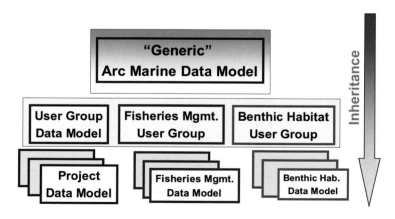

Figure 2.1 Arc Marine data model implementation hierarchy from generic features to various user groups to specific projects within a user group.

The Common Marine Data Types

The team built Common Marine Data Types through a fairly straightforward process (Breman et al. 2002). We considered examples of a wide variety of marine observations and geographic features for their fit using standard geographic features classes: points, lines, areas, rasters, and so on. A new, generic data type was defined to meet the need if these categories did not accurately represent the marine features. Generic feature classes were generated intentionally to promote the idea that these are broad categories, not specific types of marine data. In the Common Marine Data Types diagram (figure 2.2), note the Feature Point, Feature Line, and Feature Area. These features are continuations of standard GIS feature classes. The new names, such as Instantaneous Points or Location Series Points, are feature types defined specifically to meet marine user needs.

The development of new marine data types is analogous to the development of early extensions of core geographic data types to serve specialized applications in GIS. For example, we combined line features into series to form routes in a network model. We also combined multiple polygon features using a table into regions representing spatially disaggregated areas. This concept of using time series or location series tables to create new representations of geographic data is central to the development of new features in the Arc Marine data model. The development of the Common Marine Data Types can be illustrated by considering two different types of points features commonly used in coastal and marine applications: Feature Points and Measurement Points.

Marine Points

A Feature Point could be a fixed object, such as a permanent monument, a structure, or fixed buoy that does not require any specific measurement or time attribute. The standard point feature common to standard GIS applications would sufficiently represent this feature as a fixed x,y location in space and would allow for attributes to be attached or related to this feature. The feature would be considered as not having any required temporal attributes, but in a marine environment a required z-elevation value would be necessary to relate the feature to a vertical datum.

Instantaneous Points and Time Series Points

Instantaneous Points and Time Series Points extend the concept of Marine Points by allowing users to select appropriate representations of their data based on the definition of the time and location attributes. Each of these subtypes is distinguished by differences in the way they represent the time and location of the marine measurement.

Subtype: Instantaneous Points

Often the time of an observation is critical to the representation of the data and further analysis for marine GIS applications. A conductivity-temperature-depth (CTD) cast from a vessel measures salinity, temperature, and depth for a particular moment in time at a particular location and depth. Similarly, an observer spotting a right whale notes the location as well as the time of observation. Our ability to analyze and relate marine observation data to other marine features is inherently tied to our ability to locate the observation in time and

Arc Marine Common

Marine Points

Instantaneous Points | Time Series Point

Feature Points	Instant Subtype	Location Series Subtype	Time Series
ID X,Y Z	ID X,Y Z or ΔZ $m_1...m_2$ t	ID $\Delta X,Y$ ΔZ $m_1...m_2$ $t_1...t_2$	ID X,Y Z or ΔZ $m_1...m_2$ $t_1...t_{infinity}$
Examples: marker buoy, transponder, other fixed, geography	Examples: CTD, XBT, SVP casts at ΔZ, fish density, tide gauge, etc., at surface or a single Z	Examples: telemetry, bird/ mammal sighting, ship mounted ADCP	Examples: current meter, moored ADCP at ΔZ, obs. buoy, hydrophone, OBS at single Z

Survey Subtype

Examples:
aerial coastal
survey, lidar,
SCUBA/free swim obs.

Sounding Subtype

Examples:
single beam
bathy

Marine Areas

Feature Area

ID
$X_1,Y_1,X_2,Y_2...X_1,Y_1$
Z
m

Examples:
Marine boundaries
(e.g., sanctuary, MPA),
habitats,
patches, lava
flows, clipping,
masking

Time Duration Area

ID
$X_1,Y_1,X_2,Y_2...X_1,Y_1$
Z
m
$t_1...t_n$

Examples:
No-take
zones,
oil spills,
harmful algal
bloom

ACRONYMS—definitions

ADCP—acoustic doppler current profiler
ARGO—array for real-time geostrophic oceanography
BIL—band interleaved by line (for remotely sensed images or grids)
CTD—conductivity, temperature, depth
EEZ—exclusive economic zone
GeoTIFF—georeferenced tagged image file format
LIDAR—light detection and ranging
MPA—marine protected area
OBS—ocean bottom seismometer

ROV—remotely-operated vehicle
SCUBA—self-contained underwater breathing apparatus
SST—sea surface temperature
SVP—sound velocity profile
TIN—triangulated irregular network
U/W—underwater (also often refers to "underway")
VDatum—vertical datum
XBT—expendable bathythermograph

Marine Data Types

Marine Lines

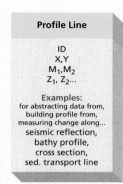

Profile Line

ID
X,Y
M_1, M_2
$Z_1, Z_2...$

Examples:
for abstracting data from,
building profile from,
measuring change along...
seismic reflection,
bathy profile,
cross section,
sed. transport line

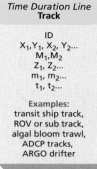

Time Duration Line
Track

ID
$X_1, Y_1, X_2, Y_2...$
M_1, M_2
$Z_1, Z_2...$
$m_1, m_2...$
$t_1, t_2...$

Examples:
transit ship track,
ROV or sub track,
algal bloom trawl,
ADCP tracks,
ARGO drifter

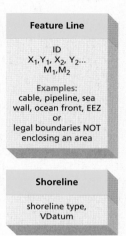

Feature Line

ID
$X_1, Y_1, X_2, Y_2...$
M_1, M_2

Examples:
cable, pipeline, sea
wall, ocean front, EEZ
or
legal boundaries NOT
enclosing an area

Shoreline

shoreline type,
VDatum

Marine Rasters/Grids/Meshes   *Derived or Placeholder*

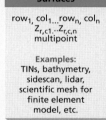

**Regularly
Interpolated
Surfaces**

$row_1, col_1...row_n, col_n$
$Z_{r,c1}...Z_{r,c,n}$
multipoint

Examples:
multibeam bathy,
sidescan, lidar,
SST, climatology,
scientific mesh,
"re-analyzed"
products
(images such as
GeoTIFF, BIL, etc.)

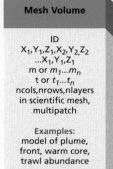

**Irregularly
Interpolated
Surfaces**

$row_1, col_1...row_n, col_n$
$Z_{r,c1}...Z_{r,c,n}$
multipoint

Examples:
TINs, bathymetry,
sidescan, lidar,
scientific mesh for
finite element
model, etc.

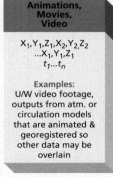

Mesh Volume

ID
$X_1, Y_1, Z_1, X_2, Y_2, Z_2$
$...X_1, Y_1, Z_1$
m or $m_1...m_n$
t or $t_1...t_n$
ncols, nrows, nlayers
in scientific mesh,
multipatch

Examples:
model of plume,
front, warm core,
trawl abundance

**Animations,
Movies,
Video**

$X_1, Y_1, Z_1, X_2, Y_2, Z_2$
$...X_1, Y_1, Z_1$
$t_1...t_n$

Examples:
U/W video footage,
outputs from atm. or
circulation models
that are animated &
georegistered so
other data may be
overlain

Figure 2.2   The Arc Marine Common Marine Data Types diagram on these two pages was developed as part of the conceptual framework for the data model. Note the "examples" (red headings), which list specific instruments, vehicles, real-world features, or products. Headings in italic eventually became abstract feature classes in the Arc Marine UML, while other headings became feature classes or subtypes. Lowercase "m" denotes a measurement in the field, uppercase "M" is a GIS geometry measure, and "t" is time.

space. So the development of a feature class subtype specifically designed to represent data tied to an instant in time is essential for a wide number of marine applications.

The Instantaneous Point subtype provides a common feature class that requires a location (x,y,z) as well as a time (t) description in addition to any measurement $(m_1...m_n)$ attributes collected at that location in space and time. Each observation in this generic data type is independent.

Subtype: Location Series

Another data type common to marine applications pertains to objects moving in the ocean environment. A vessel moving along a track, an autonomous vehicle conducting a dive, and the telemetry track of a satellite-tagged animal all represent multiple locations in space and time for a single entity. The Location Series subtype represents a series of point locations for an identified feature. The unique series identification number identifies the locations as belonging to an individual, and the related time tables establish the temporal sequence of the series. Numerous location series applications can be envisioned for marine applications. Any moving object where the time and location is recorded as a point fits into this general category. As with all of the common data types, the generic Location Series subtype could be modified and augmented to fit the specialized needs of particular marine GIS applications.

Subtype: Time Series

While Location Series provides the generic representation for moving points, the Time Series subtype provides a representation for features that stay in a fixed location but record attribute data over time. Again, numerous marine features readily fit this description. A weather buoy recording wave heights and wind speeds at a fixed location, a sea turtle nesting beach where observers record the number of hatchlings each season, and a gauging station in an estuary that records changes in salinity are all fixed geographic locations with attributes measured at different time intervals. So Time Series points can provide a common data type for a wide variety of common monitoring applications in coastal and marine environments.

Specialized point subtypes: Soundings and Survey Points

Two common types of marine point features were given specialized subtypes in the organization of the Common Marine Data Types schema. Soundings, the measurement or estimate of a depth value (z) at a location with no other attributes, is a very common point feature in marine applications and was assigned a separate subtype to represent this simple feature. A related data type, Survey Points, also measures a single defined measurement (e.g., lidar elevations) at a discrete geographic location with no other required attributes.

Line features

Lines features (indicated as data category "Feature Line" in figure 2.2) are another common feature for representing geographic data and have been extended into specialized subtypes in the Arc Marine data model. The three common line features are Profile Line, Time Duration Line, and Feature Line.

Profile Line

The Profile Line subtype provides a common data type for the representation of attributes along a linear feature. Some common examples in marine GIS applications would be a bathymetric profile constructed from a bathymetric grid (with change measures along that profile), cross sections, seismic reflections, or transport lines. Chapter 6 describes many more examples.

Time Duration Line

Just as point observations in marine applications often need to be explicitly related to the time, lines also often need to be represented with starting and stopping time as well as starting and stopping location. We developed the Time Duration Lines data type to provide marine GIS users with a common feature that requires a starting time, an ending time, and duration as core attributes. Types of common marine applications could be recording the sampling effort of a research vessel along legs of a survey, the duration of a trawl, and a segment of an autonomous vehicle track. With the required time attributes, each of these types of Time Duration Line features could be associated with other marine features based on the time of the observation along the line. This allows for a more direct method of associating dynamic environmental features (e.g., sea surface temperature—SST—or Beaufort Sea State) with the location and the appropriate period of time for the line.

Feature Line

Many marine features are most appropriately represented by standard line features. An undersea cable, a jurisdictional boundary, or a shipping lane could all be readily represented with a standard Feature Line. Feature Lines require a unique identifier; a vector of x,y coordinate pairs; as well as free-form measurement attributes unique to the particular application.

Specialized line feature: Shoreline

One category of Feature Line is so common and essential for coastal and marine applications that we provided a specialized subtype. Shoreline is a subtype of Feature Lines in that it demarcates essential boundaries of oceans and estuaries, but Shoreline definitions must also be explicitly stated (e.g., Mean Low Water versus Mean High Water) and must relate to a vertical datum to be properly represented. The specialized Shoreline subtype requires a shoreline type and a VDatum attribute to assure consistency in the representation and interpretation of shoreline features.

Marine Areas

Area features in the marine environment are divided into two common types: Feature Areas represented as static, time-independent areas, and Time Duration Areas that require changing time attributes for their representation.

Feature Area

Any marine area that can be represented by a static polygon can be appropriately represented as a Feature Area. Three straightforward examples of Feature Areas are the permanent jurisdictional area of a marine sanctuary, benthic habitat features, or the area contained within the exclusive economic zone (EEZ) of a nation. Feature Areas require a unique identifier; a vector of x,y coordinates forming the boundary; a depth (z) attribute; as well as user-defined measurement (m) attributes.

Time Duration Area

Many features of the marine environment or management responses may be ephemeral. Shellfish habitat may be demarcated as exceeding pollution thresholds for a portion of the year; seasonal area management (SAMs) and dynamic area management (DAMs) fisheries closures may be invoked for particular seasons or after specific events; and oil and gas leases may persist for specific periods of time. These three examples represent a geographic area feature tied to a specific starting and stopping time. The team developed the Time Duration Area data type to allow for this appropriate representation of marine features that persist for specified periods of time. This type of time-dependent area feature allows for users to make queries concerning overlaps in space and time. The Time Duration Area feature requires a beginning and ending time attribute in addition to the standard variables required for general area features.

Marine Rasters, Grids, Meshes

A large proportion of geospatial information used in marine applications originates as regularly interpolated surfaces. Bathymetry surfaces, oceanographic remote sensing (SST; sea surface height, SSH; or chlorophyll *a*, Chla), hydrodynamic measurements, and circulation models represent a significant proportion and volume of the data used in coastal and marine GIS and analysis. Arc Marine provides three generalized data types to represent these surface features: Regularly Interpolated Surfaces, Irregularly Interpolated Surfaces, and Mesh Volumes.

Regularly Interpolated Surfaces

Regularly Interpolated Surfaces, such as raster or image data, are a commonly used data format for many marine applications. ArcGIS GRID data, GeoTiff, Band Sequential (BSQ), and Band Interleaved (BIL) data formats represent many standard formats of currently supported raster data. In addition, a number of oceanographic and climatologic data products are distributed in hierarchically organized data formats such as network Common Data Form (netCDF) or hierarchical data format (HDF). ArcGIS (version 9.2 and beyond) will support direct read of the netCDF data format. This is further discussed in chapter 8.

Irregularly Interpolated Surfaces

Triangular irregular network (TIN) models and many finite element models form representative surfaces by identifying a minimum set of triangle facets using critical nodes and edges. The Delaney triangulation algorithm is used to validate the optimal selection of triangular surfaces. TIN models are used extensively as an efficient format for representing terrain surfaces (e.g., lidar beach surveys) or variable density nodes near shore hydrodynamic models. Again, further discussion may be found in chapter 8.

Model Meshes

A new feature type was defined to fill a special need for many marine modeling and analysis applications (particularly finite element modeling). Model Meshes allows for the representation of data as a multilayer stack of column and row mesh data. The structure of this feature allows for a flexible definition of regularly spaced mesh features, with discrete mesh node locations defined in x,y, and z dimensions. This is further discussed in chapter 7.

Animations, Movies, and Video

The final category of common data types addresses the growing need to georegister and link animations, movies, video, and other nontraditional information to spatial features for marine applications. Video footage of benthic habitats collected by an autonomous underwater vehicle (AUV), aerial surveys of seabird colonies, or fixed video cameras collecting data on port traffic will require the ability to link dynamic video data to geographic locations and specific time periods. This linkage will be derived through required x,y,z spatial locations coupled with a required time attribute (t).

Conclusion

The Common Marine Data Types concept defines broad categories of coastal and marine data representations using intentionally generic feature classes and subtypes. The goal of this design was to create a general framework that was then implemented using combinations of required attributes and relationships in Arc Marine feature classes. The Common Marine Data Types and subsequent features defined in the Arc Marine data model are intended to be general building blocks that users can modify and rename to more specific features for specific coastal and marine applications. The most important role of the Common Marine Data Types is to communicate the general framework required to represent spatially and temporally dynamic features to users in the marine GIS community. This has been and will continue to be an evolving and adaptive framework for envisioning necessary features for the marine user community and for modifying and refining each revision of Arc Marine.

References

Arctur, D., and M. Zeiler. 2004. *Designing geodatabases: Case studies in GIS data modeling.* Redlands, Calif.: ESRI Press.

Breman, J., D. J. Wright, and P. Halpin. 2002. The inception of the ArcGIS marine data model. In *Marine geography,* ed. J. Breman, 3–9. Redlands, Calif.: ESRI Press.

Laurini, R., and D. Thompson. 1992. *Fundamentals of spatial information systems.* San Diego, Calif.: Academic Press.

Zeiler, M. 1999. *Modeling our world: The ESRI guide to geodatabase design.* Redlands, Calif.: ESRI Press.

Marine surveys

Marine surveys are the backbone of Arc Marine because of the initial and critical role of data collection within a survey. All too often datasets are collected, analyzed, and "put in a GIS" after the fact. Arc Marine is designed expressly for the planning of marine surveys and the subsequent collection of data at sea. The intended result is the simplification of data management and analysis of survey data that often extends toward hundreds of data gigabytes. This chapter focuses on point datasets, the values those points represent, the measurements taken at various depths of the point, and how they all might be grouped together into a single event, often referred to as a survey. Surveys can be considered a collection of points, ranging in number from tens to billions of points. Survey types can vary, requiring a mechanism for classifying the points accordingly. This chapter also describes the use of line features (e.g., Tracks or ProfileLines) generally associated with a survey, how to store some general information about a survey (e.g., ports of call, names of scientists involved), and how to look at the data, particularly on a Track-by-Track basis. The chapter draws on two case studies: seafloor mapping and geologic sampling by the Woods Hole Science Center of the U.S. Geological Survey (USGS), in order to study the regional geologic framework of the inner continental shelf of Massachusetts; and a marine survey information geodatabase built by Photo Science, Inc., as part of a long-term USGS-led study of subsidence and sea-level rise in southeastern Louisiana (begun prior to Hurricane Katrina and ongoing).

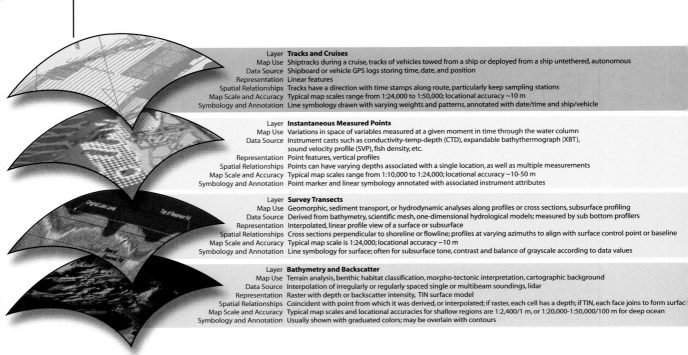

Layer	**Tracks and Cruises**
Map Use	Shiptracks during a cruise, tracks of vehicles towed from a ship or deployed from a ship untethered, autonomous
Data Source	Shipboard or vehicle GPS logs storing time, date, and position
Representation	Linear features
Spatial Relationships	Tracks have a direction with time stamps along route, particularly keep sampling stations
Map Scale and Accuracy	Typical map scales range from 1:24,000 to 1:50,000; locational accuracy ~10 m
Symbology and Annotation	Line symbology drawn with varying weights and patterns, annotated with date/time and ship/vehicle

Layer	**Instantaneous Measured Points**
Map Use	Variations in space of variables measured at a given moment in time through the water column
Data Source	Instrument casts such as conductivity-temp-depth (CTD), expandable bathythermograph (XBT), sound velocity profile (SVP), fish density, etc.
Representation	Point features, vertical profiles
Spatial Relationships	Points can have varying depths associated with a single location, as well as multiple measurements
Map Scale and Accuracy	Typical map scales range from 1:10,000 to 1:24,000; locational accuracy ~10-50 m
Symbology and Annotation	Point marker and linear symbology annotated with associated instrument attributes

Layer	**Survey Transects**
Map Use	Geomorphic, sediment transport, or hydrodynamic analyses along profiles or cross sections, subsurface profiling
Data Source	Derived from bathymetry, scientific mesh, one-dimensional hydrological models; measured by sub bottom profilers
Representation	Interpolated, linear profile view of a surface or subsurface
Spatial Relationships	Cross sections perpendicular to shoreline or flowline; profiles at varying azimuths to align with surface control point or baseline
Map Scale and Accuracy	Typical map scale is 1:24,000; locational accuracy ~10 m
Symbology and Annotation	Line symbology for surface; often for subsurface tone, contrast and balance of grayscale according to data values

Layer	**Bathymetry and Backscatter**
Map Use	Terrain analysis, benthic habitat classification, morpho-tectonic interpretation, cartographic background
Data Source	Interpolation of irregularly or regularly spaced single or multibeam soundings, lidar
Representation	Raster with depth or backscatter intensity, TIN surface model
Spatial Relationships	Coincident with point from which it was derived, or interpolated; if raster, each cell has a depth; if TIN, each face joins to form surfac
Map Scale and Accuracy	Typical map scales and locational accuracies for shallow regions are 1:2,400/1 m, or 1:20,000-1:50,000/100 m for deep ocean
Symbology and Annotation	Usually shown with graduated colors; may be overlain with contours

Introduction

At the heart of marine science and management is the survey, which focuses on the initial acquisition of marine data, and is thus concerned with the accurate sensing and collection of measurements from the marine environment and their transformation from raw to processed measurements for GIS implementation. Here, data collection is often made in two ways: (1) short-term mobile entities, such as research cruises (day operations in a small survey boat, or 24-hour operations over weeks or months on a larger research vessel), deploying various instruments, instrument platforms, remotely operated vehicles (ROVs), or submersibles; or (2) surveys that put into place longer-term, fixed entities, such as hydrophones, buoys, or various other types of moored instrumentation. These will remain in the ocean or along the shore collecting data for months or even years (the ocean observatory concept). For the mobile entities, data collection runs gather *in situ* samples, casts, or tows of various types for future laboratory analysis. These may be made at predefined sites or along predefined transects or tracklines. For fixed entities, raw datasets are sent back to shore from the hydrophones or moorings for decryption and processing. Marine surveys from these mobile and fixed entities are often made at points in space and time and may have multiple assessments of the geophysical, geological, chemical, physical, and biological properties of the marine environment. Each of these different kinds of ocean observations may also have one-to-many assessments of data quality or error.

Featured case studies

Surveys are made for a variety of purposes. Two purposes described in this chapter are the mapping of the seafloor along the inner continental shelf of Massachusetts to understand regional geology, ultimately for subsequent biological sampling and benthic habitat mapping (where and how big are the environmental impacts to the health of fisheries?), and for subsurface seismic surveying and coring of the seafloor off Louisiana to test theories about subsidence and rise of the sea level.

Brian Andrews, a researcher at the USGS Woods Hole Science Center for Coastal and Marine Geology, implemented the Massachusetts case study in cooperation with colleagues at the Massachusetts Office of Coastal Zone Management. High-resolution swath bathymetry, sidescan sonar imagery, and seismic-reflection profiles were collected at depths of 5 to 40 m in a survey area of 134 km^2 encompassing a portion of the South Essex Ocean Sanctuary between Gloucester and Nahant, Massachusetts (Andrews 2005; Barnhardt et al. 2005; figure 3.1). In addition, 100 ground-truth stations were established where bottom videos, photographic stills, and sediment grabs were collected. These represent typical geological and geophysical data collected by the Woods Hole Science Center on a regular basis throughout the New England inner continental shelf (figure 3.2). The South Essex surveys aimed to understand the geological and geophysical framework of the region to classify the seafloor into bottom types (e.g., gravel, sand, sandy silt, silty sand, cobble/boulder province), and ultimately into benthic habitat classes associated with fish species (heeding the caveats of studies such as Greene et al. 2005). A long-term goal of the study is to support the marine resource managers charged with making decisions about the use and protection of resources in South Essex, a marine-protected area. The geologic mapping is a first step toward identifying and protecting fish habitat, understanding the location and size of environmental impacts on the health of these habitats, and delineating new marine reserves as a result. From a data management standpoint, an additional question was how to synthesize the main kinds of survey data collected at sea to be the most effective at interpreting the data (in this case, interpreting the surficial geology) through subsequent analysis and map production (Andrews and Ackerman 2004). Arc Marine presented a viable solution.

Heather Mounts, senior database developer at Photo Science, Inc., (PSI) in St. Petersburg, Florida, implemented the Louisiana case study in cooperation with the USGS Florida Integrated Science Center for Coastal and Watershed Studies. Coastal geologists at the center teamed with geologists and geophysicists at the U.S. Army Corps of Engineers and the University of New Orleans to gather data on subsidence and sea-level rise within the Mississippi River delta plain and out onto the Louisiana continental shelf (figure 3.3). The devastating effects of Hurricane Katrina in August 2005 illustrate the ongoing importance of this collaborative study. The Mississippi River delta plain is subject to the highest rate of relative sea-level rise (3 feet per century) of any region in the United States, due largely to reduced sediment supply and rapid geologic subsidence and also to global atmospheric warming (Kindinger 2000). This translates to 40 sq. mi. of wetland deterioration and marshland loss per year (also the highest in the United States; Wilson and Gesch 2004) and increased potential for flooding and heightened storm impact. Subsidence and

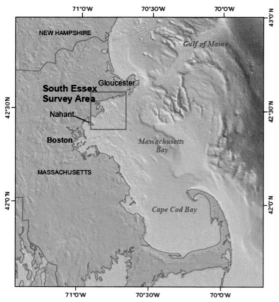

Figure 3.1   Location map of South Essex survey area, Massachusetts case study.

Courtesy of the U.S. Geological Survey.

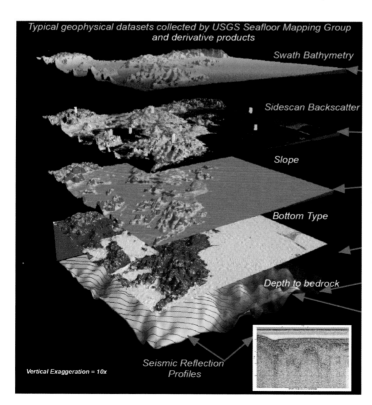

Figure 3.2   Typical datasets collected by the USGS Seafloor Mapping Group of the Woods Hole Science Center.

Courtesy of the U.S. Geological Survey.

sea-level change are two of the most critical environmental, socioeconomic, and cultural issues facing southeastern Louisiana (Kindinger 2000). Hence the data gathered (the Louisiana Sedimentary and Environmental Database or LASED) is for the use of researchers, coastal managers, and planners.

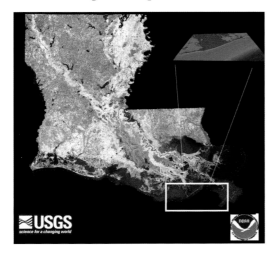

Figure 3.3   The white box outlines part of the study area for the Louisiana case study. All regions in southeast Louisiana surveyed by the USGS and their collaborators are not shown in this satellite image. Inset map at top right shows outline of 3D flyover of the region, available on the book's accompanying Web site, http://dusk.geo. orst.edu/djl/arcgis/.

Courtesy of NOAA.

Datasets needed to understand the nature and extent of geologic processes in the region have included sediment cores, seismic-reflection profiles, bathymetry, and sidescan sonar collected on several cruises and associated tide gauge data, carbon-14 dating of sediments, and satellite imagery. In 2003, the USGS enlisted PSI to incorporate the cruise logistics information and the seismic and sediment core data into an ArcGIS geodatabase. PSI built the geodatabase based on Arc Marine, choosing also to incorporate database schemas from usSEABED (a suite of software for integration of marine substrate data; Reid et al. 2001; Jenkins 2004) and the Oracle-based Florida Reconnaissance Offshore Sand Search Database (Niedoroda et al. 2004). The result has been an efficient query and retrieval mechanism for the large amount of cruise, trackline, core, and seismic data, along with other information regarding the Louisiana subsidence project. Users also can view or download core photos, core logs, interactive HTML seismic profiles, and core documents related to their query. PDF versions of these documents and image files were hyperlinked to the various feature classes.

In the parlance of Arc Marine, a ship goes out on an expedition (or cruise) of several days to weeks in duration. Within that cruise, multiple smaller trips are taken, commonly referred to as surveys. Either within a cruise or within several surveys, many specific tracks are taken (figures 3.4 and 3.5). And along a track, many point locations may be recorded with multiple variables measured at varying depths over time (figure 3.5). The following sections describe the most important feature classes and object tables in Arc Marine with regard to marine surveys, illustrating also how they were implemented in real projects by the featured case studies.

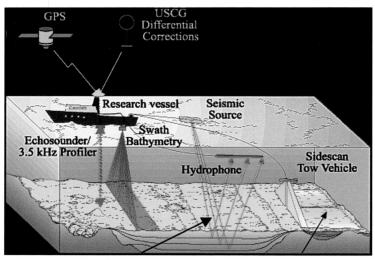

Figure 3.4   Graphic showing various survey methods and instruments at sea, including swath bathymetry, sidescan sonar, and seismic profiling.

Courtesy of the U.S. Geological Survey.

Common Marine Data Types

Marine Points

Instantaneous Points

Instant Subtype
ID X,Y Z or ΔZ $m_1...m_2$ t
Examples: CTD, XBT, SVP casts at ΔZ, fish density, tide gauge, etc., at surface or a single Z

Marine Lines

Profile Line
ID X,Y M_1,M_2 $Z_1, Z_2...$
Examples: for abstracting data from, building profile from, measuring change along... seismic reflection, bathy profile, cross section, sed. transport line

Time Duration Line **Track**
ID $X_1,Y_1, X_2, Y_2...$ M_1,M_2 $Z_1, Z_2...$ $m_1, m_2...$ $t_1, t_2...$
Examples: transit ship track, ROV or sub track, algal bloom trawl, ADCP tracks, ARGO drifter

Figure 3.5   Common Marine Data Types (from chapter 2) featured in the Massachusetts and Louisiana case studies. Headings in italics are abstract feature classes in Arc Marine. All other headings are feature classes or subtypes of feature classes.

Marine features

The superclass of Arc Marine is referred to as MarineFeature. This being a hierarchical model, all other feature classes inherit from this superclass. The MarineFeature class introduces two attributes, FeatureID and FeatureCode. Adding these attributes to this superclass ensures that they are present in all features. FeatureID is an integer field designed to be a unique identifier throughout the geodatabase. FeatureID acts as a key field for many of the relationships built into the data model. The FeatureID should be used as the key field if additional relationships involving feature classes are necessary. FeatureCode is a string field that provides a way for users to include alpha and numerical information in the identifier. If features in a feature class do not have their own code, then the user should just ignore this field. Both fields are populated by the user, as there is no tool in Arc Marine for automatically generating these values.

Under the superclass MarineFeature, three abstract classes organize the data model into feature data types. An abstract class represents an abstract concept and is never instantiated, meaning that instances of this class are not created and never appear in a geodatabase. These abstract classes are MarinePoint, MarineLine, and MarineArea. Each of these classes or groups of features is explained in detail throughout the book. This chapter will concentrate primarily on MarinePoint and its subclasses.

Point features

The class MarinePoint is further divided into two thematic subclasses, FeaturePoint and MeasurementPoint. FeaturePoint is a simple feature class for storing permanent geographic features whose spatial representation can be described with a single pair of x- and y-coordinates (e.g., a navigational buoy). This feature class adds no additional attributes and can easily be instantiated or can become a parent class from which a subclass is added. If a subclass is inserted and inherits from the FeaturePoint class, then FeaturePoint should be converted to an abstract class. In this way, only the user-defined subclass is instantiated and appears in the geodatabase. Unless FeaturePoint or other superclasses are made abstract, users will end up with unwanted feature classes in their geodatabase.

Recording varying measurements in a point feature is one of the more complex concepts of the Arc Marine data model, providing a variety of phenomena for the data model to solve. MeasurementPoint is designed to be a thematic organization for all points where measurements are taken. As an abstract class, it will never appear in a geodatabase as a feature class. Rather, two feature classes inherit from it, TimeSeriesPoint and Instantaneous-Point. However, the MeasurementPoint class adds one attribute, CruiseID, which is a key field and provides the framework for constructing a relationship class between the two subclasses (relationship classes between classes that have dependent classes are not permitted, so MeasurementPoint can never participate in a relationship) and the Cruise object class.

TimeSeriesPoint is designed as a feature class that represents point features in which time series data would be associated. For example, a moored buoy would have devices attached for measuring wave height or temperature at intervals during a long time period. The measured values of wave height or temperature would constitute the time series (please refer to chapter 5 for more information regarding time series data), and the moored buoy would be represented as a feature (instance) of the TimeSeriesPoint feature class. The TimeSeriesPoint class adds no additional attributes.

InstantaneousPoint is a feature class for storing all other point features where measurements are taken. This feature class has four subtypes (an attribute in the feature class to categorically distinguish one point from another): Instant, Sounding, Survey, and LocationSeries. This chapter describes the Survey subtype. For information on the other subtypes, please refer to chapters 4 through 6.

InstantaneousPoint is defined as a point feature that is fixed in space and time, meaning that a unique feature (and a new value for FeatureID) is defined by its x,y coordinate pair (shape) plus a single time stamp. In theory then, one InstantaneousPoint at location 669325.68, 6056605.93 with a time stamp of 24.03.1964 18:00:00 is a unique feature. A feature at the same location but with a time stamp of 24.03.1964 18:30:00 would also be a unique feature. Furthermore, two points with different x,y coordinates but with the same time stamp would be considered two unique features. The InstantaneousPoint feature class adds several additional attributes. The ZValue attribute is for storing a single depth, perhaps the sea surface or the seafloor, of the feature. However, the following section describes how point features can have multiple depths associated with them by implementing the Measurement object class. The SeriesID attribute is used as a key field for constructing a relationship class between this feature class and the Series object class. In this way, many points can belong to the same series. A series is yet another means of grouping a subset of points into a thematic organization. This is well illustrated in chapter 4. SurveyID is another key field used in the relationship class SurveyInfoHasPoints, in which zero to many points can be collected into a single survey and then defined by a single entry in the SurveyInfo table. Lastly, the PointType attribute is the subtype field in place to determine the subtype of the point. The default value for this field is 1, which identifies Instant as being the type for the point.

Measurements and virtual features

One of the greatest design challenges for Arc Marine, and specifically for point features, was developing a schema that could emulate the complex and variable ways of sampling and observing the marine environment. At each depth, there could be a variety of measuring devices, with each device recording one or more variables. Additionally, the single feature and all of the measurements recorded at each of the depths could be tagged with the same time stamp, or each measuring device could be recording different variables during an extended time period.

Measuring locations below the surface of the sea can be modeled in Arc Marine with the use of additional object classes. The Measurement object class (a table in Arc Marine) is used for storing information about the multiple depths of a feature, and the MeasuredData object class (table) can store the various values being recorded. Figure 3.6 shows the example of an InstantaneousPoint with FeatureID = 122. Six depths are associated with this point. The numbers 1 through 6 identify the Measurement. At Measurement 4, there are three measuring devices, A, B, and C. Each of these could be recording one or more variables either at a given time step or over a long time period. The values measured at a single time step might be stored in the MeasuredData table, whereas the values being recorded during a long period would be stored as a time series using the TimeSeries object classes. See chapter 5 for details on the specifics of using the TimeSeries object classes.

This phenomenon could be represented in a database by designing a schema in which each combination of x-, y-, and z-coordinates represents a unique feature. With this schema, users end up with multiple features, essentially representing the same phenomenon stacked on top of one another. From a data management perspective this schema may be difficult to manage, even though it provides some benefits from a functionality perspective. Furthermore, given the potential quantity of data being collected, having to store and replicate the x,y coordinate pairs for the same feature (one pair of coordinates for each depth) can occupy vast amounts of disk space. Granted, having multiple points at various depths and essentially representing measurements within the water column lend themselves easily to many GIS applications. However, as a means of storing data, this schema is neither efficient nor practical due to the vast amounts of replicated data. Application developers are encouraged to use the data storage mechanism of this data model and rely on software applications to stack the points at their respective depths within the water column.

With the Arc Marine schema, this phenomenon can be replicated in two ways. Both rely on the Measurement table as an intermediate table for storing the multiple depths associated with a given point feature. The outcome of this table is referred to as a "virtual feature." The Measurement table has six attributes. The first four, MeasurementID, FeatureID, FeatureClass, and ZLocation, help define the virtual feature. The other two

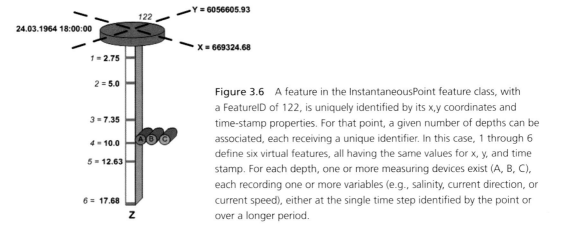

Figure 3.6 A feature in the InstantaneousPoint feature class, with a FeatureID of 122, is uniquely identified by its x,y coordinates and time-stamp properties. For that point, a given number of depths can be associated, each receiving a unique identifier. In this case, 1 through 6 define six virtual features, all having the same values for x, y, and time stamp. For each depth, one or more measuring devices exist (A, B, C), each recording one or more variables (e.g., salinity, current direction, or current speed), either at the single time step identified by the point or over a longer period.

attributes, XLocation and YLocation, assist in qualifying drift that may be introduced at a given depth. MeasurementID is meant to be a user-assigned unique identifier in this table. FeatureID is a key field used for building relationships with the FeatureID of the feature class. The value of this field should replicate the FeatureID value from the Point feature class. The FeatureClass attribute stores the name of the feature class in which the feature resides. This attribute is added to help the application developer search for a given feature by its FeatureID. It's easier to search for the matching feature with the same FeatureID if it's known in which feature class it exists. The ZLocation attribute is the below-surface-depth value associated with the feature.

The key to implementing this table (figure 3.7) correctly is that the MeasurementID remains unique. In the Measurement table, the unique combination of the FeatureID of a point and a ZLocation (depth) creates a new record in the table. A unique value for MeasurementID should be assigned to that record. The MeasurementID attribute then becomes the identifier of the "virtual feature." In the Measurements table, the FeatureID would be repeated for each depth associated with a single feature. If Feature 122 has six depths associated with it, then a value of 122 would be repeated six times for the FeatureID attribute. For each record added, the ZLocation value should change and the value of the MeasurementID should be unique.

To further the Arc Marine solution to this phenomenon, the MeasurementID is carried over to the MeasuredData table. In that table, the MeasurementID is a key field that

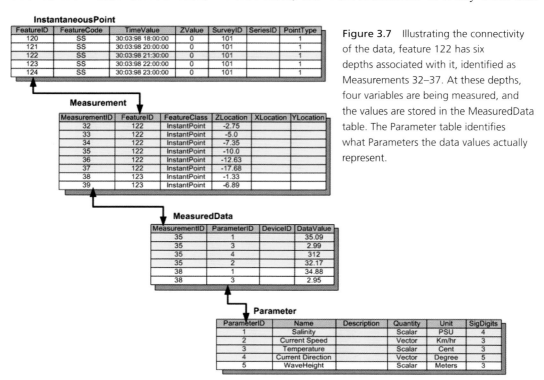

Figure 3.7 Illustrating the connectivity of the data, feature 122 has six depths associated with it, identified as Measurements 32–37. At these depths, four variables are being measured, and the values are stored in the MeasuredData table. The Parameter table identifies what Parameters the data values actually represent.

InstantaneousPoint

FeatureID	FeatureCode	TimeValue	ZValue	SurveyID	SeriesID	PointType
120	SS	30:03:98 18:00:00	0	101		1
121	SS	30:03:98 20:00:00	0	101		1
122	SS	30:03:98 21:30:00	0	101		1
123	SS	30:03:98 22:00:00	0	101		1
124	SS	30:03:98 23:00:00	0	101		1

Measurement

MeasurementID	FeatureID	FeatureClass	ZLocation	XLocation	YLocation
32	122	InstantPoint	-2.75		
33	122	InstantPoint	-5.0		
34	122	InstantPoint	-7.35		
35	122	InstantPoint	-10.0		
36	122	InstantPoint	-12.63		
37	122	InstantPoint	-17.68		
38	123	InstantPoint	-1.33		
39	123	InstantPoint	-6.89		

MeasuredData

MeasurementID	ParameterID	DeviceID	DataValue
35	1		35.09
35	3		2.99
35	4		312
35	2		32.17
38	1		34.88
38	3		2.95

Parameter

ParameterID	Name	Description	Quantity	Unit	SigDigits
1	Salinity		Scalar	PSU	4
2	Current Speed		Vector	Km/hr	3
3	Temperature		Scalar	Cent	3
4	Current Direction		Vector	Degree	5
5	WaveHeight		Scalar	Meters	3

can be repeated for each parameter being measured. This is accomplished through the MeasurementHasData relationship class, which allows a single measurement to have zero or many entries in the MeasuredData table. So, in reference to the two previous graphics, the depth of -10 for feature 122 is assigned a MeasurementID of 35, which happens to have three measuring devices, A, B, and C. For the sake of explanation, we'll say that measuring device A measures temperature, measuring device B measures salinity, and measuring device C measures current speed and direction. Consequently, in the MeasuredData table, MeasurementID 35 is repeated four times, once for each of the parameters being measured at that depth.

The Massachusetts case study by Brian Andrews is one excellent example of Arc Marine implementation. Andrews is conducting a marine geophysical survey with three concurrent acoustic measuring devices: interferometric sonar for bathymetry and backscatter, side-scan sonar for backscatter, and seismic-reflection profiling for sediment stratigraphy and structure (figure 3.4; for more details and definitions, see Barnhardt et al. 2005). The survey vessel collects data with these three sonars along predefined survey lines 100 meters apart. These lines are represented in the USGS version of the data model by a feature class called SurveyLine, an additional subclass of the ProfileLine feature class developed by Andrews. Along this SurveyLine, a swath of points is collected for bathymetry and backscatter perpendicular to the track of the ship (figure 3.4), and each swath is marked with a time stamp. Also along this survey line, seismic shot points are taken from hydrophones trailed behind the ship, and each shot point is marked with a time stamp (figures 3.4 and 3.10), which easily make the InstantaneousPoint the appropriate feature class for storing this data. At the completion of the geophysical portion of the project, the acoustic remote sensing data is "ground validated" with towed video, bottom photographs, and sediment samples (also known as "bottom grabs") (figure 3.8). The points where the bottom photos and the sediment samples are being taken are time stamped and also fit into the InstantaneousPoints feature class. However, each of these three point types represents different features with different attributes and different uses. Consequently, the data model that Andrews is implementing requires that InstantaneousPoint is made an abstract class and three new feature classes are added: SeismicShots, BottomPhotos, and SedGrabs. Each of these new classes inherits properties from InstantaneousPoint and has its own set of attributes.

Andrews then adds a SurveyLineID attribute to each of the three point feature classes that acts as a key field. It is populated with the FeatureID of the SurveyLine along which the point was recorded. He creates three new corresponding relationship classes that allow for one-to-many relationships between a SurveyLine and the three point feature classes. With this structure, Andrews can track which points are associated with which Survey-Lines (figure 3.9). He will also add the SurveyID to the SurveyLine feature class and build a relationship between this feature class and the SurveyInfo table. From this, he can manage which points belong to a specific SurveyLine feature and to which Survey the SurveyLine belongs. He also can identify which of the SurveyLine features are associated with a given measuring device.

The BottomPhotos and the SedimentGrabs feature classes each have only a single depth associated with them and will use the ZValue attribute inherited from InstantaneousPoint to store that value. However, the SeismicShots could have any number of depths associated

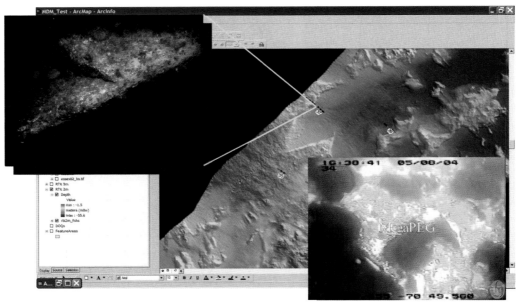

Figure 3.8 Bottom grab locations (using the BottomPhotos subclass of InstantaneousPoint) are overlaid on color hillshaded multibeam bathymetry in this ArcMap screen capture of the Massachusetts case study geodatabase. More than 590 bottom photos and 60 MPEG movies are hyperlinked to these points in the geodatabase.

Courtesy of the U.S. Geological Survey.

with them. Each depth represents a unique reflector and ultimately a unique horizon in the derived profile. These depths will be stored as Measurements, with the depth of the reflector being stored in the ZLocation attribute in the Measurement table. Additionally, Andrews has also added to the Measurements table an attribute named ReflectType that can be used to identify all of the points of a reflector type based on their classification.

Figures 3.9 and 3.10 illustrate that the SeismicShot feature with a FeatureID of 13 has four entries in the Measurement table, Measurements 1032 through 1035. Each of these Measurements is further classified according to its reflector type by use of the ReflectID attribute. Through the relationship classes that Andrews has added, he can find all of the seismic shots of a given reflector type, what survey line they are associated with, and with which survey they were recorded. He also can find all of the seismic shots along a survey line and specific reflectors within the seismic-reflection profile.

The phenomenon outlined in this chapter can be represented a second way using the TimeSeries tables. In this example, the data associated with a specific depth is a time series (a single variable being recorded over a long period at regular or irregular time steps). In the TimeSeries table, the FeatureID attribute is for storing the ID of the feature with which the specific time series should be associated. In this case, that would be the MeasurementID representing the "virtual feature" or depth of a given point feature. This case is further expanded in chapter 5.

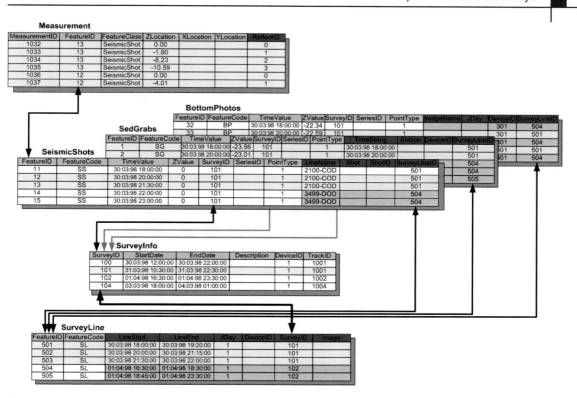

Figure 3.9   One could examine this possible data flow or connectivity for the Massachusetts case study by noting that feature 13 of the SeismicShots feature class has three associated depths, each identified as reflectors 1–3, which were collected along SurveyLine 501 and a part of Survey 101.

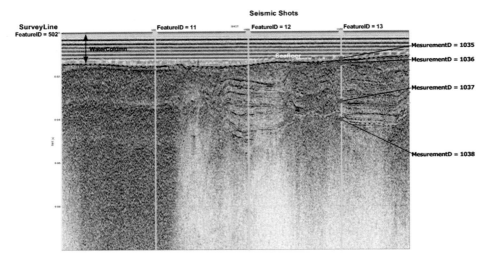

Figure 3.10   An example of a typical seismic-reflection profile from the Massachusetts case study, derived from several seismic shots (with FeatureIDs of 11, 12, and 13) along one survey line. The direction of travel of the research vessel collecting the data is from left to right. Two-way travel time below the sea surface (a proxy for depth) is indicated on the left-hand y-axis. The seafloor is indicated by the aqua blue reflector. Beneath that, other reflectors are traced in green, purple, and orange, indicative of layers of sediments or basement rock below the seafloor.

Courtesy of the U.S. Geological Survey.

With this schema, the data can be approached from two different directions. By approaching the data in the direction "from a feature to a value," a user could identify a point with several depths, drill down through those depths to select one of them, and then see any given values at that depth. Going further through the MeasuringDeviceHasData relationship class shows the measuring device being used to record the data values. Also from a depth, the user could go through the ParameterHasData relationship class and learn what parameter the value represents. Conversely, from the direction of a "parameter to a value," a user could query the Parameter table for a particular variable, such as salinity. Through the ParameterHasData relationship class (relationship classes are bidirectional), a user could find the measured values for salinity in the MeasuredData table. Furthermore, at this stage the selected set could be narrowed by selecting values within a specified range. The MeasurementHasData relationship class can then be used to find all of the "virtual features" or depths to which salinity is associated. From the Measurement table, one could find the point features associated with the Measurements and render those accordingly in ArcMap software.

Using the case being developed at the USGS and illustrated in figure 3.9, Andrews can query the SurveyInfo table for a specific survey. From that, he can find the SurveyLines included in the survey and then find the point features associated with the found SurveyLines.

He could query SurveyInfo to show him the depths (Measurements) of the second reflector (ReflectID = 2) for the lines of a given LineName in a given survey. Or, he could ask, "Where are the SurveyLines where there is more than one reflector?"

Surveys, cruises, and tracks

Surveys generally consist of collecting data for specific areas of interest during a cruise. Then by various means, surveys collect samples and measure values at many locations. The number of locations can range from as few as tens of values, as with soil samples or fish counts, to as many as billions of locations using multibeam swath mapping equipment capturing depth or backscatter values. However, surveys are usually a collection of points, no matter the number.

The Arc Marine data model uses the InstantaneousPoint feature class with subtype three to describe these points (e.g., figure 3.5). Information about the survey itself is not stored with the point data, because the same information would get repeated for each feature. Instead, the SurveyInfo object class stores that information. In that table, the SurveyID is used to distinguish between one survey and another. InstantaneousPoint also has a SurveyID attribute, so each point can be related to the survey in which they participate. The SurveyInfo table then becomes a collection of Surveys, and a Survey is a collection of points.

Furthermore, many Surveys can be associated with a Track feature. The Track feature class is a subclass of the TimeDurationLine feature class. These are linear features that generally have a beginning time stamp, an ending time stamp, and define the route taken during a survey. The TrackID attribute is used for identifying the unique Track feature. The TrackID attribute is also available in the SurveyInfo object class, allowing for collecting multiple surveys into a Track. However, Track also inherits attributes such as VehicleID and CruiseID from the TimeDurationLine. These attributes are added here as key fields for their respective tables, Vehicle and Cruise. In the Track feature class, additional attributes store information describing the Track, such as Name, Method, Description, and LocalDesc for describing the physical location. A Track is differentiated from a ProfileLine in that a Track may be merely a ship track, as when one leaves port to reach a survey site. Data may or may not be collected along that Track. However, a ProfileLine always involves the collection or derivation of data in a survey. The ProfileLine feature class is described in greater detail in chapter 6.

A Cruise is a row in the Cruise table, which describes the overall expedition (figure 3.11). Several basic attributes in the Cruise table describe the expedition, but many additional attributes could be added to meet the esoteric needs of specific users. An example of this is illustrated by the Louisiana case study, where it was vital to keep track of the descriptive information for several cruises launched over several years to the same regions along the southeastern coast of the United States and inner continental shelf (figure 3.12). In addition, Cruises can contain zero or many Tracks through the CruiseHasTracks relationship class, which uses the CruiseID attribute in both tables (figure 3.11).

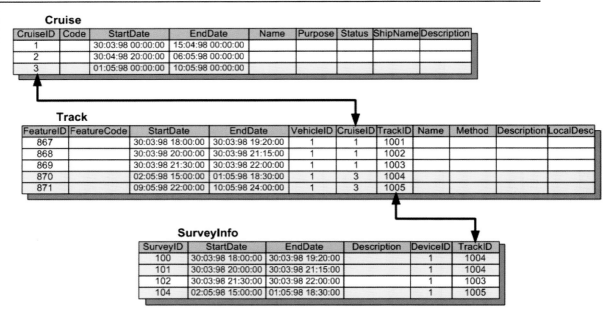

Figure 3.11   A connectivity or data flow exists between the Cruise and Track and the multiple surveys that may be conducted.

Consequently, through this data structure, a Cruise can have multiple Tracks. Each Track can have multiple Surveys. Each Survey is a collection of many points. Each point then can have multiple depths, and at each depth there might be one or more measuring devices measuring one or more variables over time. An example is a seismic line being recorded along the same positional trackline as where swath bathymetry or sidescan sonar is being collected. The three lines are spatially coincident. Yet if one device fails or a shipboard computer for a device crashes, it is still possible to collect and process data from the other two devices. Figure 3.13 from the Louisiana case study shows how a Track feature can be queried to reveal the associated Cruise information, equipment information, and shipboard science personnel responsible for collecting the data.

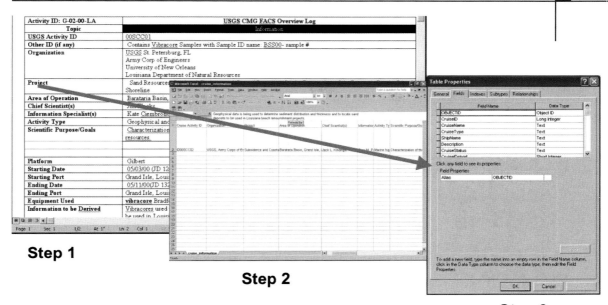

Step 1

Step 2

Step 3

Figure 3.12 Illustration from the Louisiana case study of the transfer of descriptive cruise attributes (e.g., USGS Activity ID, chief scientist, area of operation, shipboard information specialist, ship name, ports of call, names of measuring devices used) from shipboard logs to a spreadsheet to an Arc Marine Cruise object table.

Courtesy of Photo Science, Inc.

Measuring devices and vehicles

The DeviceID attribute in the SurveyInfo and MeasuringDevice object classes is a key field for developing a relationship class that joins surveys with a measuring device. The MeasuringDevice table describes the measuring devices. Andrews uses this capability to find the SurveyLines associated with a specific measuring device. To see SurveyLines representing the lines associated with the video ground validation, Andrews queries the SurveyInfo table for "DeviceID equal to 4." The result of this query provides the IDs for those Surveys. Through the SurveyKey table, the specific records in the SurveyLine feature class are returned (figure 3.13).

Arc Marine provides the Vehicle object class for storing information about the vehicle being used during a survey. The table provides a VehicleID to generate relationships between this table and the MeasuringDevice table or the Track feature class.

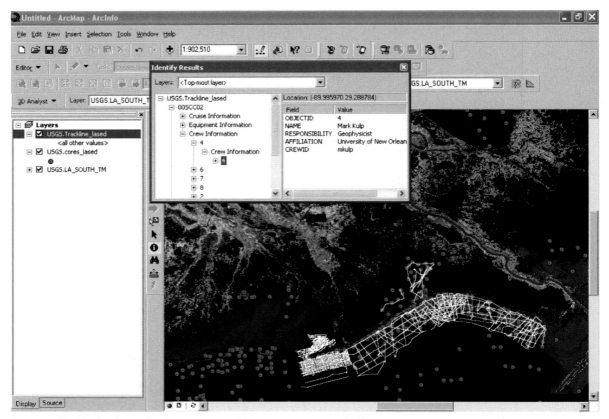

Figure 3.13   The locations of sediment cores and tracklines from several different cruises south and west of the Mississippi delta region are shown in this ArcMap screen capture from the Louisiana case study. Relationships classes from Arc Marine link cruise and track information for easier query of several different cruises. Underlay is a Landsat Thematic Mapper image.

Courtesy of Photo Science, Inc., and the U.S. Geological Survey.

Conclusion

The previous descriptions and examples illustrate how Arc Marine can provide an excellent framework to organize, manage, query, and retrieve data from marine surveys. The Massachusetts case study showed how Arc Marine ensured the integrity of data from the planning stages of a survey and the collection of data at sea to the analysis and final publication of the data and maps. Using Arc Marine at sea at the beginning of the survey made the rest of the data collection, processing, and analysis much easier because the schema had already been defined and populated with relationships. These relationships, along with valid attribute domains and database rules (behavior), reduced errors during the data entry phase at sea and the analysis phases at sea and onshore. Existing relationship classes and database rules simplified data management throughout the project. More importantly, they facilitated geologic interpretation and modeling. Both case studies illustrate the benefits of a standardized Arc Marine schema for organizations that routinely collect, process, and analyze the same types of data, thereby facilitating collaboration across a larger network of users who can easily transport and transfer the resulting geodatabase.

The case studies were provided as examples, but there are many possible variations for other kinds of surveys (Massachusetts and Louisiana were largely geological and geophysical in nature). As mentioned in chapter 1, the Arc Marine data model is a starting point on which to build and leverage the needs and expertise of the user.

Arc Marine class definitions featured in this chapter

FEATURE CLASSES	**InstantaneousPoint** is a point feature class representing features that are single observations in time and space. The x- and y-coordinates, plus a time stamp, create the unique feature. An InstantaneousPoint can have multiple ZValues by implementing a relationship to the Measurement object class.		
	Subtype	Survey	
	Notes	InstantaneousPoint is a subclass of the superclass MeasurementPoint.	
	Properties	None	
	Fields	FeatureID	A geodatabase-wide unique identifier and key field for participating in relationships
		FeatureCode	A user-defined code used for identifying a feature
		CruiseID	A key field for relating this feature class to a Cruise
		TimeValue	The time stamp for the point
		ZValue	A single depth value for the point
		SurveyID	A foreign key to the SurveyInfo object class
		SeriesID	A key field for relating this feature to the Series table
		PointType	Defines the subtype to be one of the following: 1 = Instant (default value) 2 = Sounding 3 = Survey 4 = LocationSeries
	Track is a linear feature class representing the path and event associated with a specific tangent from the expedition.		
	Subtype	None apply	
	Properties	HasM = True HasZ = True	
	Notes	Track is a subclass of TimeDurationLine. In TimeDurationLine, the beginning of the line starts at a given time stamp and the end of the line has a different time stamp. A Track can also have a relationship with the Cruise object class via the CruiseID field. The relationship, CruiseHasTracks, is characterized by a Cruise and can have zero or many Tracks.	
	Fields	FeatureID	A geodatabase-wide unique identifier and key field for participating in relationships
		FeatureCode	A user-defined code used for identifying a feature
		StartDate	The beginning time stamp for the feature
		EndDate	The ending time stamp for the feature
		VehicleID	A key field for relating this feature to the Vehicle table
		CruiseID	A key field for relating this feature to the Cruise table
		TrackID	An identifier for a Track feature
		Name	The name of a specific Track
		Method	Text describing the method for a specific Track
		Description	Text describing the Track
		LocalDesc	Text describing the locale of the Track

FEATURE CLASSES (cont'd)	**ProfileLine** is a feature class representing linear features that are not physical features themselves but rather features interpolated along the line from another source—for example, a profile interpolated from a bathymetry survey.		
	Subtype	None apply	
	Properties	HasM = True HasZ = True	
	Notes		
	Fields	FeatureID	A geodatabase-wide unique identifier and key field for participating in relationships
		FeatureCode	A user-defined code used for identifying a feature
		CruiseID	A key field for relating this feature class to a Cruise
OBJECT CLASSES	**SurveyInfo** is an object class designed for storing information about a specific survey.		
	Notes		
	Fields	SurveyID	A key field for relating this table to a feature class
		StartDate	The beginning date of the survey
		EndDate	The ending date of the survey
		Description	A general description of the survey
		DeviceID	A key field for relating a survey with a Measuring device
		TrackID	A key field for relating a survey with a Track
	Measurement is an object class designed for extending a single feature with multiple depths.		
	Notes	Measurements are designed for storing multiple depths for a single feature. This is done by creating a new and unique identifier for the feature—in this case MeasurementID—for every unique combination of FeatureID and ZLocation. In this table, FeatureID is repeated for every depth (ZLocation) associated with the feature.	
	Fields	MeasurementID	A unique identifier for the feature created by combining unique combinations of FeatureID and ZLocation
		FeatureID	A key field relating to the FeatureID of the feature
		FeatureClass	The name of the feature class that the relating feature participates in
		ZLocation	The value representing the depth being associated with the feature
		XLocation	The x-coordinate of the feature for the given depth
		YLocation	The y-coordinate of the feature for the given depth

41

OBJECT CLASSES (cont'd)	**Cruise** is an object class that stores the characteristics of a ship for the duration of an expedition.		
	Notes		
	Fields	CruiseID	An identifier for a given cruise
		Code	A user-defined code for a given cruise
		Name	The name of the cruise
		Purpose	The purpose of the cruise
		Status	Defines the status of the cruise
		Description	A general description of the cruise
		StartDate	The beginning time stamp for the cruise
		EndDate	The ending time stamp for the cruise
		ShipName	The name of the ship participating in the cruise
	MeasuredData is an object class that stores recorded values for a given parameter.		
	Notes		
	Fields	MeasurementID	A key field for relating this table to the Measurement table
		ParameterID	A key field for relating this table to the Parameter table
		DeviceID	A key field for relating this table to the MeasuringDevice table
		DataValue	The recorded value
	MeasuringDevice is an object class that stores information pertaining to the device taking the measurements.		
	Notes		
	Fields	DeviceID	A key field for relating this table to either another table or feature class
		Name	The name of the measuring device
		Description	A description of the measuring device
		VehicleID	A key field relating this table to the Vehicles table
	Parameter is an object class that stores information about the parameters being measured.		
	Notes	This table can be used as a mechanism for querying a geodatabase for a specific parameter and then finding values of a particular type in related tables or as a lookup table of parameter types for a particular value.	
	Fields	ParameterID	The unique identifier of a specific parameter
		Name	The name of a parameter
		Description	The description of a parameter
		Quantity	The quantity type for a parameter. This is solved by the use of a coded value domain: 1 = Other 2 = Scalar 3 = Vector
		Unit	The unit of measure for a parameter
		Significant Digits	The number of significant digits defining the precision of this parameter

RELATIONSHIPS	CruiseHasTracks	1 : *	One Cruise can have zero or many Tracks
	SurveyInfoHasPoints	1 : *	One Survey can have zero or many points
	MeasurementHasData	1 : *	One Measurement can have zero or many MeasuredData values
	MeasuringDeviceHasData	1 : *	One MeasuringDevice can have zero or many MeasuredData values
	ParameterHasData	1 : *	One Parameter can have zero or many MeasuredData values

References

Andrews, B. 2005. Geologic seafloor mapping using the Arc Marine Data Model. *Proceedings of the ESRI International User Conference 25*, Map Gallery Poster, http://dusk.geo.orst.edu/djl/arcgis/docs/AdrewsUSGSPoster_ESRI_UC_05.pdf.

Andrews, B., and S. Ackerman. 2004. Geologic seafloor mapping: Marine Data Model case study. *Proceedings of the ESRI International User Conference 24*, Abstract 1877. http://gis.esri.com/library/userconf/index.html.

Barnhardt, W. A., B. D. Andrews, and B. Butman. 2005. *High-resolution geologic mapping of the inner continental shelf: Nahant to Gloucester, Massachusetts.* U.S. Geological Survey Open-File Report, 2005-1293. Woods Hole, Mass.: USGS Woods Hole Science Center.

Greene, G. H., J. J. Bizarro, J. E. Tilden, H. L. Lopez, and M. D. Erdey. 2005. The benefits and pitfalls of geographic information systems in marine benthic habitat mapping. In *Place matters: Geospatial tools for marine science, conservation and management in the Pacific Northwest,* ed. D. J. Wright and A. J. Scholz, 34–47. Corvallis, Ore.: Oregon State University Press.

Jenkins, C. J. 2004. *Report for the U.S. Geological Survey & University of Colorado Collaboration in usSEABED-dbSEABED: 2003–4.* Boulder, Colo.: Institute for Arctic and Alpine Research (INSTAAR) Technical Report. http://instaar.colorado.edu/~jenkinsc/dbseabed/.

Kindinger, J. L. 2000. *Subsidence and sea-level rise in southeast Louisiana: Implications for coastal management and restoration.* U.S. Geological Survey Open-File Report, 00–132. St. Petersburg, Fla.: USGS Center for Coastal & Watershed Studies.

Niedoroda, A. W., L. Hatchett, and J. Donoghue. 2004. *Reconnaissance level regional sand search of the Florida Panhandle.* Tallahassee, Fla.: URS Corporation unpublished consulting report. http://ross.urs-tally.com/reports.asp.

Reid, J. A., C. J. Jenkins, M. E. Field, J. V. Gardner, M. Zimmermann, C. E. Box, and T. A. Kneeshaw. 2001. usSEABED: Database efforts in marine surficial sediments of the US EEZ. *Eos, Transactions of the American Geophysical Union* 82(47), Fall Meeting Supplement: F593.

Wilson, R. W., and D. Gesch. 2004. Merging bathymetric-topographic data to common vertical datum for Louisiana. *Proceedings of the ESRI International User Conference* 24, Abstract 2065. http://gis.esri.com/library/userconf/index.html.

Chapter acknowledgments

Dawn Wright, Oregon State University

Michael Blongewicz, DHI Water & Environment

Brian Andrews, USGS Woods Hole Science Center for Coastal and Marine Geology, Woods Hole, Massachusetts—Geologic Seafloor Mapping Case Study

Heather Mounts, Photo Science, Inc., St. Petersburg, Florida—Louisiana Subsidence Case Study

Marine animal data applications

This chapter describes how Arc Marine can be used to associate the movements of various species of marine animals (horizontally on the sea surface and vertically through the water column) with important environmental parameters such as sea surface temperature, chlorophyll a concentration, bathymetry, and coastal geology. Five case studies demonstrate the importance of this association by way of InstantaneousPoints, LocationSeriesPoints, TimeDurationLines, TimeDurationAreas, FeatureAreas, and rasters. The first case study examines the movements of humpback whales in the North Atlantic during summer, while the second examines the impact of the Stellwagen Bank National Marine Sanctuary on humpback whale abundance. The third study examines the migration of loggerhead sea turtles (tracked by satellite transmitters) and its association with surface chlorophyll a concentration off the coast of North Carolina and out into the western Atlantic. The fourth study analyzes the vertical dive profiles of loggerhead turtles in association with deeper chlorophyll a and bathymetry around the Cayman Islands. The final study examines the populations of harbor seals and the locations of where they leave the water (haul-out) onto rock ledges, as a function of time. These case studies rely on the use of the extensive data holdings in the Ocean Biogeographic Information System-Spatial Ecological Analysis of Megavertebrate Populations (OBIS-SEAMAP) and have significant implications, discussed later in this chapter, for marine animal conservation and management.

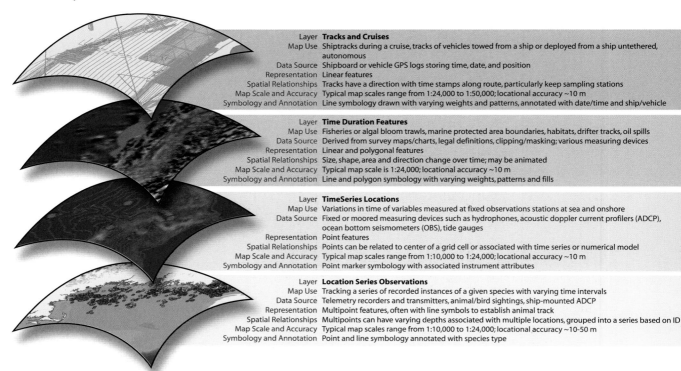

Layer Tracks and Cruises
Map Use Shiptracks during a cruise, tracks of vehicles towed from a ship or deployed from a ship untethered, autonomous
Data Source Shipboard or vehicle GPS logs storing time, date, and position
Representation Linear features
Spatial Relationships Tracks have a direction with time stamps along route, particularly keep sampling stations
Map Scale and Accuracy Typical map scales range from 1:24,000 to 1:50,000; locational accuracy ~10 m
Symbology and Annotation Line symbology drawn with varying weights and patterns, annotated with date/time and ship/vehicle

Layer Time Duration Features
Map Use Fisheries or algal bloom trawls, marine protected area boundaries, habitats, drifter tracks, oil spills
Data Source Derived from survey maps/charts, legal definitions, clipping/masking; various measuring devices
Representation Linear and polygonal features
Spatial Relationships Size, shape, area and direction change over time; may be animated
Map Scale and Accuracy Typical map scale is 1:24,000; locational accuracy ~10 m
Symbology and Annotation Line and polygon symbology with varying weights, patterns and fills

Layer TimeSeries Locations
Map Use Variations in time of variables measured at fixed observations stations at sea and onshore
Data Source Fixed or moored measuring devices such as hydrophones, acoustic doppler current profilers (ADCP), ocean bottom seismometers (OBS), tide gauges
Representation Point features
Spatial Relationships Points can be related to center of a grid cell or associated with time series or numerical model
Map Scale and Accuracy Typical map scales range from 1:10,000 to 1:24,000; locational accuracy ~10 m
Symbology and Annotation Point marker symbology with associated instrument attributes

Layer Location Series Observations
Map Use Tracking a series of recorded instances of a given species with varying time intervals
Data Source Telemetry recorders and transmitters, animal/bird sightings, ship-mounted ADCP
Representation Multipoint features, often with line symbols to establish animal track
Spatial Relationships Multipoints can have varying depths associated with multiple locations, grouped into a series based on ID
Map Scale and Accuracy Typical map scales range from 1:10,000 to 1:24,000; locational accuracy ~10-50 m
Symbology and Annotation Point and line symbology annotated with species type

Introduction

Associating marine animal observations with environmental data is a common practice in conservation research. This approach enables researchers to describe and predict animal habitat based on environmental conditions. The Arc Marine data model framework easily facilitates the linking of environmental data spatially and temporally to other features. Animal observations are often collected concurrent with related data. When dealing with fishery or endangered species issues, it is often useful to relate these observations to permanent or ephemeral political boundaries (e.g., protected areas, temporary closures, oil spills). With the increased availability of remotely sensed data, more biologists and managers are correlating these data sources to animal observations that are coincident in space and time. This has provided an extremely diverse and useful data resource.

This chapter presents research from the Marine Geospatial Ecology Lab of the Nicholas School of the Environment and Earth Sciences at Duke University. Program researchers examined Arc Marine data types relevant to marine animal data applications using data provided through the OBIS-SEAMAP project (Halpin et al. 2006). OBIS-SEAMAP (http://seamap.env.duke.edu/) is an online archive of georeferenced data on marine mammals, seabirds, and sea turtles collected by scientific contributors globally via boat, plane, beach, and telemetry tags. Given the highly migratory nature of these taxa, the time and place of their observation is critical for associating the environmental conditions to describe habitat. Demonstrated below are the visualization and analytical advantages of using specific Arc Marine data types across five case studies: (1) cetacean surveys, (2) marine protected area, (3) sea turtle tagging, (4) sea turtle dive profiles, and (5) seal haul-outs (places where seals leave the water). See table 4.1 for a summary of the data types used per case study. Also important for the case studies are FeatureAreas, which may be used to represent static marine boundaries around marine protected areas (MPAs) or other kinds of restricted areas at sea (figures 4.1a and b).

Case study	Arc Marine data types
1. Cetacean surveys	• InstantaneousPoint: species observations • TimeDurationLines: ship track
2. Marine protected area	• TimeDurationAreas: marine protected area
3. Sea turtle tagging	• LocationSeriesPoint: individual animal locations • TimeDurationLines: animal track
4. Sea turtle dive profiles	• LocationSeriesPoint with z-value: individual animal locations at depth
5. Seal haul-outs	• TimeSeriesPoint: animal haul-out ledges

Table 4.1   Arc Marine data types implemented by case study.

Common Marine Data Types

Marine Points
Instantaneous Points

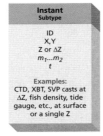

Instant
Subtype

ID
X,Y
Z or ΔZ
$m_1...m_2$
t

Examples:
CTD, XBT, SVP casts at
ΔZ, fish density, tide
gauge, etc., at surface
or a single Z

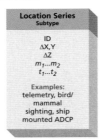

Location Series
Subtype

ID
$\Delta X,Y$
ΔZ
$m_1...m_2$
$t_1...t_2$

Examples:
telemetry, bird/
mammal
sighting, ship
mounted ADCP

Marine Lines

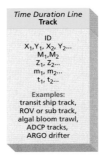

Time Duration Line
Track

ID
$X_1,Y_1, X_2, Y_2...$
M_1,M_2
$Z_1, Z_2...$
$m_1, m_2...$
$t_1, t_2...$

Examples:
transit ship track,
ROV or sub track,
algal bloom trawl,
ADCP tracks,
ARGO drifter

Marine Rasters/Grids/Meshes

**Regularly
Interpolated
Surfaces**

$row_1, col_1... row_n, col_n$
$Z_{r,c1}...Z_{r,c,n}$
multipoint

Examples:
multibeam bathy,
sidescan, lidar,
SST, climatology,
scientific mesh,
"re-analyzed"
products
(images such as
GeoTIFF, BIL, etc.)

a

Figure 4.1a and b Portions of the main Common Marine Data Types diagram (from chapter 2) representing the various combinations of marine data types as explained in the case studies below. Headings in italics are abstract feature classes in Arc Marine. All other headings are feature classes or subtypes of feature classes.

A series of points

As initially described in the discussion of marine surveys in chapter 3, Arc Marine presents a hierarchical structure for organizing the various feature classes, with MarineFeature being atop the hierarchical structure from which three abstract subclasses, MarinePoint, MarineLine, and MarineArea, inherit. The use of feature classes from each of these is described below.

This chapter looks at another implementation of the InstantaneousPoint feature class, which inherits from the superclass MarinePoint. The LocationSeries subtype of the InstantaneousPoint feature class is designed for representing features where the x- and

Common Marine Data Types

Marine Points

Time Series Point

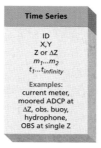

Marine Areas

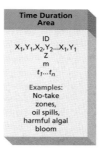

b

y-coordinates of the feature changes for different time stamps. Specifically, it is meant to be applied to the tracking of marine animals, where the animal is the feature being tracked but obviously is not fixed at a single location. Rather, the movement of the animal is being recorded with the use of telemetry over a long duration of time, and each recording includes a new x- and y-coordinate—a new point feature and time stamp. The InstantaneousPoint feature class provides the attribute TimeValue for recording the time stamp of when the location is being recorded. It is the combination of TimeValue plus the x- and y-coordinates that denotes the unique feature. The ZValue attribute allows for the storage of a single depth, the sea surface, for example. The SurveyID attribute is a key field used in the relationship class SurveyInfoHasPoints to link the features of this feature class with the SurveyInfo object class and in essence is a unique survey. The SeriesID is a key field provided to construct a relationship between the features of InstantaneousPoint with a row in the object class Series. The PointType attribute is the subtype attribute denoting the type of InstantaneousPoint. For the LocationSeries subtype, this value is set to 4.

One of the principal concepts introduced by the LocationSeries subtype is that many instances of the feature class represent the same object—marine animal, in this case. To track or group the multiple instances of a specific animal being added to the Instantaneous-Point feature class, a mechanism was required to support the identification of the points that were essentially the same animal or to thematically group like features. In Arc Marine, this mechanism is the Series object class. The case studies presented in this chapter note that researchers use this to track several sightings of an individual animal.

The Series object class is a simple table containing only the SeriesID attribute. This attribute is the key field for linking the Series object class to any other feature class that implements that attribute. Given that each new sighting is recorded with a new x- and y-coordinate and time stamp, through the SeriesID that unique animal can be identified, and all of its sightings can be mapped accordingly. Currently in Arc Marine, this includes the InstantaneousPoint and TimeDurationArea feature classes. Although a relationship class has not been added to Arc Marine, the structure for establishing a relationship is in place in that both classes have the SeriesID attribute. Users can easily extend the Series class to store the attributes necessary for grouping the features. Additionally, since the SeriesID attribute is included in the InstantaneousPoint feature class, Arc Marine does not limit the use of this to the LocationSeries subtypes.

Tracks and cruises

This chapter also looks at the use of the TimeDurationLine feature class. TimeDurationLine is never instantiated in a geodatabase but rather is an abstract subclass of MarineLine. TimeDurationLine is designed for features where data values along the line would change over time. The TimeDurationLine feature class introduces four attributes in addition to the FeatureID and FeatureCode inherited from the MarineFeature superclass. The StartDate attribute denotes the time stamp for the beginning of the line, whereas the attribute End-Date denotes the time stamp for the end of the line. The next two attributes, VehicleID and CruiseID, are key fields for linking this feature class to their respective object classes.

The TimeDurationLine has one instantiable subclass called Track, which was initially introduced in chapter 3. In the Track feature class, the properties HasZ and HasM have been implemented so that the linear feature could have varying depths (ZValues) along the line. Furthermore, the HasM property provides for the feature having a linear measurement system along the feature. In this case, the units of the linear measurement system would be based on time, and the StartDate and EndDate attributes inherited from TimeDurationLine define the extent of the measurement system. Consequently, locations along the line can be interpolated based on a time stamp between the time extent. Track introduces several new attributes in addition to those inherited from the TimeDurationLine class. A complete description of those can be found in chapter 3.

An accompanying object class of the Track feature class is Cruise, which was also introduced in chapter 3. Cruise defines an expedition, which contains one or more instances of Track and is connected to Track through the CruiseHasTracks relationship class. The CruiseHas-Tracks relationship is a one-to-many and uses the CruiseID from the Cruise object class as the origin field and the CruiseID that Track inherits from TimeDurationLine as the destination field. The Cruise object class also delivers several additional fields for describing a given cruise.

Area features

MarineArea, as with MarineLine and MarinePoint, also inherits from the superclass MarineFeature, acquiring the FeatureID and FeatureCode attributes. MarineArea is an abstract class for the purpose of organizing the area feature classes. Two subclasses to MarineArea delivered in Arc Marine can be instantiated: FeatureArea and TimeDurationArea.

FeatureArea is a simple polygon feature class for the purpose of adding feature classes that represent physical features that can be represented with polygonal geometry. FeatureArea adds no new attributes in addition to the FeatureID and FeatureCode inherited from MarineArea. FeatureArea is dealt with extensively in chapter 6.

The TimeDurationArea feature class is also a subclass of MarineArea that can be instantiated. This feature class is designed to hold polygonal features whose geometry changes over time. The concept behind TimeDurationArea is similar to the LocationSeries subtype of the InstantaneousPoint feature class. The concept involves a polygonal feature changing shape, requiring new geometry and new instances in the feature class at various time steps, while still representing the same feature. This is also similar to the ESRI coverage data structure implementation of regions, which allows for a thematic grouping of multiple polygons into a collection that can be referenced by a single attribute. Consequently, TimeDurationArea uses the Series table for collecting similar features through the use of the SeriesID. TimeDurationArea adds the attribute SeriesID as a key field for relating to the Series object class, along with StartDate (the beginning time stamp for a given feature) and EndDate (the ending time stamp for a given feature). Some applications may require one or both of the date fields.

A simple example to illustrate the use of the TimeDurationArea feature class along with the Series table is the example of an oil spill. A polygon represents the boundary of the oil spill and denotes the feature at a given point in time. The boundary has a specific geometry, and the StartDate is populated with a time stamp (not all applications will use the StartDate and the EndDate). At a point in time in the future, the geometry denoting the boundary of the oil spill will change, the time stamp will be recorded, and a new record or feature will be added to the TimeDurationArea feature class. This process is repeated multiple times in the future, with each instance receiving new polygonal geometry and a time stamp. The mechanism for identifying the polygons as being from the same oil spill is the Series table (figure 4.1a and b). Each of the instances added to TimeDurationArea also receive the same value for the SeriesID attribute. The Series table serves as a lookup table, defining the attributes of the feature that the many polygons represent.

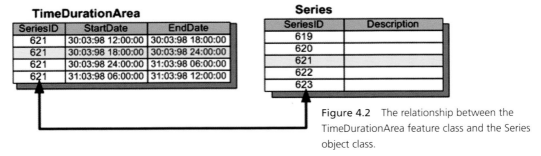

Figure 4.2 The relationship between the TimeDurationArea feature class and the Series object class.

Featured case studies

Cetacean surveys

Introduction: This case study correlated environmental data with observations of marine mammals during boat and aerial surveys. The relationship between animals and their environment provides critical knowledge to inform key conservation issues such as assessment of potential anthropogenic impacts and improved marine protected area design (Hooker et al. 1999; Hyrenbach et al. 2000). In particular, the study found sea surface temperature (SST) a useful variable in defining the limits of a species range (Mikol 1997) and in delineating marine protected area boundaries (Hyrenbach et al. 2000). More specifically, this case study investigated observations of humpback whales *(Megaptera novaeangliae)* in the North Atlantic during summer to identify the range of SSTs where the mammals are found. The humpback whale migrates to feeding grounds in high-latitude waters in summer (Mackintosh 1965). Predicting species habitat is complicated and beyond the scope of this book. However, the general environmental envelope of the species (Walker and Cocks 1991) can be quantified simply.

Data: The National Oceanic and Atmospheric Administration Northeast Fisheries Science Center (NOAA NEFSC) conducted 13 shipboard and aerial surveys from 1991 to 2002 in U.S. waters in the northern Atlantic. The surveys have been archived at OBIS-SEAMAP (figure 4.3). The surveys primarily wanted to estimate abundance of cetacean species. The NEFSC datasets contain 6,477 cetacean observations from 1991 to 2002, including 188 humpback whale sightings. Each set of the sightings for a specific month and year is synchronized with the remotely sensed SST image for that month and year. The values from the SST data layer are then sampled at each of the sighting locations. This process is repeated across all months and years. Maximum and minimum temperature values define the thermal envelope for humpback whales in the northeast Atlantic.

Each dataset produces cetacean sighting data along with locations of the ships/aircraft. Cetacean sightings are point events with location and time. They also include identification of species sighted and number observed. In OBIS-SEAMAP, species are coded with

1 - 13 out of 13 datasets found						birds	mammals	turtles
Datasets are grouped by source organization in alphabetic order. Click provider name to expand/hide datasets of the provider. Collapse all				years				
dataset name	map	platform	effort	begin	end	birds	mammals	turtles
NOAA Northeast Fisheries Science Center (NEFSC)								
NEFSC 1992 aj9201		boat	yes	1992	1992		1238	1
NEFSC 1995 AJ9501 (Part I)		boat	yes	1995	1995		150	
NEFSC 1995 AJ9501 (Part II)		boat	yes	1995	1995		1401	
NEFSC 1995 pe9501		boat	yes	1995	1995		433	7
NEFSC 1999 aj9902		boat	yes	1999	1999		1021	5
NEFSC Aerial Survey - Experimental 2002		plane	yes	2002	2002		332	7
NEFSC Aerial Survey - Summer 1995		plane	yes	1995	1995		304	71
NEFSC Aerial Survey - Summer 1998		plane	yes	1998	1998		422	282
NEFSC Harbor Porpoise Survey 1991		boat	yes	1991	1991		770	1
NEFSC Survey 1991		boat	yes	1991	1991		80	
NEFSC Survey 1997		boat	yes	1997	1997		60	
NEFSC Survey 1998 1		boat	yes	1998	1998		492	13
NEFSC Survey 1998 2		boat	yes	1998	1998		309	6

Figure 4.3   Thirteen datasets from NOAA Northeast Fisheries Science Center are registered in OBIS-SEAMAP (http://seamap. env.duke.edu/datasets). The datasets are downloadable in comma-separated values (CSV) format and ESRI shapefiles.

Courtesy of National Marine Fisheries Services.

the taxonomic serial number from the Integrated Taxonomic Information System (http:// www.itis.usda.gov/). The ship and aircraft locations are used to construct track lines. Sea surface temperatures along the ship/aircraft tracks are picked up and summarized to determine if the survey areas—more specifically the linear locations where the ships/aircraft traveled—affected the environmental envelope. All the NEFSC datasets provide survey effort data, which sums up to 1,626.8 effort hours.

Loading data into Arc Marine: Datasets of observations and effort were downloaded from the OBIS-SEAMAP site (http://seamap.env.duke.edu/datasets) in shapefile format. The general information of the NEFSC ship and aerial surveys were stored in an Arc Marine Cruise table. OBIS-SEAMAP distinguishes individual surveys by unique dataset identification numbers, which were used to populate the CruiseID field in the Cruise table. CruiseID became the key to relate the dataset and its observations as well as its ship/aircraft tracks.

The InstantaneousPoint feature class (figure 4.4) represented sighting locations. Researchers loaded the features in the shapefiles into InstantaneousPoint. They recorded dates and times of the sightings in the TimeValue field in InstantaneousPoint.

In Arc Marine, all attributes other than time and location are managed in separate tables. These attributes differ from the simpler data attributes attached to point observations in the shapefiles downloaded from OBIS-SEAMAP. The MarineEvent feature class can be used as an attribute table for InstantaneousPoint. Animal observations from ship/aerial surveys are, however, structurally different from data that MarineEvent was intended to hold. While MarineEvent can hold a single value (in the DataValue field), animal sightings typically include many parameters, such as species identification, animal count, sea state, and others. A survey can also record multiple values for one parameter. For example, it may record animal counts (parameter) based on three different observers or estimated values (e.g., low, high, and best estimate).

Although users can modify the MarineEvent table to better fit animal sightings data, the researchers chose to create a new table. Thus, they created and loaded the Animal-Sightings table with the attributes from the shapefiles. It contains CruiseID, taxonomic serial

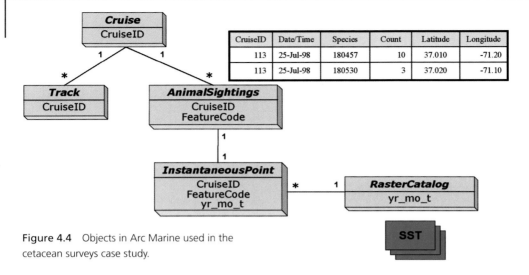

CruiseID	Date/Time	Species	Count	Latitude	Longitude
113	25-Jul-98	180457	10	37.010	-71.20
113	25-Jul-98	180530	3	37.020	-71.10

Figure 4.4 Objects in Arc Marine used in the cetacean surveys case study.

numbers of species sighted, animal counts, and unique ID that distinguishes sightings from multiple datasets. Researchers defined relationship classes to link AnimalSightings to InstantaneousPoint.

Intuitively, ship and aircraft tracks were stored as a Track feature class. Datasets provided by OBIS-SEAMAP are accompanied by polyline shapefiles of the track when available. A Relationship Class was created to link Track to Cruise with CruiseID as a key. Environmental data such as SST is available in various formats from a variety of providers. Fortunately, for well-recognized data such as NOAA/NASA Pathfinder Advanced Very High Resolution Radiometer (AVHRR) Sea Surface Temperature (podaac-www.jpl.nasa.gov/sst/), converters from the original data format to ESRI GRID format are usually available. Once converted to ESRI GRID format, the creation of a raster catalog provided a convenient way to store these datasets in Arc Marine. A raster catalog can be related to objects in a geodatabase, allowing users to select one of the raster layers based on currently selected vector features. For example, a relationship class would allow users to select an SST layer in the catalog corresponding to point sightings in a specific month and year.

This case study used monthly sea surface temperature images that were compiled in a raster catalog. To create a relationship in general, it is advisable to add a new field that has key values pointing to the raster catalog and the related object (AnimalSightings in this case). In this study, a field holding year and month (e.g., 2001/07) was added to match sightings with monthly SST layers. The relationship class allows users to select an SST layer in the catalog that corresponds to sightings in a specific month and year.

Loading raster images into the raster catalog was straightforward because the layers already existed as ESRI rasters. After loading all the layers into the raster catalog, researchers populated the newly added relationship field with appropriate values. They did this by adding the raster catalog to an ArcMap document and using the Calculate Values function on the field in the attribute table (figure 4.5). They saved the calculation formula for future use.

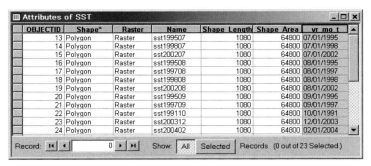

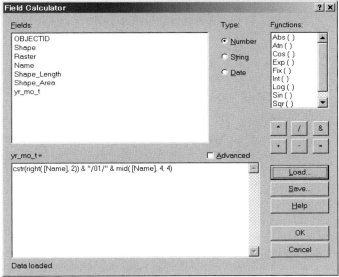

Figure 4.5 Fields can be added to the raster catalog using the Field Calculator as a convenient way to fill in the values. This example shows the added field "yr_mo_t," a key relating SST to InstantaneousPoint.

Analysis with Arc Marine: The NEFSC datasets contain sightings of species (figure 4.6). Thus, the first step of the study was to extract humpback whale sightings. Researchers did this by using Select by Attribute on the AnimalSightings table with the humpback whale's ITIS number (180530) as a criterion. The result was saved as a layer for future use.

A specific month and year was selected from the humpback whale layer (e.g., July 1998). The corresponding SST layer in the catalog was selected by following the relationship class from InstantaneousPoint (in this case, the humpback whale layer) to the SST raster catalog. As spatial analysis tools cannot operate directly on a raster layer in the raster catalog, the layer itself needed to be added to an ArcMap document. Users can do this by specifying the raster name in the following manner: CatalogName\Raster.OBJECTID=xx, where CatalogName is the name of the raster catalog and xx is the ObjectID of the raster layer. The humpback whale and the SST layers were then entered as inputs to the Sample tool to extract SST values where sightings in a specific month and year occurred. Researchers

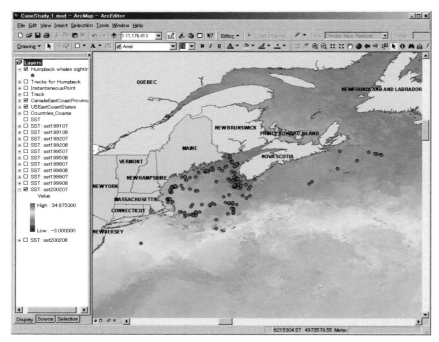

Figure 4.6 Researchers recorded 188 sightings of humpback whales in the NEFSC datasets from 1991 to 2002. The humpback whale sightings were first selected from the AnimalSightings table (not shown on the map) using Select by Attribute, then the selection was linked to InstantaneousPoint via a relationship class.

Courtesy of National Marine Fisheries Services.

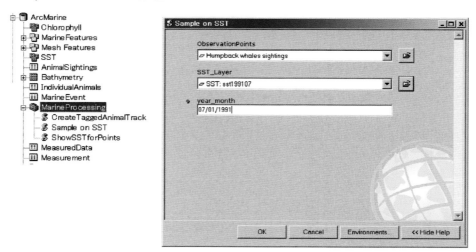

Figure 4.7 ArcToolBox can contain user-defined geoprocessing toolboxes where useful scripts can be added. The script named "Sample on SST" automates filtering of humpback whale sightings by a specified year and month and passes the selection to the Sample tool to obtain the SST in the specified year and month.

saved the results in a table, which contains sighting locations (latitude and longitude) and corresponding sea surface temperature values.

As the procedure described above needed to be repeated for all combinations of month and year, researchers developed a geoprocessing script with the Python scripting language to streamline the procedure (figure 4.7). To make the best use of Arc Marine, a toolbox was created and the script was added as a tool in the toolbox. After repeating the procedure for all combinations of month and year, researchers combined the resulting tables and used the R statistical package to summarize the data.

Researchers sampled sightings and SST along the ship/aircraft surveys in the same way. Starting from the humpback whale layer, which is a subset of the InstantaneousPoint, they used relationship classes to identify the cruises in which humpback whales were sighted. Cruise table has a relationship to Track, so it was straightforward to select ship/aircraft tracks for the cruises selected (figure 4.8). The selected tracklines were buffered with an arbitrarily determined strip width of 1 km. For each combination of year and month, the tracklines were further filtered with the year and month and overlaid on the corresponding SST layer. The Zonal Statistics as Table tool was used to calculate statistics of the SST layer where it was traversed by the buffered trackline polygon.

Results: Humpback whales were observed during the summer months of July and August in 1991, 1992, 1995, 1998, 1999, and 2002. Latitudes of observations ranged from 39.7 to 44.9 degrees north. Excluding exceptional values in August 1992 and July 1995, the mean sea surface temperature ranged from 11.8°C to 16.8°C (table 4.2 and figure 4.9). The SST along the ship/aircraft tracklines ranged from 2.8°C to 27.7°C. A closer look reveals that the humpback whale was never sighted where the water temperature was above 23.2°C

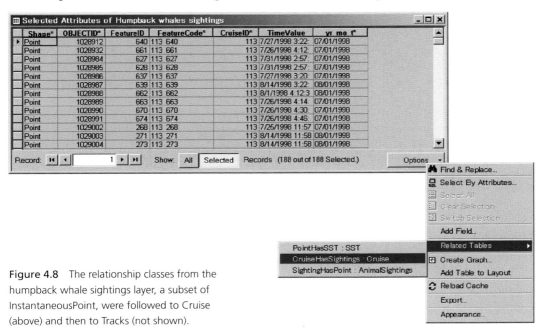

Figure 4.8   The relationship classes from the humpback whale sightings layer, a subset of InstantaneousPoint, were followed to Cruise (above) and then to Tracks (not shown).

		'91/07	'91/08	'92/07	'92/08	'95/07	'95/08	'98/07	'98/08	'99/07	'99/08	'02/07	'02/08
Whales	Mean	12.07	13.84	11.77	10.42	23.17	15.12	16.84	16.51	13.84	14.44	15.70	15.67
	Standard error	0.19	0.62	0.00	1.70	0.00	0.68	0.30	0.70	0.86	0.29	0.62	0.00
	Minimum	11.85	10.87	11.77	7.50	23.17	9.67	13.20	10.42	12.97	10.95	8.10	15.67
	Maximum	12.45	16.05	11.77	14.85	23.17	19.35	18.82	19.95	14.70	18.97	18.67	15.67
	Count	3	7	1	5	1	27	29	16	2	36	15	2
	Confidence level (95.0%)	0.81	1.51	N/A	4.73	N/A	1.41	0.61	1.48	10.99	0.59	1.32	0.00
Tracks	Mean	11.61	13.40	11.89	13.86	24.28	17.76	19.11	16.38	14.15	14.63	18.07	15.07
	Standard error	0.17	0.14	0.27	0.12	0.12	0.12	0.12	0.15	0.31	0.12	0.11	0.20
	Minimum	8.17	-3	9	6.59	18.89	4.57	-3	2.84	12.97	5.77	-3	10.72
	Maximum	16.12	19.27	14.32	17.25	27.67	26.32	25.57	21.75	17.10	18.97	23.62	22.64
	Count	113	277	19	253	255	1183	722	350	15	260	452	111

Table 4.2 Monthly (July and August) summary of sea surface temperature (°C) where humpback whales were sighted and ships/aircraft traveled.

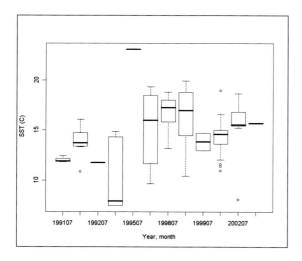

Figure 4.9 Statistical box plot showing monthly SST (°C) where whales were sighted.

(the highest temperature where the whale was sighted is 23.17°C). However, according to a t-test, the mean SST for the sightings was not statistically different from the tracklines, suggesting the environmental envelope found in this study (11.8–16.8°C) was restricted by the areas surveyed.

Discussion: Humpback whales were observed during summer months where water temperatures ranged from 11.8°C to 16.8°C. However, researchers could not conclude that whales do not range in waters beyond this temperature range. Broader areas should be surveyed to answer this question. Humpback whales were never sighted in surface temperature above 23.2°C, whereas the survey tracklines covered waters with surface temperatures up to 27°C. More detailed statistics may suggest that the upper limit of the environmental envelope is about 23°C in summer feeding grounds. The environmental envelope is defined with various variables. For example, the water depth can be associated with feeding behavior (Sardi et al. 2005). This can be examined by using bathymetry data in place of the SST layers in this case study. Prey such as krill, while more difficult to detect, tends to be a strong predictor of habitat (Bryant et al. 1981).

To make analytical processes simple and focus the reader's attention on Arc Marine, this case study used "raw" SST images, which can contain inaccurate values due to cloud cover. For example, three of the year-and-month combinations reported -3°C as a minimum water temperature for tracklines, which should have been eliminated before the analysis. For more accurate analyses, appropriate quality control procedures should be taken.

Marine protected area

Introduction: This example is similar to the cetacean survey case study with the addition of the TimeDurationArea feature class, representing a dynamic marine sanctuary boundary. The study aimed to examine the impact of a marine sanctuary on cetacean abundance. This kind of study can be used to evaluate marine protected areas.

Data: The case study focuses on Stellwagen Bank National Marine Sanctuary. The sanctuary, covering more than 800 square miles in Massachusetts Bay, was established in 1992 (http://stellwagen.noaa.gov/). Endangered right whales, humpback whales, and many other cetaceans frequent the sanctuary, making it one of the top 10 whale-watching sites in the world, according to World Wildlife Fund (Hoyt 1991). Researchers obtained the sanctuary boundary as a polygon shapefile from the NOAA National Marine Sanctuaries Web site (http://sanctuaries.noaa.gov/).

Researchers first extracted from the shapefile the cetacean sightings and ship/aerial survey tracks that occurred within the boundaries of the sanctuary. The sightings and tracks were further divided into those that occurred before and after the designation of the sanctuary. Next, researchers calculated the total number of sightings and observation effort hours before and after the sanctuary was designated. Comparison of sighting counts per hour before and after the sanctuary establishment gives a rough estimate of the effectiveness of the sanctuary in marine mammal abundance.

Loading data into Arc Marine: Loading of the NEFSC marine mammals observations into Arc Marine is described in the first case study with cetacean surveys. Since this second case study focuses on the species abundance before and after the sanctuary establishment, the sanctuary is considered to be an object that turns on and off over time (it is initially off and then turns on once the sanctuary is designated). This type of feature can be stored as a TimeDurationArea (figure 4.10).

It is good practice to create a new feature class for each time-area closure because of the potential for thematically different time sensitive features (e.g., sanctuaries and fishery closures function differently and will have different attributes). Researchers created a new MarineSanctuaries feature class for this case study and inherited properties from

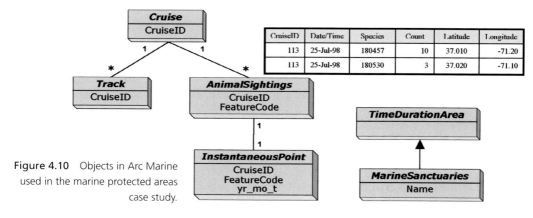

Figure 4.10 Objects in Arc Marine used in the marine protected areas case study.

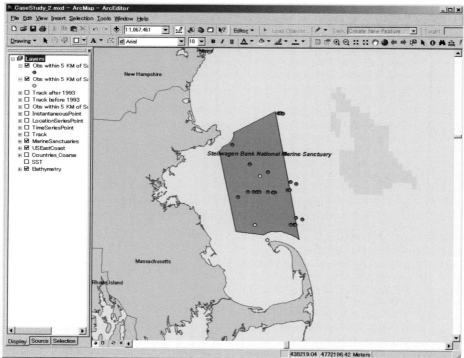

Figure 4.11 Spatial query allows the user to filter the sighting points that fall in the sanctuary boundary (blue polygon). Case study 2 arbitrarily designated a 5-km buffer, assuming animals in the buffer would occur in the sanctuary. The filtered sightings were split into those dated either before (yellow dots) or after (red dots) the sanctuary was established. The results were saved as separate layers.

Courtesy of National Marine Fisheries Services.

TimeDurationArea, with a new field added to hold sanctuary names. Only one polygon was loaded in to the class representing the boundary of Stellwagen Bank National Marine Sanctuary, though it could contain the boundaries of more than one sanctuary.

Analysis with Arc Marine: The NEFSC datasets contained observations encompassing much of the U.S. North Atlantic. Researchers first extracted the sightings that fell in the boundary of the sanctuary (figure 4.11). This was done by spatial query on MarineSanctuaries and InstantaneousPoint. The resulting selection was split into those dated before and after the establishment of the sanctuary. The two selections were saved as separate layers. The observation datasets associated with the selected points (species and count) were found using a relationship class, which extracted related rows from AnimalSightings. This process was repeated for observation points before and after the sanctuary establishment. The resulting sighting datasets were exported to a file in CSV format for later calculation.

To calculate sighting rates, ship/aircraft tracklines were imported as a Track feature class and related to the AnimalSightings table via the Cruise table (see first case study). Observations were matched with AnimalSightings and the appropriate cruises and tracklines were identified, following the relationship class. Since this process brought up all the tracks for the cruises, they needed to be constrained to those that passed the sanctuary boundary (figure 4.12). This query was similar to the process used to select InstantaneousPoint data falling within the sanctuary. Next, the effort hours were determined by calculating the difference between StartDate and EndDate in Track. Observation counts were the number of rows in the selection by species. Observation rates were obtained by dividing the counts by hours of effort.

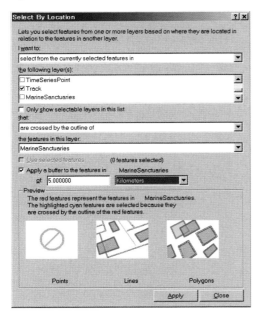

Figure 4.12   After following the relationship classes from AnimalSightings to Cruise to Track, a spatial query extracted the tracks passing over the sanctuary boundary.

Before				After			
Species	**Sightings**	**Animals**	**Sighting/hour**	**Species**	**Sightings**	**Animals**	**Sighting/hour**
Fin whale	1	1	0.5128	Fin whale	1	1	0.2474
Humpback whale	1	1	0.5128	Fin/Sei whale	1	1	0.2474
Unidentified large whale	1	1	0.5128	Humpback whale	12	22	2.9693
All cetacean	3	3	1.5384	Minke whale	2	3	0.4949
				Unidentified large whale	2	2	0.4949
				White-sided dolphin	4	86	0.9898
				All cetacean	22	115	5.4437

Table 4.3   Sighting rates of cetaceans before and after the establishment of the sanctuary.

Results: Overall, 1.95 hours of effort were reported before designation of the sanctuary in 1992, with three whale species sighted during that time, yielding an observation rate of 1.5 per hour (table 4.3). A total of 4.04 hours of effort were reported after the establishment of the sanctuary with 22 cetacean species observed for a rate of 5.4 observations per hour. In particular, the endangered humpback whale (*Megaptera novaeangliae*) exhibited a much higher observation rate after the sanctuary was established. By contrast, the observation rate for the fin whale (*Balaenoptera physalus*), another endangered species in this area, exhibited no increase.

Discussion: Due to the deficiency of the sightings before the establishment of the sanctuary, the direct comparison of the sighting rates before and after the event is not statistically relevant. Only 1.95 effort hours occurred before the event, and those are concentrated in October, when migratory species such as humpback whales may have left the area for wintering areas to the south. On the other hand, the sightings after the event were recorded during summer surveys (July and August), when the humpback whale is likely to be more abundant, with two exceptions sighted in early September.

Prey productivity affects humpback whale abundance, which was reported to have increased dramatically during 1992–93 in the northern Gulf of Maine. Fewer whales were found nearshore, but larger herring stocks were found offshore (Blaylock et al. 1995). Further analysis should help to explain these anomalous events.

Sea turtle tagging

Introduction: Researchers from the Duke University Marine Laboratory, in cooperation with the NOAA Southeast Fisheries Science Center (SEFSC), are studying interactions between sea turtles and commercial fisheries in North Carolina by tracking sea turtles using satellite transmitters (Read et al. 2004). Transmitter data is archived at OBIS-SEAMAP (http://seamap.env.duke.edu/datasets/detail/316), including location data for 6 green (*Chelonia mydas*) and 19 loggerhead (*Caretta caretta*) sea turtles from October 2003 to May 2006.

Loggerhead turtles migrate long distances between their natal beaches and oceanic habitats. However, their behaviors and habitats used in pelagic regions are not well known (Polovina et al. 2004). It is generally believed that juveniles forage mainly in the open ocean, while large adults forage in coastal waters, with a few exceptions (Hawkes et al. 2006). This case study examines the migration of two satellite tagged loggerhead turtles and their relation to remotely sensed chlorophyll *a* concentration. Chlorophyll *a* is a potential indicator of loggerhead prey abundance (Polovina et al. 2004).

Data: Of 19 loggerhead turtles whose locations were recorded in the Duke University Marine Laboratory dataset, two were selected for the study, one of which mainly stayed in the coastal region off North Carolina, while the other migrated into pelagic waters. Chlorophyll *a* concentration datasets used in the study were obtained from the Sea-viewing Wide Field-of-view Sensor (SeaWiFS, NASA Goddard Space Flight Center). The turtle locations were grouped on a monthly basis and each group overlain with the chlorophyll *a* concentration image for that month. The concentration values underlying the turtle locations were sampled and summarized.

Loading data into Arc Marine: Each tagged animal had a number of associated characteristics such as nickname, species, age, size, and gender. This information was stored in a Series table, a template with just two fields defined: OBJECTID and SeriesID. For this case study, researchers created a new table named IndividualAnimals, inheriting from the Series table the generic fields, plus the additional fields of nickname, species, age, size, gender, and taxonomic serial number. LocationSeriesPoint was used for the location data from the tagged animals (figure 4.13). Monthly chlorophyll *a* concentration datasets from SeaWiFS were stored in a raster catalog. See the first case study for more details about the raster catalog and how to load grids.

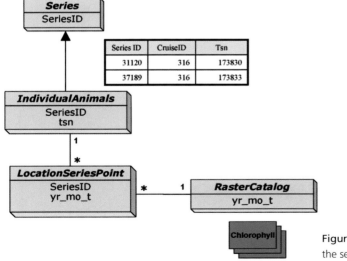

Figure 4.13   Objects in Arc Marine used in the sea turtle tagging case study.

Analysis with Arc Marine: The two study animals were selected from the IndividualAnimals table and linked to all corresponding location data in LocationSeriesPoint using the relationship class. The resulting locations were saved as a layer for later use for each individual animal. Monthly chlorophyll *a* concentration images were added to an ArcMap document for all corresponding month and year combinations for each individual turtle. The location data and chlorophyll image were entered as inputs to the Zonal Statistics as Table tool to summarize the chlorophyll *a* concentration values coincident with each location. This process was repeated for all combinations of year and month for both turtles. The results were combined in a spreadsheet in order to compare and contrast data related to coastal and oceanic movements.

Results: The loggerhead turtle that migrated to pelagic waters traveled more than 1,500 km away from its release location near the Outer Banks, North Carolina. It started its journey in October 2003 and reached the furthest point in April 2005 (figure 4.14). It returned to coastal waters in May 2005. As the turtle migrated from the coastal region to pelagic waters, the mean chlorophyll *a* concentration decreased from 0.94 mg/m^3 in October to 0.21 mg/m^3 in February.

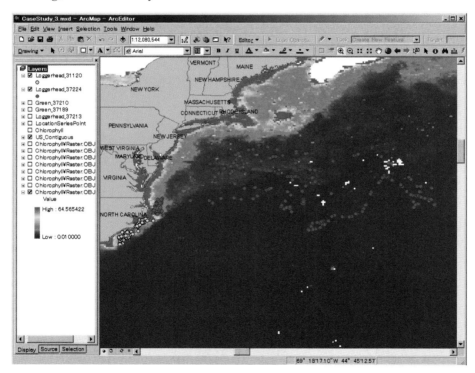

Figure 4.14   Basemap of the sea turtle tagging case study showing the movements of two loggerheads, one of which migrated to oceanic regions (red dots) and the other staying in coastal regions (yellow dots). Chlorophyll *a* concentration image for October 2003 is shown as an underlay.

Data courtesy of Catherine McClellan, Duke University Marine Lab.

Day	Deepest Dive	Bathymetry	Chlorophyll
2004/06/23	26	-3,388.50	0.09
2004/06/24	30	-4,644.00	0.09
2004/06/25	72	-4,763.66	0.08
2004/06/26	72	-5,452.50	0.09
2004/06/27	36	-5,395.25	0.11
2004/06/28	44	-2,526.00	0.07
2004/06/29	52	-2,365.00	0.1
2004/06/30	72	-2,980.00	0.1
2004/07/01	88	-3,499.71	0.07
2004/07/02	104	-2,009.66	0.07
2004/07/03	30	-1.00	
2004/07/05	10	-1.00	0.06
2004/07/06	10		
2004/07/07	10	-82.00	0.07
2004/07/08	10	-201.00	
2004/07/09	10	2.50	0.07
2004/07/10	10	-37.66	0.06
2004/07/11	5	4.00	0.04
2004/07/12	26	-1,214.00	0.09
2004/07/14	30	-2,968.50	0.06
2004/07/15	52	-2,899.66	0.05
2004/07/16	30	-2,627.66	0.06
2004/07/17	60	-2,878.50	0.08

Table 4.4 Summary of chlorophyll *a* concentrations on a monthly basis for the two loggerhead turtles. P-values of t-test between mean concentrations for oceanic and coastal loggerheads are also shown.

The loggerhead using only coastal waters remained within 80 km of the coastline near the Outer Banks during fall and traveled south during the winter. The sampled chlorophyll concentrations spanned a relatively small range from 0.47 to 0.66 mg/m^3 (table 4.4), with the higher mean chlorophyll *a* concentrations occurring during October and November 2003. Monthly mean chlorophyll *a* concentration was significantly different between coastal and pelagic loggerhead locations from winter to spring (p-values: 0.001, 0.012, 0.043, and 0.020 from December to April, respectively).

Discussion: The chlorophyll *a* concentration in the Mid-Atlantic Bight (MAB) has a clear annual cycle with higher concentration in winter and lower concentration in summer (Yoder et al. 2001). Although the coastal loggerhead in this study stayed south of MAB, assuming that the trend of chlorophyll *a* concentration in MAB is applied to the water off Outer Banks, it is speculated that the animal left the region when the concentration lowered in spring to a place with higher concentration. However, an additional examination indicated that the concentration off the Outer Banks in spring and in the area where the animal stayed in spring were not different enough to prove this speculation (0.72 mg/m^3 in south of Outer Banks and 0.70 mg/m^3 off Outer Banks in February 2004).

The oceanic loggerhead foraged under lower chlorophyll *a* concentration than the coastal loggerhead. This observation is not inconsistent with the life history characteristics of the loggerhead whereby young loggerheads mainly eat prey floating on sea surface (Polovina et al. 2004; Hawkes et al. 2006). SST provides another variable potentially influencing turtle movements (Polovina et al. 2004). The association of turtle movements with SST can be analyzed with Arc Marine in a similar manner to this case study (see also the first case study in this chapter).

Sea turtle dive profiles

Introduction: This case study examined dive profile data obtained from a loggerhead sea turtle outfitted with a data-relay satellite transmitter. Attention is focused on the association between the dive profile and surrounding environmental data, including bathymetry and chlorophyll *a* concentration.

When Christopher Columbus discovered the Cayman Islands in 1503, the sea turtle population was estimated at more than 6.5 million turtles, and turtle fishing ("turtling") came to form the basis of the economy and culture of the Cayman Islands. By the beginning of the nineteenth century, however, commercial exploitation had driven the sea turtle nesting population in the Cayman Islands to the brink of extinction. Turtles do still come to the islands to nest (Aiken et al. 2001), and waters around the islands serve as important feeding grounds for green *(Chelonia mydas)* and hawksbill *(Eretmochelys imbricata)* sea turtles.

Several conservation efforts have been put into effect recently on the islands. For example, with the help of schools and the local community, the Cayman Islands Department of Environment and the Marine Turtle Research Group (http://www.seaturtle.org/mtrg/) have begun a satellite telemetry project to track sea turtles. It is vital to understand the ecology of sea turtles for better conservation management. Many studies have been conducted regarding migration, feeding, and diving of sea turtles worldwide (Whiting and Miller 1998; Polovina et al. 2004; Hawkes et al. 2006).

Data: The telemetry data of sea turtles foraging around the Cayman Islands is registered in and downloadable from OBIS-SEAMAP (http://seamap.env.duke.edu/datasets/detail/350). Of the five sea turtles returned from the query (loggerhead and green sea turtles), a loggerhead for which a complete dive profile was available was chosen for the study. Dive profile data is not, however, publicly available from OBIS-SEAMAP at this time. Turtle locations obtained from the satellite transmitter were mapped and the dive profile (depth) was used to visualize movements in three-dimensional (3D) space in the ArcGlobe application in ArcGIS 3D Analyst.

Two environmental datasets were compared to the dive profile data. Monthly chlorophyll *a* concentration datasets used in the study were obtained from SeaWiFS. Bathymetry datasets were obtained from the 2-minute Gridded Global Relief Data (ETOPO2; U.S. Department of Commerce, NOAA, National Geophysical Data Center, 2001). These environmental datasets were sampled at turtle locations and their values summarized by date. The dive profile was also used to calculate daily maximum dive depth. Depth was compared with summarized environmental data to find any potential relationships.

Loading data into Arc Marine: Locations from the tagged loggerhead were loaded into LocationSeriesPoint as described in the previous case study. The only difference was that a new field, ZValue, was added to LocationSeriesPoint to hold the dive depth. Bathymetry and monthly chlorophyll *a* concentrations for June and July 2004 were added to Arc Marine as rasters (figure 4.15).

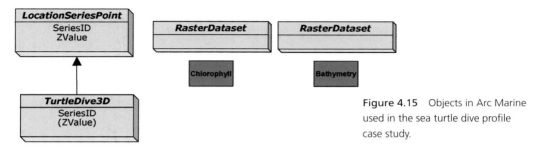

Figure 4.15   Objects in Arc Marine used in the sea turtle dive profile case study.

Although not essential to the analysis, visualization of the turtle dive in a 3D space offers excellent visual context for researchers and target audiences. For this purpose, researchers used ESRI ArcGlobe, which can take bathymetry data as an input to display the track, with the dive profile in perspective view (figure 4.16). There are two ways to visualize turtle dive data in three dimensions. A simple way is to use the ZValue field in LocationSeriesPoint as bathymetry data. In the Show Properties dialog box for the shapefile in ArcGlobe, go to the Elevation tab, check "Use constant value or expression", and select the ZValue field from the combination box below it. Alternatively, LocationSeriesPoint can be converted to a 3D feature class with the Features to 3D tool available in the 3D Analyst toolbar. In this case, ArcGlobe is able to recognize a 3D feature class and automatically render it as a 3D feature. This case study took the latter approach.

Analysis with Arc Marine: The telemetry data from the tagged loggerhead was available from June 23, 2004, to July 17, 2004 (figure 4.17). The Zonal Statistics as Table tool was used to sample environmental values of the pixels under each turtle location for each environmental data layer, including one bathymetry layer and two monthly chlorophyll *a* layers (June and July 2004). The tool returned minimum, maximum, and mean data values by month. The maximum dive depth by date was calculated from the ZValue field. The results were combined in a tabular format for graphical display.

Results: The loggerhead in this study was tagged on June 28, 2004, and traveled approximately 90 km southeast of Grand Cayman, before turning around and heading back to Grand Cayman Island in a large, interesting loop (figure 4.18). The turtle returned to nest on Grand Cayman on July 3 and spent 10 days near the island before heading

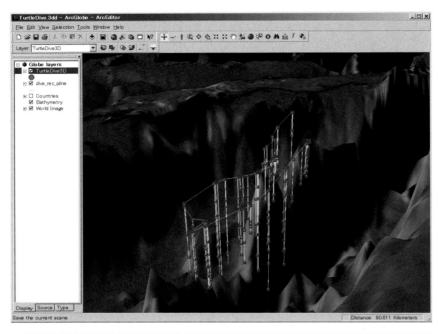

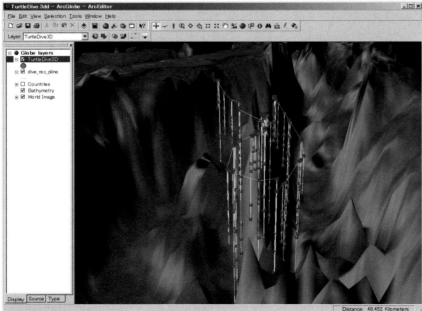

Figure 4.16   Visualization of the turtle dive in 3D ArcGlobe space. LocationSeriesPoints were converted to a 3D feature class, and ETOPO2 grids were used for bathymetry and elevation.

Courtesy of Brendan J. Godley Marine Turtle Research Group, Centre for Ecology and Conservation, University of Exeter in Cornwall, United Kingdom.

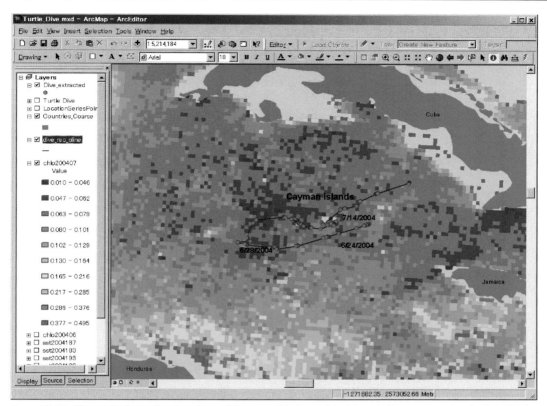

Figure 4.17   Route of a loggerhead turtle overlain on a grid of monthly chlorophyll *a* concentration for July 2004.

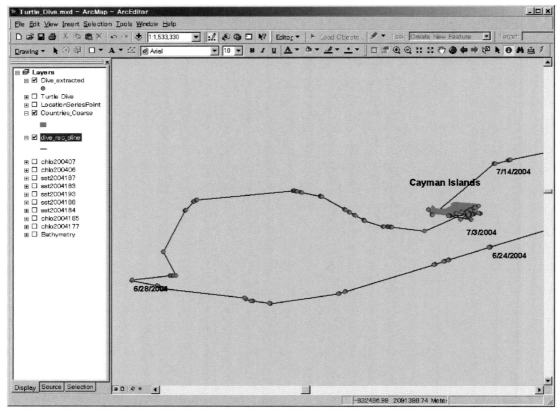

Figure 4.18   Closer view of loggerhead turtle movement in blue (with dive points in red) and Grand Cayman Island shown in green.

Courtesy of ESRI Data & Maps, 2005.

eastward. The maximum daily dive depth ranged from 5 meters to 104 meters (table 4.5 and figure 4.19). These results are consistent with those reported for loggerheads in the Pacific, which spend most of their time near the surface, at depths less than 100 m (Polovina et al. 2004). The turtle remained in shallow waters when near Grand Cayman, exhibiting deeper dives in pelagic waters. Since detailed statistical analyses are beyond the scope of the book, no clear tendency among turtle dive depth and chlorophyll *a* concentration was observed. However, it might be speculated that the loggerhead dived deeper as chlorophyll *a* concentration became lower as slight synchronization between them could be seen (figure 4.19).

Discussion: One may speculate that loggerheads dive deeper to seek prey where chlorophyll *a* concentrations are lower. This study did not find clear association between the turtle dive depth and the chlorophyll *a* concentration. However, the monthly chlorophyll *a* imagery is probably not an appropriate temporal scale to test this hypothesis. Finer temporal resolution data (e.g., 8-day) unfortunately had too many cloud-covered data gaps to be usable here.

Day	Deepest Dive	Bathymetry	Chlorophyll
2004/06/23	26	-3,388.50	0.09
2004/06/24	30	-4,644.00	0.09
2004/06/25	72	-4,763.66	0.08
2004/06/26	72	-5,452.50	0.09
2004/06/27	36	-5,395.25	0.11
2004/06/28	44	-2,526.00	0.07
2004/06/29	52	-2,365.00	0.1
2004/06/30	72	-2,980.00	0.1
2004/07/01	88	-3,499.71	0.07
2004/07/02	104	-2,009.66	0.07
2004/07/03	30	-1.00	
2004/07/05	10	-1.00	0.06
2004/07/06	10		
2004/07/07	10	-82.00	0.07
2004/07/08	10	-201.00	
2004/07/09	10	2.50	0.07
2004/07/10	10	-37.66	0.06
2004/07/11	5	4.00	0.04
2004/07/12	26	-1,214.00	0.09
2004/07/14	30	-2,968.50	0.06
2004/07/15	52	-2,899.66	0.05
2004/07/16	30	-2,627.66	0.06
2004/07/17	60	-2,878.50	0.08

Table 4.5   Daily maximum dive depth (m) and the corresponding bathymetry (m) and chlorophyll *a* concentration (mg/m³). Blank cells indicate no data available.

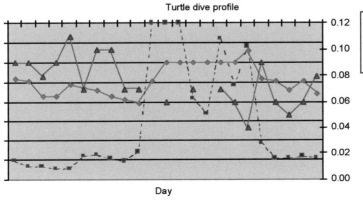

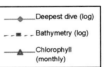

Figure 4.19   Time series trend of daily maximum dive depth, bathymetry, and chlorophyll *a* concentration. Dive depth and bathymetry are log-scaled.

71

While the loggerheads stayed in shallow waters around the island, they may have been foraging for benthic invertebrates, which are a dominant prey for loggerheads (Plotkin et al. 1993). On the other hand, the seafloor was far deeper than the turtle could dive when it traveled away from the island. Thus, it is thought that the loggerhead fed on prey other than benthic invertebrates. The currents and eddies may play an important role in gathering floating organisms as prey for sea turtles in their pelagic stage (Mortimer and Carr 1987). Sea surface current data may therefore be considered for future analysis with Arc Marine.

Seal haul-outs

Introduction: This case study examined the abundance of adult harbor seals over time. Such a time series analysis is essential to understanding long-term population dynamics of seals in the area (Thompson et al. 2005). Seal populations in the northwest Atlantic are thriving, yet relatively few resources are available for seal research projects in the region. The east coast of the United States lacks a management plan for seals, primarily because managers do not have information on the spatial distribution of the species, and more specifically, where haul-out sites are located (Dow 2005).

Data: To address this management issue, aerial surveys were conducted from 1981 to 2001 to collect seal and pup counts along the coastline of Maine (Gilbert et al. 2005). The archived data collected is downloadable from OBIS-SEAMAP (http://seamap.env.duke.edu/datasets/detail/315). Gray seals *(Halichoerus grypus)* and harbor seals *(Phoca vitulina)* haul out on islands and rock ledges in the area. Aerial surveys were used in the survey area to count the number of seals on ledges each day by species. To provide a sampling unit to estimate the seal abundance, researchers arbitrarily grouped ledges into regions based on proximity. Final abundance values are summed by region.

Loading data into Arc Marine: Ledges were represented in the Arc Marine data model by nonmobile points where data accumulates over time. Each ledge was given a numeric identification code. Each region, comprising a group of ledges in close proximity to one another, was identified by a five-letter code. Regional boundaries were not explicitly defined. A convex hull polygon encompassing all the ledges in a region was created to visualize each. A region code linked a region and its member ledges. The time series of the seal counts were presented in tabular format, with each row providing date, species, and life stage from one survey. Time series data was linked to ledges using "LedgeID."

Ledges were represented in Arc Marine by the TimeSeriesPoint feature class. Point features for the ledges were created as a shapefile from latitude and longitude values from the survey dataset. The FeatureArea feature class was used to hold the region polygons (figure 4.20). Before loading the ledge points and region polygons into the appropriate feature classes in the geodatabase, a common field must be present or created to link them. In this case, the region code was the key and was stored in the FeatureCode field. There was no need to customize the TimeSeriesPoint and FeatureArea feature classes for this case study.

After loading the features into the feature classes, a relationship class was created to relate TimeSeriesPoint to FeatureArea. Since a region contained many ledges, the cardinality of the relationship was one to many (1:M). In order to calculate abundance trends by species and life stage, two fields were created for these attributes in the seal count

TimeSeries. TimeSeries was related to TimeSeriesPoint with FeatureID as a key, which stored ledge IDs.

Analysis with Arc Marine: With the relationship classes properly defined, seal counts were selected for a specific region (figure 4.21) by selecting a region of interest, opening the

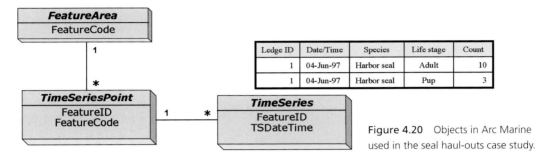

Ledge ID	Date/Time	Species	Life stage	Count
1	04-Jun-97	Harbor seal	Adult	10
1	04-Jun-97	Harbor seal	Pup	3

Figure 4.20   Objects in Arc Marine used in the seal haul-outs case study.

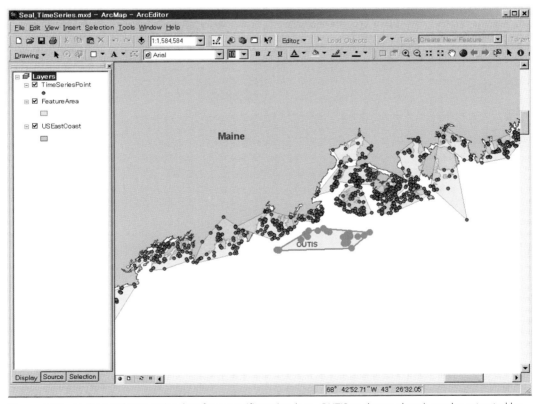

Figure 4.21   Harbor seal time series data for a specific region (e.g., OUTIS as shown above) may be extracted by way of relationship classes.

Data courtesy of James Gilbert.

attribute table and selecting Options>Related Tables. The appropriate relationship class was selected from the ledges attribute table and again for TimeSeries.

At this point, the selected seal counts mixed the two seal species and two life stages. To separate each species (e.g., harbor seal) and life stage (adult), Select by Attribute was performed on TimeSeries, with "Select from current selection" selected from Method. The adult harbor seal abundance trend was calculated from the resulting selection of TimeSeries. This was accomplished by right-clicking any field in the attribute table and selecting Summarize... . The summary statistics were saved as a table and stored in the geodatabase.

A graph of the summary statistics was created via Tools>Graphs>Create... (figure 4.22). The graph definition, including references to the summary statistics table, was saved in the ArcMap document. In general, it is a good practice to store the table in the geodatabase and overwrite it every time Summarize... is conducted. In this way, the graph definition is reusable for other regions, saving several steps in the graph creation wizard.

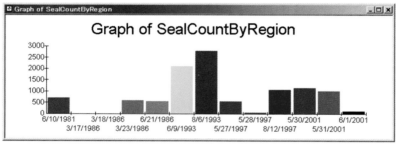

Figure 4.22 Sample graph of abundance trend for adult harbor seals in a region (region code: OUTIS). The selection in TimeSeries is summarized by TSDateTime, and the result is saved as SealCountByRegion in Arc Marine.

Results and discussion: Six regions were compared, with all but one (BHBIH) displaying a similar trend (figure 4.23). Counts from the survey in May–June, 1993, to that in May–June, 2001, were similar for the five regions, while the BHBIH region exhibited an inverse trend. Since the BHBIH lies near the BHBMR and BHBSI regions and the other three (BOSHB, CASB, and CELPT) are also close together, this difference is likely not attributable to geographical location alone. Thompson et al. (1997) suggested that sea counts during the pupping season provide the best estimates of abundance, as it represents a time when a large part of the population aggregates. Looking only at surveys during the pupping season (May–June; Dow 2005), all regions display a similar trend, suggesting that the harbor seal population has increased over time.

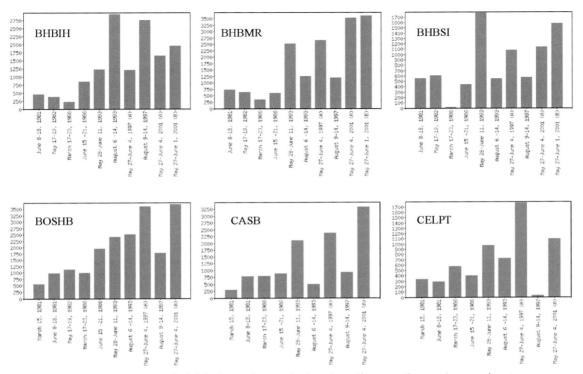

Figure 4.23   Time series of adult harbor seal counts in six regions. The upper three regions are close to each other geographically, as are the lower three.

Conclusion

The case studies in this chapter demonstrate that the Arc Marine data model lets users directly establish spatial and temporal relationships to analyze marine animals within a dynamic ocean environment. These case studies depict the use of InstantaneousPoints, LocationSeries Points, TimeDurationLines, TimeDurationAreas, FeatureAreas, and raster data within the Arc Marine structure. While each of the case studies highlights different issues, the central theme that ties these applications together is the use of temporal and spatial relationships to link marine animal observations to their environmental context. This linkage in space and time is essential for scientific analysis and management of critical ocean species.

Arc Marine class definitions featured in this chapter

FEATURE CLASSES	**InstantaneousPoint** is a point feature class representing features that are single observations in time and space. The x- and y-coordinates, plus a time stamp, create the unique feature. An InstantaneousPoint can have multiple ZValues by implementing a relationship to the Measurement object class.		
	Subtype	LocationSeries	
	Notes	InstantaneousPoint is a subclass of the superclass MeasurementPoint.	
	Properties	None	
	Fields	FeatureID	A geodatabase-wide unique identifier and key field for participating in relationships
		FeatureCode	A user-defined code used for identifying a feature
		CruiseID	A key field for relating this feature class to a Cruise
		TimeValue	The time stamp for a given point
		ZValue	A single depth value for the point
		SurveyID	A foreign key to the SurveyInfo object class
		SeriesID	A foreign key to the Series object class
		PointType	Defines the subtype to be one of the following: 1 = Instant (default value) 2 = Sounding 3 = Survey 4 = LocationSeries
	Track is a linear feature class representing the path and event associated with going on a specific tangent from the expedition.		
	Subtype	None apply	
	Properties	HasM = True HasZ = True	
	Notes	Track is a subclass of TimeDurationLine. The TimeDurationLine is designed as a feature where the beginning of the line starts at a given time stamp and the end of the line has a different time stamp. A Track can also have a relationship with the Cruise object class via the CruiseID field. The relationship, CruiseHasTracks, is characterized by a Cruise and can have zero or many Tracks.	
	Fields	FeatureID	A geodatabase-wide unique identifier and key field for participating in relationships
		FeatureCode	A user-defined code used for identifying a feature
		StartDate	The beginning time stamp for the feature
		EndDate	The ending time stamp for the feature
		VehicleID	A key field for relating this feature to the Vehicle
		CruiseID	A key field for relating this feature to the Cruise
		TrackID	An identifier for a Track feature
		Name	The name of a specific Track
		Method	Text describing the method for a specific Track
		Description	Text describing the Track
		LocalDesc	Text describing the locale of the Track

FEATURE CLASSES (cont'd)	**TimeDurationArea** is a class representing area features that have a beginning time stamp and an ending time stamp.		
	Subtype	None apply	
	Properties	HasM = True HasZ = True	
	Notes	The TimeDurationArea is a feature class representing area features that have varying x,y,z locations and a beginning and ending time stamp.	
	Fields	FeatureID	A geodatabase-wide unique identifier and key field for participating in relationships
		FeatureCode	A user-defined code used for identifying a feature
		SeriesID	A foreign key to the Series object class
		StartDate	The beginning time stamp for the feature
		EndDate	The ending time stamp for the feature
OBJECT CLASSES	**SurveyInfo** is an object class designed for storing information about a specific survey.		
	Notes		
	Fields	SurveyID	A key field for relating this table to a feature class
		StartDate	The beginning date of the survey
		EndDate	The ending date of the survey
		Description	A general description of the survey
		DeviceID	A key field for relating a survey with a Measuring device
		TrackID	A key field for relating a survey with a Track
	Series is an object class designed for storing information about a group of features that could be collected into a series.		
	Notes		
	Fields	SeriesID	A key field for relating this table to a feature class
	Cruise is an object class that defines the characteristics of a ship for the duration of an expedition.		
	Notes		
	Fields	CruiseID	An identifier for a given cruise
		Code	A user-defined code for a given cruise
		Name	The name of the cruise
		Purpose	The purpose of the cruise
		Status	Defines the status of the cruise
		Description	A general description of the cruise
		StartDate	The beginning time stamp for the cruise
		EndDate	The ending time stamp for the cruise
		ShipName	The name of the ship participating in the cruise

OBJECT CLASSES (cont'd)	**MeasuredData** is an object class used for storing recorded values for a given parameter.		
	Notes		
	Fields	MeasurementID	A key field for relating this table to the Measurement table
		ParameterID	A key field for relating this table to the Parameter table
		DeviceID	A key field for relating this table to the MeasuringDevice Table
		DataValue	The recorded value
	MeasuringDevice is an object class used for storing information pertaining to the device taking the measurements.		
	Notes		
	Fields	DeviceID	A key field for relating this table to either another table or feature class
		Name	The name of the measuring device
		Description	A description of the measuring device
		VehicleID	A key field relating this table to the Vehicles table
	Parameter is an object class that stores some basic information about the parameters being measured.		
	Notes	This table can be used in a couple of different ways. It can be used as a mechanism for querying a geodatabase for a specific parameter and then finding values of a particular type in related tables. Alternatively, it can be used as a lookup table of parameter types for a particular value.	
	Fields	ParameterID	The unique identifier of a specific parameter
		Name	The name of a parameter
		Description	The description of a parameter
		Quantity	The quantity type for a parameter. This is solved by the use of a coded value domain: 1 = Scalar, 2 = Vector
		Unit	The unit of measure for a parameter
		Significant Digits	The number of significant digits defining this parameter

RELATIONSHIPS	**SurveyInfoHasPoints**	1 : *	One Survey can have zero or many points
	CruiseHasTracks	1 : *	One Cruise can have zero or many Tracks

References

Aiken, J. J., Brendan J. Godley, A. C. Broderick, T. Austin, G. Ebanks-Petrie, and G. C. Hays. 2001. Two hundred years after a commercial marine turtle fishery: The current status of marine turtles nesting in the Cayman Islands. *Oryx* 35:145–51.

Blaylock, R. A., J. W. Hain, L. J. Hansen, D. L. Palka, and G. T. Waring. 1995. U.S. *Atlantic and Gulf of Mexico marine mammal stock assessments.* NOAA Technical Memorandum NMFS-SEFSC-363. Miami, Fla.: Martin County Engineering Department.

Bryant, P. J., G. Nichols, T. B. Bryant, and K. Miller. 1981. Krill availability and the distribution of humpback whales in southeastern Alaska. *Journal of Mammalogy* 62:427–30.

Dow, W. E. 2005. *Digital atlas of seal haul-out sites in Maine: 1981–2001.* M.E.M. Thesis, Durham, N.C.: Duke University.

Gilbert, J. R., G. T. Waring, K. M. Wynne, and N. Guldager. 2005. Changes in abundance of harbor seals in Maine, 1981–2001. *Marine Mammal Science* 21:519–35.

Halpin, P. N., A. J. Read, B. D. Best, K. D. Hyrenbach, E. Fujioka, M. S. Coyne, L. B. Crowder, S. A. Freeman, and C. Spoerri. 2006. OBIS-SEAMAP: Developing a biogeographic research data commons for the ecological studies of marine mammals, seabirds, and sea turtles. *Marine Ecology Progress Series 01114* 316:239–46.

Hawkes, L. A., A. C. Broderick, M. S. Coyne, M. H. Godfrey, L. F. Lopez-Jurado, P. Lopez-Suarez, S. E. Merino, N. Varo-Cruz, and Brendan J. Godley. 2006. Phenotypically linked dichotomy in sea turtle foraging requires multiple conservation approaches. *Current Biology* 16:990–95.

Hooker, S. K., H. Whitehead, and S. Gowans. 1999. Marine protected area design and the spatial and temporal distribution of cetaceans in a submarine canyon. *Conservation Biology* 13:592–602.

Hoyt, E. 1991. *Whale-watching around the world: A survey.* Unpublished report. Bath, United Kingdom: Whale and Dolphin Conservation Society, 12.77410.

Hyrenbach, K. D., K. A. Forney, and P. K. Dayton. 2000. Marine protected areas and ocean basin management. *Aquatic Conservation-Marine and Freshwater Ecosystems* 10:437–58.

Mackintosh, N. A. 1965. *The stocks of whales.* London: Fishing News (Books), Ltd.

Mikol, B. 1997. *Temperature directed fishing: How to reduce bycatch and increase productivity.* Marine Advisory Bulletin No. 48. Fairbanks, Alaska: Alaska Seagrant College Program, University of Alaska, Fairbanks.

Mortimer, J. A., and A. Carr. 1987. Reproduction and migrations of the Ascension-Island green turtle *(Chelonia-mydas). Copeia* 1987(1): 103–13.

Plotkin, P. T., M. K. Wicksten, and A. F. Amos. 1993. Feeding ecology of the loggerhead sea-turtle Caretta-Caretta in the northwestern Gulf of Mexico. *Marine Biology* 115:1–5.

Polovina, J. J., G. H. Balazs, E. A. Howell, D. M. Parker, M. P. Seki, and P. H. Dutton. 2004. Forage and migration habitat of loggerhead (Caretta caretta) and olive ridley (Lepidochelys olivacea) sea turtles in the central North Pacific Ocean. *Fisheries Oceanography* 13:36–51.

Read, A., B. Foster, C. McClellan, and D. Waples. 2004. *Habitat use of sea turtles in relation to fisheries interactions.* Final report, North Carolina Fishery Resource Grant Program Project 02-FEG-05. Raleigh, N.C.: North Carolina Sea Grant.

Sardi, K. A., M. T. Weinrich, and R. C. Connor. 2005. Social interactions of humpback whale (Megaptera novaeangliae) mother/calf pairs on a North Atlantic feeding ground. *Behaviour* 142:731–50.

Thompson, D., M. Lonergan, and C. Duck. 2005. Population dynamics of harbour seals *Phoca vitulina* in England: Monitoring growth and catastrophic declines. *Journal of Applied Ecology* 42:638–48.

Thompson, P. M., D. J. Tollit, D. Wood, H. M. Corpe, P. S. Hammond, and A. Mackay. 1997. Estimating harbour seal abundance and status in an estuarine habitat in north-east Scotland. *Journal of Applied Ecology* 34:43–52.

Walker, P. A., and K. D. Cocks. 1991. Habitat-A procedure for modeling a disjoint environmental envelope for a plant or animal species. *Global Ecology and Biogeography Letters* 1:108–18.

Whiting, S. D., and J. D. Miller. 1998. Short term foraging ranges of adult green turtles (Chelonia mydas). *Journal of Herpetology* 32:330–37.

Yoder, J. A., J. E. O'Reilly, A. H. Barnard, T. S. Moore, and C. M. Ruhsam. 2001. Variability in coastal zone color scanner (CZCS) chlorophyll imagery of ocean margin waters off the U.S. East Coast. *Continental Shelf Research* 21:1191–1218.

Chapter acknowledgments

Patrick N. Halpin, Nicholas School of the Environment & Earth Sciences, Duke University

Ei Fujioka, Michael S. Coyne, and **Ben D. Best,** Nicholas School of the Environment & Earth Sciences, Duke University

Implementing time series and measurements

GIS has recently made great improvements in its ability to implement the temporal dimension (e.g., Langran 1992; Miller 2005). The improvements resulted partly from continued demands from user groups and partly from technological advances. This chapter describes how the Arc Marine data model sorts out the complexity of storing time-varying data, thereby providing users with a logical means of accessing the data for query, display, analysis, and map production.

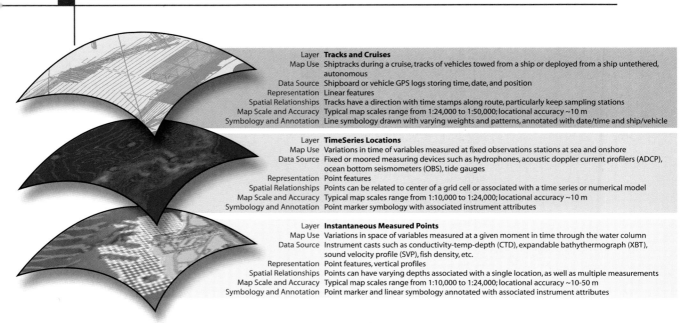

Layer **Tracks and Cruises**
Map Use Shiptracks during a cruise, tracks of vehicles towed from a ship or deployed from a ship untethered, autonomous
Data Source Shipboard or vehicle GPS logs storing time, date, and position
Representation Linear features
Spatial Relationships Tracks have a direction with time stamps along route, particularly keep sampling stations
Map Scale and Accuracy Typical map scales range from 1:24,000 to 1:50,000; locational accuracy ~10 m
Symbology and Annotation Line symbology drawn with varying weights and patterns, annotated with date/time and ship/vehicle

Layer **TimeSeries Locations**
Map Use Variations in time of variables measured at fixed observations stations at sea and onshore
Data Source Fixed or moored measuring devices such as hydrophones, acoustic doppler current profilers (ADCP), ocean bottom seismometers (OBS), tide gauges
Representation Point features
Spatial Relationships Points can be related to center of a grid cell or associated with a time series or numerical model
Map Scale and Accuracy Typical map scales range from 1:10,000 to 1:24,000; locational accuracy ~10 m
Symbology and Annotation Point marker symbology with associated instrument attributes

Layer **Instantaneous Measured Points**
Map Use Variations in space of variables measured at a given moment in time through the water column
Data Source Instrument casts such as conductivity-temp-depth (CTD), expandable bathythermograph (XBT), sound velocity profile (SVP), fish density, etc.
Representation Point features, vertical profiles
Spatial Relationships Points can have varying depths associated with a single location, as well as multiple measurements
Map Scale and Accuracy Typical map scales range from 1:10,000 to 1:24,000; locational accuracy ~10-50 m
Symbology and Annotation Point marker and linear symbology annotated with associated instrument attributes

Introduction

Adding a temporal dimension to geographic data makes it more complex. However, users can better re-create the natural state of a feature and visualize the measured values at a given point in time once they have added a temporal perspective to the dataset.

For example, once they sort out the complexity, users could query a geodatabase for water temperature values during a given month of a specified year and then compare those values with the values of the same month in a different year. Additionally, users could track changes of a feature over time or the generation of statistics for a time period in order to compare those results against statistics generated for a separate time period. Furthermore, the symbology for those features could change as the values change from one point in time to another.

This chapter focuses on the element of time during the process of values being recorded at varying positions and varying depths. That element of time might be a fixed stamp, or it might be collected continually over longer periods, generating what is commonly referred to as a time series. Given that the dataset varies over time, the intent is to let users query and view their data at one period of time or another. In marine applications, this can include looking at the speed and direction of currents in order to understand sediment transport; discerning how daily and monthly fluctuations in sea surface temperature (SST) may correlate to phytoplankton distributions and fish migrations; and tracking the motion of an oil spill, a hydrothermal plume, or a warm core ring. All of these scenarios have an important element of time, and the data to support them is often based on measurements taken at varying depths.

Featured case study

The main case study for this chapter was implemented by researchers at the Marine Institute, Galway, Ireland, in collaboration with developers at ESRI Ireland, and is still ongoing. The marine resources of Ireland (220 million acres) constitute more than ten times its land area, resulting in a huge impact on the Irish economy currently in excess of 3 billion Euros in revenue and employing more than 44,000 people (Marine Institute 2005). The national Marine Institute of Ireland coordinates and promotes marine research, development, and conservation along with associated services (such as data integration, and access). All of this is provided with the goal of promoting economic development. The Marine Institute also collaborates on marine activities with a multitude of other government departments, agencies, industries, and research institutes in Ireland. As a result, it must deal with a plethora of datasets collected in a diverse range of formats and at varying standards and scales. Before it adopted Arc Marine, the Marine Institute stored and managed the majority of its datasets independently of each other, resulting in inadequate overview and management of national archives (Hennessy et al. 2006) in ways that included the following:

- An increased risk of data loss or corruption of files since they were not managed and controlled within a single database management system.
- Not exploiting the full scientific value of the data due to the inability to readily integrate data from multiple sources, due to the diverse current data storage arrangements.
- Responses to incoming requests for information involving a significant investment of time and effort, despite having the data readily available. For example,
  - What is the average summer temperature of Galway Bay?
  - How much have Irish waters warmed up over the last decade?
  - Is there any correlation between algal bloom events in Cork Harbor and variations in water temperature?

To address these issues, the Marine Institute developed a geodatabase called the Marine Data Repository (and the accompanying interface for querying the geodatabase called Map Viewer). The geodatabase was implemented with the Arc Marine structure and powered by Microsoft SQL Server 2000 and ArcSDE technology. The loading of data into the Marine Data Repository presented an initial challenge due to the large volumes of data involved (nearly 120 million data records) and the various transformations needed from the source formats. As a solution, the Marine Institute has used geoprocessing tools with Python scripts for the automatic loading of data. These ETL (Extract, Transform, and Load) scripts ran the SQL Server procedures necessary for the automatic import of the datasets and their transformations from source formats. Use of ETL scripts also keeps track of the various Arc Marine FeatureIDs and MeasurementIDs that are assigned, as these identifiers are vital for managing the various relationships within the geodatabase and ensuring the integrity of the data.

Figure 5.1 shows the extent of current holdings in the Marine Data Repository by geographic coverage and oceanographic subdiscipline. The initial implementation of Arc Marine focused on underway and conductivity-temperature-depth (CTD) data from one of the Marine Institute's research vessels (the R/V Celtic Explorer), international CTD data collected from Irish territorial waters, physical data from the Irish Marine Data buoy platforms,

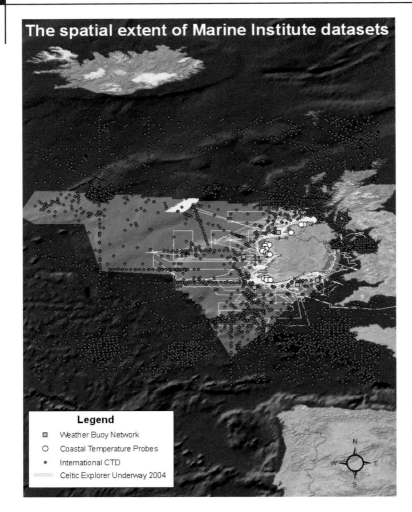

The spatial extent of Marine Institute datasets

Legend
- ▣ Weather Buoy Network
- ○ Coastal Temperature Probes
- ◆ International CTD
- ⎯ Celtic Explorer Underway 2004

Figure 5.1 The extent of chemical and physical oceanographic data stored by the Marine Institute in the Marine Data Repository.

© Marine Institute, Ireland.

and nutrient monitoring and temperature data from coastal temperature probes, which were extremely time varying.

Time-varying data

The Arc Marine data model essentially has three structures for storing time-varying data. This chapter addresses two of those, while chapter 7 will cover the third. As presented in chapter 3, the InstantaneousPoint feature class is the best way to store time-varying data. This point feature class contains a time stamp as an attribute, and then through a series of relationship classes, the data values to be recorded at that location and time stamp

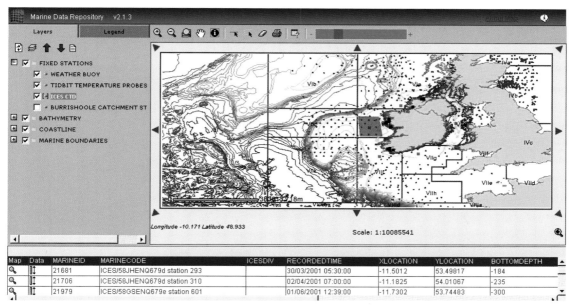

Figure 5.2   The results of a query for CTD sampling stations from the Marine Institute's Map Viewer Web GIS application (developed for the Marine Institute by ESRI Ireland and based on the Microsoft .NET framework).

© Marine Institute, Ireland.

are stored in an object class called MeasuredData. For any new measurement value being recorded, a new record is added to the MeasuredData table. TheMeasurementID attribute is then carried over to identify where that value had been recorded. This structure can easily be associated with the storage of CTD data where multiple variables are being measured and collected at multiple depths for a single instant in time (figure 5.2).

A time series is the second way to store time-varying data. The time steps can be regular, meaning that the distance between one time step and the next is consistent throughout the time series, or it can be irregular, where values are measured at random intervals. The values can represent virtually any phenomenon that may change over time.

The Arc Marine data model lets users associate the time series with a spatial feature so that the spatial and temporal components can be combined in query, display, and analysis.

Measurement points

Introduced during the discussion of marine surveys in chapter 3, MeasurementPoint is an abstract class acting to thematically organize point feature classes that store features where measurements are being recorded. It has two subclasses that can be instantiated,

InstantaneousPoint and TimeSeriesPoint. The InstantaneousPoint feature class was also initially introduced in chapter 3, but the focus was on its use for storing survey data. Features of the InstantaneousPoint feature class are defined as being fixed in space and time. This means that a unique feature is defined by its x- and y-coordinate and a single time stamp. There are four subtypes available for this feature class, Instant, Sounding, Survey, and LocationSeries, with Instant being the default. Although the subtypes are treated and act the same, this chapter will focus on the use of the Instant subtype. Refer to chapter 3 for the complete description of this data structure.

The TimeSeriesPoint feature class, like the InstantaneousPoint feature class, is a subclass of MeasurementPoint. This feature class introduces no new attributes and is designed to be a general feature class for the variety of features established for collecting data over long periods of time. Features of TimeSeriesPoint are generally associated with a time series, whereas the use of InstantaneousPoint is associated with a single time stamp. Although Arc Marine does not limit the association of time series to any feature class, regardless of its geometry, the TimeSeriesPoint feature class is offered in this data model as a template. For example, a moored buoy might have several measuring devices attached for measuring values of wave height, sea surface temperature, wind speed, and direction. Where the moored buoy would be represented as a feature of the TimeSeriesPoint feature class, the values for each of these variables being recorded over a long period of time would be stored as an individual time series. Arc Marine then provides the framework in which these time series can be associated with the correct buoy feature.

Features of TimeSeriesPoint or InstantaneousPoint can have multiple depths. In the previous example of the moored buoy, additional measuring devices might be cabled together at varying depths below the sea surface to record additional data such as salinity, water column temperature, current speed, and direction. These would be stored as a time series and associated with the moored buoy feature at their recorded depth. As with InstantaneousPoint, users accomplish this through the Measurement object class. A section later in this chapter titled Measurements details how users manage this within Arc Marine.

In the case study developed by the Marine Institute of Ireland, the InstantaneousPoint and TimeSeriesPoint feature classes are the only feature classes of Arc Marine that are implemented. However, the Institute has extended a number of object classes extensively to accommodate its applications and to make the collected data available to all staff members (figure 5.4). The additional tables have been grouped into either "Activities" (an organizational mechanism based on the collection activity), "Organizations," "Contacts," or "Platforms," all of which describe who owns the data, who to contact about accessing data, and where a data collection is being performed. The Marine Institute uses InstantaneousPoint to store its research vessel underway data, as well as datasets such as CTD casts collected from the vessel. TimeSeriesPoint is used for storing its offshore weather buoy, nutrient monitoring, and coastal temperature probe locations. Both the InstantaneousPoint and TimeSeriesPoint feature classes have an ActivityID attribute added for relating the features to the Activity table (figure 5.4). In this way, the institute is able to make its datasets more readily available and to derive value-added products such as monthly climatologies (hence information, and data).

Common Marine Data Types

Marine Points

Instantaneous Points

Time Series Point

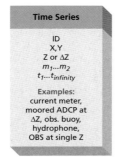

Marine Lines

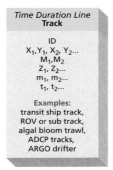

Marine Areas

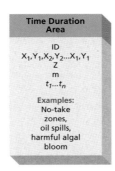

Figure 5.3   Portion of the main Common Marine Data Types diagram (from chapter 2) representing the marine data types featured in this chapter and implemented in the Marine Institute case study. Headings in italics are abstract feature classes in Arc Marine. All other headings are feature classes or subtypes of feature classes.

TimeSeries

The data structure for the TimeSeries classes implemented in Arc Marine is the same data structure introduced and implemented in the Arc Hydro data model (Arctur and Zeiler 2004; Maidment et al. 2002). Using data over time is just one aspect in common between the Arc Hydro and Arc Marine data models, and for the sake of constancy it was important to this effort that a new data structure for dealing with time-varying data not be introduced. The TimeSeries group consists of two object classes and one relationship class. The first table, TimeSeries, is the table in which the data values are actually stored. This table consists of four fields, FeatureID, TSTypeID, TimeValue, and DataValue. The value of FeatureID identifies the feature associated with the time series and is used as a key field for developing any relationships between this table and a feature class. The TSTypeID is a key field for the relationship class TSTypeHasTimeSeries between the TimeSeries table and the

87

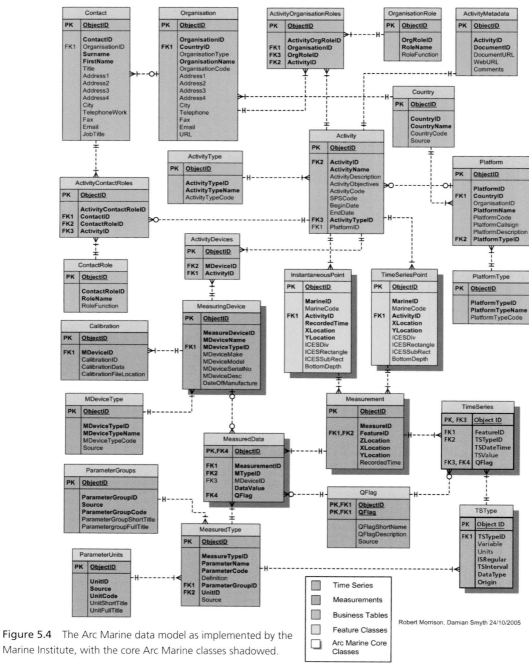

Figure 5.4 The Arc Marine data model as implemented by the Marine Institute, with the core Arc Marine classes shadowed.

© Marine Institute, Ireland.

TSType

TSTypeID	Variable	Units	IsRegular	TSInterval	DataType	Origin
1	WaveHeight	Centigrade	1	1Hour	Instantaneous	Recorded
2	Temperature	Centigrade	1	1Hour	Instantaneous	Recorded
3	Wind Speed	Centigrade	1	1Hour	Instantaneous	Recorded
4	Wind Direction	Centigrade	1	1Hour	Instantaneous	Recorded

TSTypeHasTimeSeries

TimeSeries

FeatureID	TSTypeID	TimeValue	DataValue
5008701	2	30:08.2004 04:00:00	16.73
5008701	2	30:08.2004 05:00:00	16.75
5008701	2	30:08.2004 06:00:00	16.75
5008701	2	30:08.2004 07:00:00	16.79
5008701	2	30:08.2004 08:00:00	16.85
5008701	2	30:08.2004 09:00:00	17.33
5008701	2	30:08.2004 10:00:00	17.40

Figure 5.5   The structure of the TSType table, the TimeSeries table, and the relationship between them.

TSType table. It identifies the record in the TSType table, which defines the parameters of the time series. TSDateTime is the field (and is of a Date type that includes time) for storing the time steps. TSValue is the field storing the corresponding data values. These last two columns essentially make the time series matrix.

The TSType table is used for storing parameters that describe the time series data (figure 5.5). TSType acts as a lookup table for all data values stored in the TimeSeries table. Consequently, the TSTypeID is meant to be a unique identifier for each "type" of time series in a geodatabase and acts as a key field for relating to the TimeSeries table. How a user defines a type of time series should be flexible. The TimeSeries table provides several options. The Variable field is a string field that identifies the measured data. Examples of this include wave height, temperature, and salinity. The Units field is a string field that stores information with the units of measure for the collected data. The IsRegular field is a Boolean field identifying whether the time step interval is regular or irregular. TSInterval defines the time interval between two time steps of a Regular time series. For irregular time series, TSInterval is undefined. The values of TSInterval are defined in a coded value domain called TSIntervalType and include values such as 1Minute, 2Minute through 30Minutes, 1Hour, 2Hour, 1Day, and 1Month. The DataType field determines how the type of stored data has been recorded and uses a coded value domain that includes Instantaneous, Cumulative, Incremental, Average, Maximum, and Minimum data. The Origin field uses a coded valued domain of either Recorded or Generated. A Generated origin generally refers to a time series created from a model, whereas a Recorded time series consists of actual measured values.

There is no defined relationship class between the TimeSeriesPoint feature class and the TimeSeries table. This presumes that when users implement the TimeSeries feature class, it would be converted to an abstract class and inherited by a user-specified subclass. For example, users might build specific feature classes for the points representing weather buoys and another feature class for temperature probes. The two subclasses of TimeSeriesPoint would inherit from that class. Through this process, the FeatureID is present in each of the feature classes and in the TimeSeries table. With this attribute, a relationship is implied.

Accessing and applying time series data

Accessing and using time series data stored in a geodatabase is the same as accessing any other table in the geodatabase. Users can query the set of tables and graph the results. Depending on the question, users can query the table based on a combination of the ID of the feature, time period, and type of data, essentially providing the capability to query for a particular variable in space and time. For example, users might query the TSType table for a specific type of data, such as temperature. Then the selection set of the TimeSeries table is updated via the relationship class TSTypeHasTimeSeries. This results in a selection set of the TimeSeries table for the values representing temperature data. Based on the FeatureID or a specific time period, and using values within a specified range, users can expand the query by selecting from the current selection set of records. This results in isolating the identifiers of the features where temperatures for a given time period and of a particular value or value range are associated.

However, going beyond this query example usually requires some additional processing. For example, to highlight features in the ArcMap data view associated with these time series, users need to build an additional relationship between the feature class and the TimeSeries table, using FeatureID as the key field. As described above, the FeatureID exists in both the feature class and TimeSeries table. Once this relate has been built, the associated features can be highlighted. However, a relate doesn't allow for the use of the TimeSeries values for rendering in ArcMap. Additionally, a Join in ArcMap doesn't support a one-to-many relationship between a feature and all of the records included in a time series. Users could generate Summary Statistics for the selected set of the TimeSeries table as the input. This produces statistics for each unique FeatureID and TSType combination. The output table from that process could then be joined to the feature class, which then could be used to update the symbology of that feature class. Using the example of the moored buoy, we might presume that a user has several instances of these features, which have been collecting temperature data for the past year. Once that data has been imported into the Time-Series table, the user could go through a similar process outlined above and update the display categorically for those TimeSeries points based on the statistical results.

Advanced applications for managing time series data are starting to be developed and made available as extensions to ArcMap. For example, DHI Water & Environment, an international consulting and research organization, has recently released an extension to ArcMap called the Temporal Analyst for ArcGIS (see the book's companion Web sites for more details). With this extension, users can easily import time series data into a geodatabase from a variety of sources, associate the time series with features, and then access the time series data for various plotting, reporting, and analytical processes (figure 5.6). The Temporal Analyst extension provides this functionality on a collection of time series data, individual time series, or by directly accessing the time series data from the ArcMap data frame by right-clicking the feature and selecting the time series of interest (figure 5.7). The DHI Temporal Analyst extension also provides an analysis environment in which several advanced temporal processes are available, such as filling gaps in the data, resampling, synchronization, creating distribution curves, scatter curves, and double mass curves.

More advanced spatiotemporal analysis, through the use of tools such as statistical calculations and a temporal calculator, are also available through the Temporal Analyst extension. Within the analysis environment, the example outlined above is a matter of a few mouse clicks. Once the time series of interest are added to the analysis environment of the Temporal Analyst extension, they can be selected and the Compute Scalar(s) From Time Series dialog box can be opened (figure 5.8). In the Compute Scalar(s) From Time

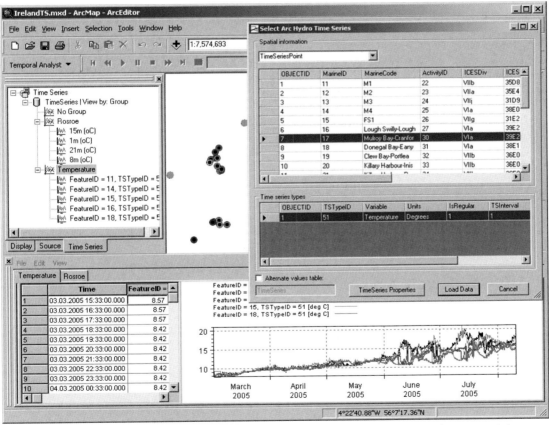

Figure 5.6   The DHI Temporal Analyst extension provides access to Temperature data stored in an Arc Marine geodatabase. The Marine Institute provided this geodatabase. As an example, the geodatabase shows temperature data associated with temperature probes stored in the TimeSeriesPoint feature class.

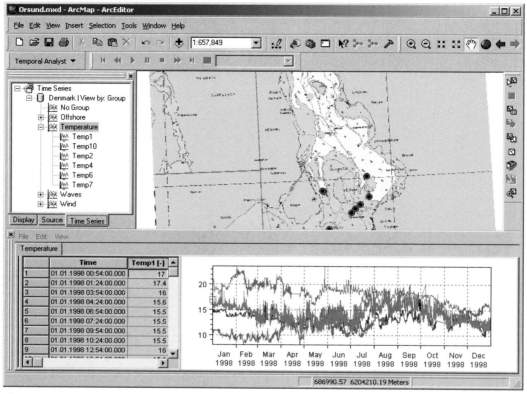

Figure 5.7 The DHI Temporal Analyst extension as used in ArcMap to plot a collection of temperature time series data collected in the Kattegat Strait between Denmark and Sweden and stored in the geodatabase.

Series dialog box, the time period of interest is specified, and the Time Weighted Average is selected for the statistical operation. This operation produces a feature class that is a replica of the features associated with the input time series and with the statistical value added to the attribute table. This attribute can then be used to determine the categorical distribution and symbology for the new feature layer, as seen in figure 5.8. The new feature layer, in this case a point feature layer, can alternatively be used as input for interpolating a statistical surface using the inverse distance weighted (IDW) function of the ArcGIS Spatial Analyst extension (figure 5.9).

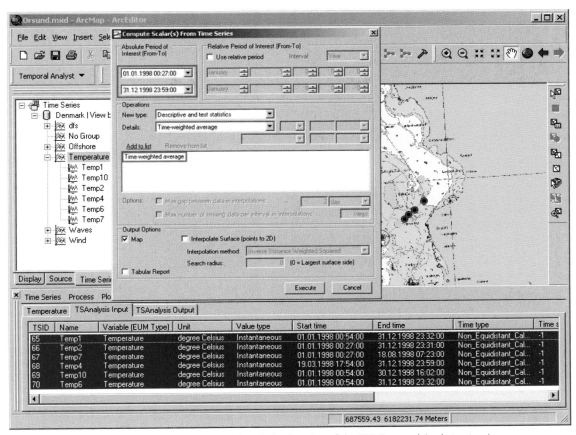

Figure 5.8 The Compute Scalar(s) From Time Series function of the DHI Temporal Analyst extension calculates the time-weighted average of the selected time series.

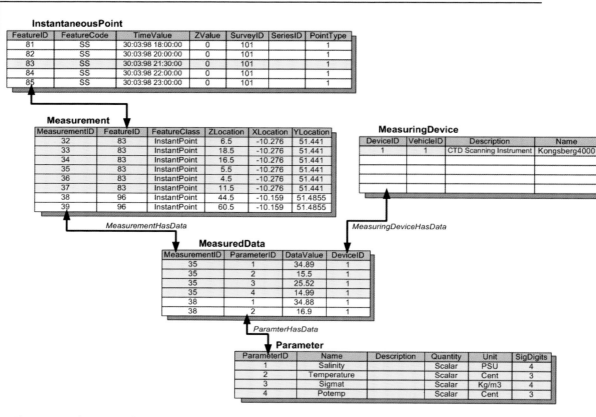

InstantaneousPoint

FeatureID	FeatureCode	TimeValue	ZValue	SurveyID	SeriesID	PointType
81	SS	30:03:98 18:00:00	0	101		1
82	SS	30:03:98 20:00:00	0	101		1
83	SS	30:03:98 21:30:00	0	101		1
84	SS	30:03:98 22:00:00	0	101		1
85	SS	30:03:98 23:00:00	0	101		1

Measurement

MeasurementID	FeatureID	FeatureClass	ZLocation	XLocation	YLocation
32	83	InstantPoint	6.5	-10.276	51.441
33	83	InstantPoint	18.5	-10.276	51.441
34	83	InstantPoint	16.5	-10.276	51.441
35	83	InstantPoint	5.5	-10.276	51.441
36	83	InstantPoint	4.5	-10.276	51.441
37	83	InstantPoint	11.5	-10.276	51.441
38	96	InstantPoint	44.5	-10.159	51.4855
39	96	InstantPoint	60.5	-10.159	51.4855

MeasuringDevice

DeviceID	VehicleID	Description	Name
1	1	CTD Scanning Instrument	Kongsberg4000

MeasurementHasData

MeasuringDeviceHasData

MeasuredData

MeasurementID	ParameterID	DataValue	DeviceID
35	1	34.89	1
35	2	15.5	1
35	3	25.52	1
35	4	14.99	1
38	1	34.88	1
38	2	16.9	1

ParamterHasData

Parameter

ParameterID	Name	Description	Quantity	Unit	SigDigits
1	Salinity		Scalar	PSU	4
2	Temperature		Scalar	Cent	3
3	Sigmat		Scalar	Kg/m3	4
4	Potemp		Scalar	Cent	3

Figure 5.9 The results of computing the Time Weighted Average of the Temperature time series and associating that scalar value to the point features associated with the time series. The scalar value is used to determine the symbology for the measuring stations and further used as the input value for interpolating an IDW surface using ArcGIS Spatial Analyst.

Limitations to the TimeSeries classes

The Arc Marine development team understood the importance of integrating this data model with the data models of similar applications. Since a data structure for time series had already been published with the Arc Hydro data model, it was natural that Arc Marine should implement the same data structure. However, Arc Hydro team members did not have a lot of experience combining spatial and temporal data when they were developing the data structure for time series. It was important to keep the data structure simple with the ability to resolve simple queries for locating a feature with a given variable or type of time series and for a specified time period. Arc Marine meets that requirement. However, since the development of Arc Hydro, and with the advent of other technologies, the use of temporal and spatial data has increased beyond query and graphing. We have more experience and knowledge about the best ways to manage temporal data, and advances have exposed some limitations to the original time series data structure.

By having the FeatureID attribute included in the TimeSeries table along with the TSTypeID attribute, a feature can only be associated with a single instance of a time series of a given type. For example, stream flow can be associated with a gauging station. Generally, a gauging station will be associated with a single stream flow time series. This may be sufficient for mere data collection and input. However, in other instances, the time series might represent a forecast scenario, a modeling result, or a user might have several versions based on a particular event or different time periods. In those cases, the type of time series replicated for each instance of that feature would be identical and would also need to be associated with multiple versions of a similar time series.

Because a time series is a matrix, the FeatureID is repeated for every time step of a time series in the TimeSeries table. This precludes having a specific time series associated with more than one feature. That can be resolved by duplicating the time series matrix and populating the FeatureID for each record with a new value; but that is not good database management and not recommended.

To solve these limitations, first add an additional field to the TimeSeries table, called TimeSeriesID. This field distinguishes one time series (a collection of rows in the TimeSeries table) from another, and is populated with the same value for each row being included. Second, add a simple table that has just three attributes, TimeSeriesID, FeatureID, and FeatureClass. This table acts as a turntable or attributed relationship class, in which the TimeSeriesID and FeatureID are key fields through which two relationship classes would link to the TimeSeries table and to the feature class, and match up with the TimeSeriesID and FeatureID, respectively. In the turntable, the TimeSeriesID and FeatureID are populated with any number of combinations, and any combination can be repeated any number of times. The FeatureClass attribute is not required, but aids in identifying the feature class where the FeatureID is located.

Measurements

As previously illustrated in chapter 3, features can have multiple depths associated with them, where various variables are being recorded or measured. These measuring locations below the surface can be modeled in Arc Marine with the use of the Measurement table or what has been termed Measurements. The Measurement table provides the capability of having multiple depth locations for a specific feature. It has a FeatureID attribute designed to be used in a one-to-many relationship, between itself and the TimeSeriesPoint or InstantaneousPoint feature classes, for example. This table is where one point feature can have many entries, each describing a unique depth. The Measurement table also has a MeasurementID designed as a unique identifier for each Measurement in the geodatabase. Every combination of FeatureID and ZLocation creates a unique MeasurementID. For this reason, it is imperative to the integrity of the data that MeasurementID remains unique throughout the entire geodatabase.

When associating time series to a depth location for a given feature via the Measurement table, the value of the MeasurementID needs to be inserted as the value of the FeatureID in the TimeSeries table. Measurement acts as a virtual feature, which can be treated in a similar manner to physical features, while adding yet another dimension. In the temperature query example previously outlined, a query was made for temperature data, and the corresponding features were identified. Now, the depths of those features can be identified rather than simply identifying the associated features. Referring back to the DHI Temporal Analyst extension, if the Measurement table is populated, then making an association between a time series and a Measurement is supported. Likewise, as illustrated in figure 5.10, the time series associated with a Measurement can be retrieved.

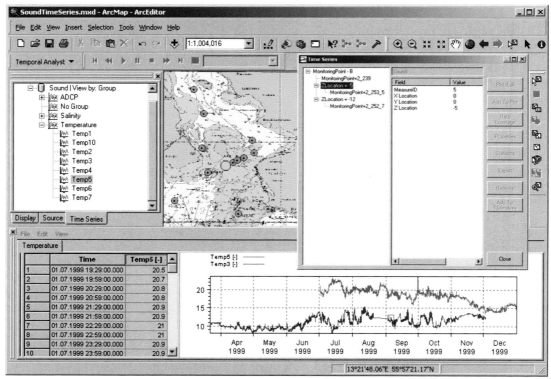

Figure 5.10 The DHI Temporal Analyst extension allows users to access and view the time series associated with the Measurements of a TimeSeriesPoint.

MeasuredData

The Arc Marine development team designed the MeasuredData table as an alternative to time series tables to store recorded or measured values for multiple variables. The generic table included in Arc Marine is available to store undefined values. The Parameter table, which defines these variables, can be accessed from the MeasuredData table via the ParameterHasData relationship class (figure 5.11).

The MeasuredData table has a MeasurementID attribute, which is the key field used in the relationship class MeasurementHasData. The relationship links the MeasuredData table with the Measurement table. This mechanism associates measured or recorded values with the depth of a point feature. The MeasurementID is repeated in this table for each variable measured at a specific depth.

For example, using this table to store the data from a CTD cast, the location of the cast would be represented as an InstantaneousPoint (denoted as x,y coordinates plus a time step). The various depths where variables were being recorded would be stored as Measurements in the Measurement table. The MeasuredData table would include an entry for each of the recorded variables for each Measurement. Figure 5.11 shows an example that includes entries for Salinity, Temperature, Sigma-t (water density), and Potemp (potential temperature) at each Measurement. Only the values appear in the table. The ParameterID is a key

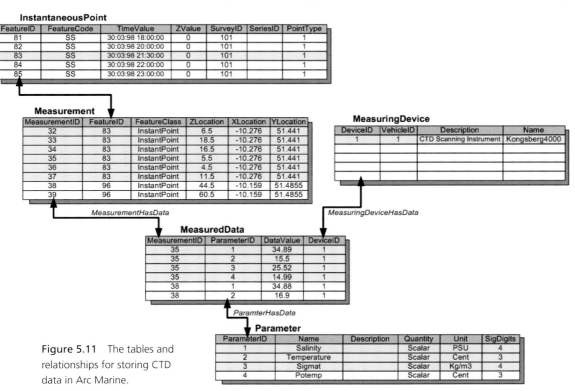

Figure 5.11   The tables and relationships for storing CTD data in Arc Marine.

InstantaneousPoint

FeatureID	FeatureCode	TimeValue	ZValue	SurveyID	SeriesID	PointType
81	SS	30:03:98 18:00:00	0	101		1
82	SS	30:03:98 20:00:00	0	101		1
83	SS	30:03:98 21:30:00	0	101		1
84	SS	30:03:98 22:00:00	0	101		1
85	SS	30:03:98 23:00:00	0	101		1

Measurement

MeasurementID	FeatureID	FeatureClass	ZLocation	XLocation	YLocation
32	83	InstantPoint	6.5	-10.276	51.441
33	83	InstantPoint	18.5	-10.276	51.441
34	83	InstantPoint	16.5	-10.276	51.441
35	83	InstantPoint	5.5	-10.276	51.441
36	83	InstantPoint	4.5	-10.276	51.441
37	83	InstantPoint	11.5	-10.276	51.441
38	96	InstantPoint	44.5	-10.159	51.4855
39	96	InstantPoint	60.5	-10.159	51.4855

MeasurementHasData

MeasuringDevice

DeviceID	VehicleID	Description	Name
1	1	CTD Scanning Instrument	Kongsberg4000

MeasuringDeviceHasData

MeasuredData

MeasurementID	ParameterID	DataValue	DeviceID
35	1	34.89	1
35	2	15.5	1
35	3	25.52	1
35	4	14.99	1
38	1	34.88	1
38	2	16.9	1

ParamterHasData

Parameter

ParameterID	Name	Description	Quantity	Unit	SigDigits
1	Salinity		Scalar	PSU	4
2	Temperature		Scalar	Cent	3
3	Sigmat		Scalar	Kg/m3	4
4	Potemp		Scalar	Cent	3

field in the relationship class ParameterHasData, which connects this table to the Parameter table to identify the collected data type. This process is more efficient and flexible than adding an attribute to the MeasuredData table for each measured variable in the geodatabase.

The Marine Institute implements this structure for managing and archiving its CTD data. The institute designed a Web-based Map Viewer (figure 5.2) to make these datasets readily and easily available to its user base internal and external to the institute and in response to requests from other government agencies. The Map Viewer includes a Query Tool for easier access to the institute's complex storage structure (figure 5.12). The Query tool allows users to search the geodatabase using a number of different criteria:

Location	User-defined areas or manually entered coordinates
Time	Date ranges or recurring time periods, for example, every January
Depth	Either single values or depth ranges
Parameter	Select from one or more parameter groups

Advanced search criteria include the following:

Parameters	Select individual parameters associated with a group
Data Sources	Matches this list to Activities, allowing users to restrict the search to datasets of interest
Filter	Search for user-defined values or ranges of values

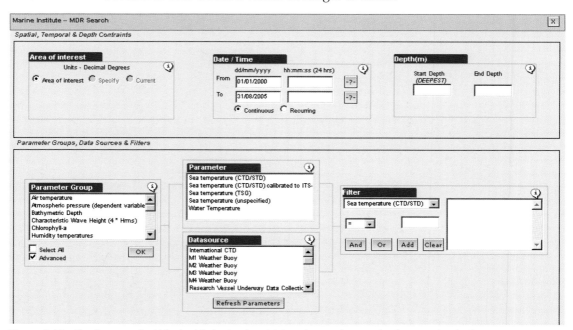

Figure 5.12   The Query tool within the Marine Institute's Map Viewer. The complex functionality facilitates searches on location, time, depth, and individual parameters. Additional filters on individual parameter values can be applied to focus the search.

© Marine Institute, Ireland.

Figure 5.13 shows the Vertical Measure feature within the Marine Institute's Map Viewer. For a given feature, this tool can display the results of a Join between the Measurement table and matching values of the MeasuredData table. The result is a listing of all measured CTD values at each depth.

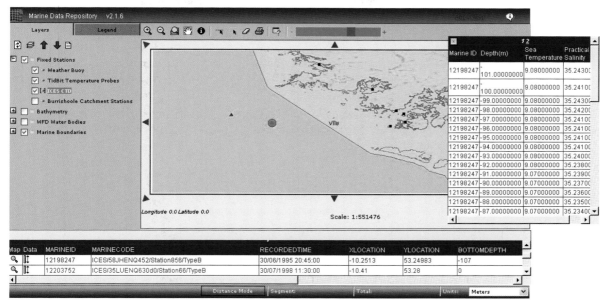

Figure 5.13   Result of a query using the Vertical Measure feature within the Query tool of the Marine Institute's Map Viewer, showing a listing of measured CTD values at varying depths, suitable for constructing a vertical profile. The CTD records are similar to the display in figure 5.2.

© Marine Institute, Ireland.

Conclusion

This chapter focused on the element of time, as short-term time stamps or longer-term time series, in conjunction with oceanographic measurements made at varying positions and depths. The case study of the Marine Institute of Ireland, through its Marine Data Repository, showed several examples of how Arc Marine can be effectively implemented with a variety of time- and space-varying measurements such as CTD casts or data collected from buoys or probes. It was further shown that with an extension such as the DHI Temporal Analyst, these point features can be associated with time series for plotting, querying, summary statistics, resampling, interpolating, weighted averaging, and more. These examples show that after sorting out the complexities of multidimensional data, the data model actually facilitates the building of applications that simplify access and allow for advanced processing. With the initial success of integrating physical and chemical oceanographic data into the Marine Data Repository, the inclusion of fisheries, biotoxin, and other biological datasets is planned for the near future. These datasets will likely be incorporated into additional Arc Marine feature classes such as TimeDurationLines for fisheries hauls and TimeDurationAreas for harmful algal blooms.

The Marine Institute is still in the initial stages of its implementation of Arc Marine, with the maintenance of current data and the input of new data along with efforts to expand the geographic coverage for future holdings. Once the Marine Data Repository has been operational for a period of time, it is anticipated that enhancements and modifications will become clear based on user feedback. Meanwhile, the work represents a significant step forward for the Marine Institute in its management of data assets and delivery of improved information services. According to Hennessy et al. (2006), the implementation of Arc Marine has done the following:

- Provided a design template that would otherwise have been much more time-consuming to create and taken considerably longer to implement
- Forced issues such as varying data quality and standards to be addressed and resolved
- Put in place a single, secure, centralized, spatially enabled database on one server, thereby reducing the support requirements compared with a host of databases and formats previously used
- Allowed the integration of diverse marine datasets, facilitating a more holistic approach to the exploration and analysis of data
- Extended the services available from the institute to the wider scientific community, facilitating greater access to and dissemination of data and, over time, information
- Facilitated the future expansion of its management system regarding loaded data and software tools available to enhance analysis

Arc Marine class definitions featured in this chapter

FEATURE CLASSES	**InstantaneousPoint** is a feature class representing features that are single observations in time and space. The x- and y-coordinates, plus a time stamp, create the unique feature. An InstantaneousPoint can have multiple ZValues by implementing a relationship to the Measurement object class.		
	Subtype	Survey	
	Notes	InstantaneousPoint is a subclass of the superclass MeasurementPoint.	
	Properties	None	
	Fields	FeatureID	A geodatabase-wide unique identifier and key field for participating in relationships
		FeatureCode	A user-defined code used for identifying a feature
		CruiseID	A key field for relating this feature class to a Cruise
		TimeValue	The time stamp for the point
		ZValue	A single depth value for the point
		SurveyID	A foreign key to the SurveyInfo object class
		SeriesID	A key field for relating this feature to the Series table
		PointType	Defines the subtype to be one of the following: 1 = Instant (default value) 2 = Sounding 3 = Survey 4 = LocationSeries
	TimeSeriesPoint is a feature class representing features that are fixed in space (x,y) and have an association with an instance of the TimeSeries.		
	Subtype	None apply	
	Properties	None apply	
	Notes	A TimeSeriesPoint is a subclass of the superclass MeasurementPoint and can have multiple ZLocations by implementing the Measurement object class.	
	Fields	FeatureID	A geodatabase-wide unique identifier and key field for participating in relationships
		FeatureCode	A user-defined code used for identifying a feature
		CruiseID	A key field for relating this feature to the Cruise table
	ProfileLine is a feature class representing linear features that are not physical features themselves but rather features interpolated along the line from another source—for example, a profile interpolated from a bathymetry survey.		
	Subtype	None apply	
	Properties	HasM = True HasZ = True	
	Notes	None available	
	Fields	FeatureID	A geodatabase-wide unique identifier and key field for participating in relationships
		FeatureCode	A user-defined code used for identifying a feature

FEATURE CLASSES (cont'd)	**FeatureLine** is a feature class representing fixed or dynamic linear features.		
	Subtype	None apply	
	Properties	None available	
	Notes		
	Fields	FeatureID	A geodatabase-wide unique identifier and key field for participating in relationships
		FeatureCode	A user-defined code used for identifying a feature
OBJECT CLASSES	**SurveyInfo** is an object class designed for storing information about a specific survey.		
	Notes		
	Fields	SurveyID	A key field for relating this table to a feature class
		StartDate	The beginning date of the survey
		EndDate	The ending date of the survey
		Description	A general description of the survey
		DeviceID	A key field for relating a survey with a Measuring device
		TrackID	A key field for relating a survey with a Track
	Measurement is an object class designed for extending a single feature with multiple depths.		
	Notes	Measurements are designed for storing multiple depths for a single feature. This is done by creating a new and unique identifier for the feature, in this case MeasurementID, for every unique combination of FeatureID and ZLocation. In this table, FeatureID is repeated for every depth (ZLocation) associated with the feature.	
	Fields	MeasurementID	A unique identifier for the feature created by combining unique combinations of FeatureID and ZLocation
		FeatureID	A key field relating to the FeatureID of the feature
		FeatureClass	The name of the feature class in which the relating feature participates
		ZLocation	The value representing the depth being associated with the feature
		XLocation	The x-coordinate of the feature for the given depth
		YLocation	The y-coordinate of the feature for the given depth.

OBJECT CLASSES (cont'd)	**TSType** is an index of the types of time series data stored in the TimeSeries table.		
	Notes		
	Fields	TSTypeID	The identifier for a type of time series
		Variable	The type of data being described by the time series
		Units	The units of measurement
		IsRegular	Whether the units have a regular or irregular time step
		TSInterval	The interval between two time steps
		DataType	The type of time series. This is solved by the use of a coded value domain: 1 = Instantaneous 2 = Cumulative 3 = Incremental 4 = Average 5 = Maximum 6= Minimum
		Origin	The origin of the time series. This is solved by the use of a coded value domain: 1 = Recorded 2 = Generated
	TimeSeries is an object class that stores the time-varying attributes of features.		
	Notes		
	Fields	FeatureID	A key field for relating this time series to a feature class
		TSTypeID	A key field for relating this time series to an entry in the TSType table
		TSDateTime	The data and time stamp of a time series value
		TSValue	The measured value for the time step
	Cruise is an object class that defines the characteristics of a ship for the duration of an expedition.		
	Notes		
	Fields	CruiseID	An identifier for a given cruise
		Code	A user-defined code for a given cruise
		Name	The name of the cruise
		Purpose	The purpose of the cruise
		Status	Defines the status of the cruise
		Description	A general description of the cruise
		StartDate	The beginning time stamp for the cruise
		EndDate	The ending time stamp for the cruise
		ShipName	The name of the ship participating in the cruise

OBJECT CLASSES (cont'd)	**MeasuredData** is an object class that stores recorded values for a given parameter.		
	Notes		
	Fields	MeasurementID	A key field for relating this table to the Measurement table
		ParameterID	A key field for relating this table to the Parameter table
		DeviceID	A key field for relating this table to the MeasuringDevice Table
		DataValue	The recorded value
	MeasuringDevice is an object class that stores information pertaining to the device taking the measurements.		
	Notes		
	Fields	DeviceID	A key field for relating this table to either another table or feature class
		Name	The name of the measuring device
		Description	A description of the measuring device
		VehicleID	A key field relating this table to the Vehicles table
	Parameter is an object class that stores information about the parameters being measured.		
	Notes	This table can be used as a mechanism for querying a geodatabase for a specific parameter and then finding values of a particular type in related tables. Or it can be used as a lookup table of parameter types for a particular value.	
	Fields	ParameterID	The unique identifier of a specific parameter
		Name	The name of a parameter
		Description	The description of a parameter
		Quantity	The quantity type for a parameter. This is solved by the use of a coded value domain: 1 = Other 2 = Scalar 3 = Vector
		Unit	The unit of measure for a parameter
		Significant Digits	The number of significant digits defining the precision of this parameter

RELATIONSHIPS	**CruiseHasTracks**	1 : *	One Cruise can have zero or many Tracks
	SurveyInfoHasPoints	1 : *	One Survey can have zero or many points
	MeasurementHasData	1 : *	One Measurement can have zero or many MeasuredData values
	MeasuringDeviceHasData	1 : *	One MeasuringDevice can have zero or many MeasuredData values
	ParameterHasData	1 : *	One Parameter can have zero or many MeasuredData values
	TSTypeHasTimeSeries	1 : *	One TSType can have one or more TimeSeries

References

Arctur, D., and M. Zeiler. 2004. *Designing geodatabases: Case studies in GIS data modeling.* Redlands, Calif.: ESRI Press.

Hennessy, M., D. Smyth, and T. Alcorn. 2006. *Building a spatial data warehouse for the Marine Institute.* Unpublished Technical Report. Galway, Ireland: Marine Institute.

Langran, G. 1992. *Time in geographic information systems.* London: Taylor & Francis.

Maidment, D., V. Merwade, T. Whiteaker, M. Blongewicz, and D. Arctur. 2002. Time series. In *Arc Hydro: GIS for water resources,* ed. D. Maidment, 141–66. Redlands, Calif.: ESRI Press.

Marine Institute. 2005. Ireland's ocean economy and resources. *Marine Foresight Series 4 Technical Report.* Galway, Ireland: Marine Institute.

Miller, H. J. 2005. A measurement theory for time geography. *Geographical Analysis* 37(1): 17–45.

Chapter acknowledgments

Dawn Wright, Oregon State University

Michael Blongewicz, DHI Water & Environment

Martina Hennessy, Damian Smyth, and **Trevor Alcorn,** Marine Institute, Galway, Ireland

Rob Morrison, ESRI Ireland

Nearshore and coastal/ shoreline analysis

This chapter discusses the linear feature classes in the Arc Marine data model and their varied implementation in mapping important entities such as present and historical shorelines, sediment budget profiles, alongshore hurricane tracks, nearshore SCUBA survey transects, and jurisdictional boundaries. Concepts are illustrated by a coastal engineering/resource management case study in Florida and a coastal evolution/sediment budget case study in Denmark. While linear features themselves are certainly important, observations, measurements, and samples along with these features are also critical. Two nearshore studies of coral reef fish and invertebrates in Hawai'i demonstrate the utility of the Survey subtype of the InstantaneousPoint feature class and the SurveyInfo object table.

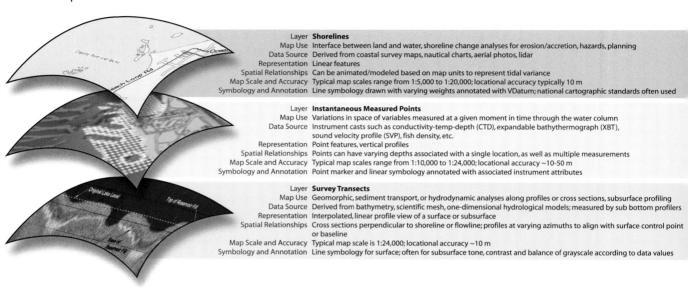

Layer **Shorelines**
Map Use Interface between land and water, shoreline change analyses for erosion/accretion, hazards, planning
Data Source Derived from coastal survey maps, nautical charts, aerial photos, lidar
Representation Linear features
Spatial Relationships Can be animated/modeled based on map units to represent tidal variance
Map Scale and Accuracy Typical map scales range from 1:5,000 to 1:20,000; locational accuracy typically 10 m
Symbology and Annotation Line symbology drawn with varying weights annotated with VDatum; national cartographic standards often used

Layer **Instantaneous Measured Points**
Map Use Variations in space of variables measured at a given moment in time through the water column
Data Source Instrument casts such as conductivity-temp-depth (CTD), expandable bathythermograph (XBT), sound velocity profile (SVP), fish density, etc.
Representation Point features, vertical profiles
Spatial Relationships Points can have varying depths associated with a single location, as well as multiple measurements
Map Scale and Accuracy Typical map scales range from 1:10,000 to 1:24,000; locational accuracy ~10-50 m
Symbology and Annotation Point marker and linear symbology annotated with associated instrument attributes

Layer **Survey Transects**
Map Use Geomorphic, sediment transport, or hydrodynamic analyses along profiles or cross sections, subsurface profiling
Data Source Derived from bathymetry, scientific mesh, one-dimensional hydrological models; measured by sub bottom profilers
Representation Interpolated, linear profile view of a surface or subsurface
Spatial Relationships Cross sections perpendicular to shoreline or flowline; profiles at varying azimuths to align with surface control point or baseline
Map Scale and Accuracy Typical map scale is 1:24,000; locational accuracy ~10 m
Symbology and Annotation Line symbology for surface; often for subsurface tone, contrast and balance of grayscale according to data values

Introduction

The coast (or shore) represents one of the most important linear features on earth, marking the interface between land, sea, and the overlying atmosphere, and between different levels of government, judicial responsibility, or research management (see overviews in Bartlett 2000 and Sherin 2000). The shoreline is also used as a baseline for delimiting nearshore boundaries such as state territorial waters, exclusive economic zones (EEZs), and marine protected areas (MPAs). Only in the past century has the need to establish maritime territorial claims been proposed, and only within the past few decades have protocols been internationally adopted for drawing such lines in the ocean to create maritime boundaries (see overview of Palmer and Pruett 2000). And disconnected lines in the nearshore are used for data collection (transects, tracklines, vehicle tows, and the like). This is important in a navigation framework such as the ArcGIS International Hydrographic Organization (IHO) S-57 data model for electronic nautical charts (http://support.esri.com/datamodels) or the U.S. Hydrographic Data Content Standard for Inland and Coastal Waterways (http://www.fgdc.gov/standards/projects/FGDC-standards-projects/coastal-and-inland-waterways/).

Byrnes et al. (1991) cite five critical factors to consider when mapping coastal and nearshore linear features: coastal and ocean processes, relative sea level, sediment budget, climate, and human activities. This chapter discusses the linear feature classes in the Arc Marine data model and their varied implementation in mapping some of these important factors (figure 6.1). Oftentimes, the interest is not primarily in the linear features and attributes describing the lines (as is typically implemented in terrestrial applications that look at electrical networks, roads, and rivers, for example) but rather in what occurs or is observed along that line. Generally, it is a point measurement, sample, or observation taken at some location along that line (such as the SurveyPoint in figure 6.1) that is of interest.

Common Marine Data Types

Marine Points

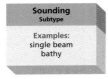

Marine Lines

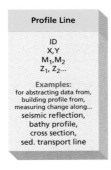

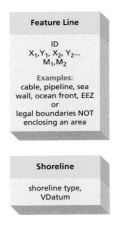

Marine Areas

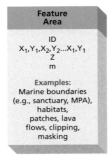

Figure 6.1   Portion of the main Common Marine Data Types diagram (from chapter 2) representing the marine data types featured in this chapter and implemented in the case studies. All headings are feature classes or subtypes of feature classes.

Featured case studies

Two case studies from the west coast of the Big Island of Hawai'i illustrate the key role of the Survey subtype of the InstantaneousPoint feature class in Arc Marine to integrate, manage, and retrieve nearshore datasets. The first case study, implemented by Oregon State University graduate student Alyssa Aaby, used Arc Marine to integrate available nearshore fish species information from private and public sources around the main eight Hawaiian Islands (figure 6.2; Aaby 2004). Aaby integrated spatial information on near-shore fish species into Arc Marine to identify patterns of spatial habitat use and gaps in conservation. Recent studies have shown that the most effective marine protected areas represent a full range of habitat types (Leslie et al. 2003; Carr et al. 2003). The study used the querying ability of Arc Marine to evaluate the habitat use patterns of specific nearshore reef fish along the west coast of the island of Hawai'i (figure 6.3) by identifying correlations between regional-scale spatial information and fine-scale spatial information. This is important because available scientific research has not yet evaluated the current status of nearshore marine habitat use in western Hawai'i at the large scales needed by resource

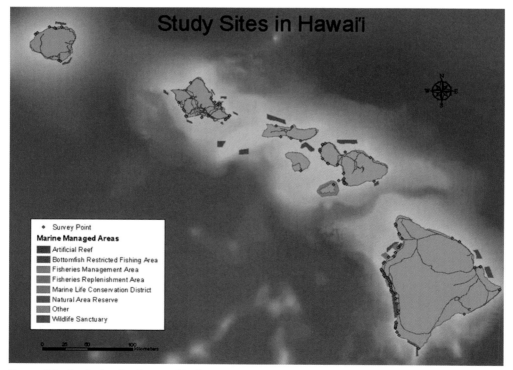

Figure 6.2   Study sites for data used in the western Hawai'i reef fish case study. Map from Aaby (2004), which also contains full documentation on data sources, some of which are proprietary.

Courtesy of Alyssa Aaby, University of Hawai'i and National Park Service (NPS).

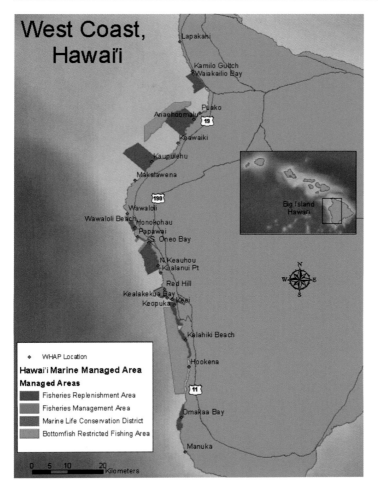

Figure 6.3 Western Hawai'i Aquarium Project (WHAP) study sites used in the western Hawai'i reef fish case study.

Courtesy of Alyssa Aaby, University of Hawai'i and the National Park Service (NPS).

managers. While most marine studies have been conducted at very small scales, management units are usually on the scale of a single island, and resource evaluation therefore should reflect this larger scale (Friedlander and Brown 2003). By determining which combinations of habitat types are necessary for survival, the efficacy of the network of MPAs in western Hawai'i can be evaluated.

Similarly, Lisa Wedding, marine GIS database manager/research assistant; Dr. Larry Basch, senior marine scientist; and their colleagues at the Pacific Islands Coral Reef Program (PICRP) and the Pacific Islands Network Inventory and Monitoring Program, both of the National Park Service (NPS), implemented Arc Marine as a pilot project to develop new geodatabase standards and protocols for moving their data holdings to the geodatabase structure. The geodatabase gives resource managers and biologists at Pacific Islands National Parks the ability to easily access, view, and integrate different datasets (e.g., from inventory, monitoring, and research efforts) to generate maps and graphics; perform simple

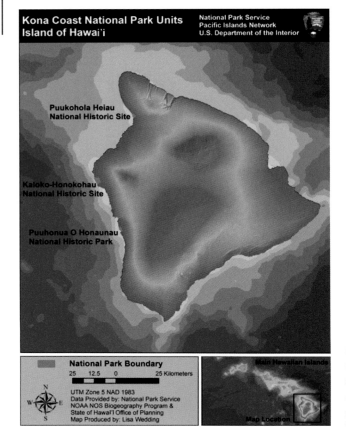

Figure 6.4 Location of the national park units on the west coast of Hawai'i that served as study sites for the Hawaiian NPS case study.

Map produced by Lisa Wedding, University of Hawai'i. Courtesy of National Park Service (NPS).

analyses; and make well-informed, science-based decisions about marine management and conservation actions (Wedding and Basch 2006). Specific tasks include comparing inventories between the parks, tracking research efforts within and across parks (from local and regional to national levels), and monitoring ecological change in parks over time. As such, the geodatabase is not limited to marine data but includes watersheds, land-use practices, subsistence fisheries use, and other terrestrial data. The idea is to increase work efficiency, eliminating the need to sacrifice time and resources to implement a database on their own. The parks in question are on the west coast of Hawai'i: the Pu'ukohola Heiau National Historic Site (PUHE), the Kaloko-Honokohau National Historical Park (KAHO), and the Pu'uhonua o Honaunau National Historical Park (PUHO), all of which are connected by the 175-mile long corridor of the Ala Kahakai National Historic Trail (ALKA) (figure 6.4). The initial efforts focused on this network of national parks and surrounding areas nearshore because of the many ongoing marine research, inventory, and monitoring studies there.

A third case study focused on the central Atlantic coast of Florida in Martin County (figure 6.5), where Kathy Fitzpatrick, coastal engineer of the Martin County Engineering

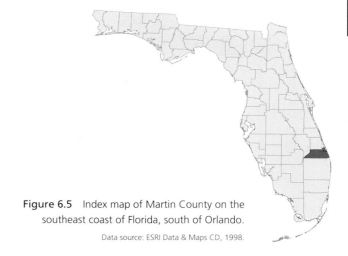

Figure 6.5   Index map of Martin County on the southeast coast of Florida, south of Orlando.

Data source: ESRI Data & Maps CD, 1998.

Department; Heather Mounts, senior database developer at Photo Science, Inc., (PSI) in St. Petersburg, Florida; and Rob Hudson, project manager of PSI, used Arc Marine to store and query an extensive variety of datasets by way of FeatureLine, Shoreline, and FeatureArea (as explained in sections below), and several kinds of raster layers. The Coastal Division of the Martin County Engineering Department houses and maintains data from 21 miles of shoreline and 114 miles of inland waterways. It also maintains data on beach nourishment and management projects, water inlet management, water quality monitoring programs, and the construction and management of several nearshore artificial reefs. The region includes two major inland waterways: the Atlantic Intracoastal (AIWW) and Okeechobee Waterways (OWW). The AIWW runs north–south within the Indian River Lagoon, designated a Lagoon of National Significance partly because it provides essential habitat to juvenile sea turtles, West Indian manatee, and many ocean fish species. Endangered sea turtles also rely heavily on nearby beaches for nesting sites. Effective management requires rapid access to this information coupled with the capability for rapid analysis, particularly regarding hurricane recovery projects (two hurricanes hit Martin County in 2004). Shoreline hardening, coastal development projects, and public lands management are areas of growing concern within the county. Each project represents a substantial and long-term financial investment in the planning, permitting, construction, and monitoring phases of the recovery projects. Using Arc Marine as a guide, the county has been building a sustainable, standardized, and documented coastal GIS to meet local needs while contributing and conforming to evolving state and national coastal geospatial initiatives (Fitzpatrick et al. 2004).

   Ann Skou of DHI Water & Environment implemented the chapter's fourth and final case study. This study is more complex, involving historical coastline evolution, measurements of bathymetry for cross-shore profiles, and simulation of sediment transport rates with the use of numerical models. Recently, the municipality of Køge, Denmark, announced plans to construct a new harbor to support cargo traffic, directly competing with the Copenhagen harbor a few kilometers to the north. The new harbor will rise between an existing harbor to the south and a yacht harbor to the north. Køge is situated along the inner side of Køge bay on the east coast of Zealand, the main island of Denmark. The area has weak currents, and the waves, which are the driving force behind sediment transport, approach the coast almost perpendicularly, resulting in small net transport rates. This has left the bay with a reasonably sandy and stable coastline.

In studies such as this, modelers need to know if the sediment transport is nonexistent overall or if the harbor entrance is just beyond the active transport zone. Even if the harbor doesn't have any problems with sedimentation, the adjacent coastline will be affected because the harbor will block the longshore sediment transport. In this case, where the municipality of Køge plans to more than double the size of the harbor, planners must consider the impact of the adjacent coastline. The volume of upstream sediment and downstream erosion could increase by extending the harbor (if indeed longshore transport does exist), which would change the stability orientation of the coastline and thus the coastline location. Danish authorities require these kinds of investigations before they proceed on such projects.

To investigate the morphological conditions in the area, DHI used its MIKE Marine GIS software (http://www.dhisoftware.com/general/Marine_overview.htm) to examine the coastline and preprocess input data for DHI LITPACK software. LITPACK is a numerical modeling software that applies a unique deterministic approach to a wide range of coastal zone management applications. It simulates wave and current scenarios along coastlines and combines these simulations into predictions of coastal profiles and long-term coastal evolution. The MIKE Marine GIS is an ArcMap extension that consists of a suite of tools to manage, display, and analyze marine-based model data in ArcGIS, relying on a geodatabase with an extended version of Arc Marine for its data structure. DHI has extended Arc Marine's core classes with additional feature classes, object classes, and relationship classes necessary to accommodate the storing of model data. Using MIKE Marine GIS to store, process, and present the data smoothed the workflow and facilitated a better understanding of the investigation findings to nontechnical and technical users.

Linear features and surveys

Similar to chapter 3, which first introduced the superclass MarineFeature and the subsequent point feature subclasses, this chapter focuses on the various linear feature classes, which also inherit from the MarineFeature superclass. MarineLine is an abstract class used to categorically group all of the linear feature classes. Under MarineLine there are three subclasses to be implemented: FeatureLine, ProfileLine, and TimeDurationLine.

FeatureLine is an instantiable feature class that inherits the attributes FeatureID and FeatureCode from MarineFeature but does not introduce new attributes. It is meant simply to be a template for storing physical linear features such as maritime boundaries, sea walls, cables, pipelines, and navigational chart lines. Consequently, Arc Marine also introduces a subclass to FeatureLine called Shoreline. The Shoreline feature class introduces one new attribute, VDatum, which stores the vertical datum used in identifying the specified shoreline. Arc Marine does not define what a shoreline is, but provides an efficient storing mechanism for information making that determination.

The ProfileLine feature class inherits from MarineLine but adds no new attributes beyond the FeatureID and FeatureCode obtained through the inheritance. However, the properties HasM and HasZ have been enabled so that the feature can have a linear measurement system and a depth value that can change along the line. ProfileLine represents a linear feature designed for data interpolation along the distance of the line based on another data source, specifically surveys. The concept behind this collection of classes is that users can associate a ProfileLine with one or many Surveys and can associate a Survey with one or many features of the ProfileLine feature class. Essentially, this emulates a many-to-many relationship, where many features in one class (ProfileLine) can be associated with many instances in a second class (SurveyInfo). To replicate this multiplicity, an additional table called SurveyKey is inserted between the two classes. This table contains two key fields, SurveyID and FeatureID, which are used to relate back to their respective sources, ProfileLine and SurveyInfo. Users can repeat the values for these two fields in SurveyKey in any number of instances, allowing multiple combinations of the same values. FeatureID stores its value in the ProfileLine feature class. FeatureID will repeat each time it associates with a Survey. The value of SurveyID, which identifies a specific

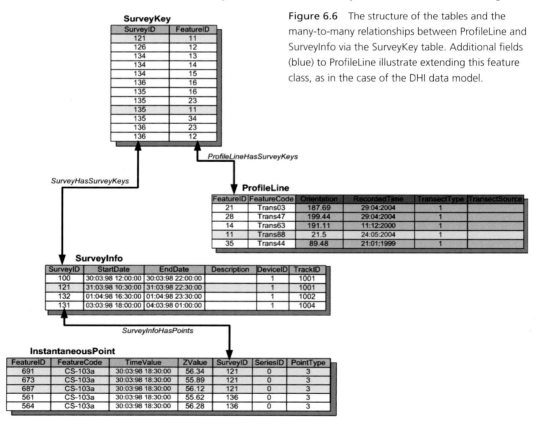

Figure 6.6   The structure of the tables and the many-to-many relationships between ProfileLine and SurveyInfo via the SurveyKey table. Additional fields (blue) to ProfileLine illustrate extending this feature class, as in the case of the DHI data model.

SurveyKey

SurveyID	FeatureID
121	11
126	12
134	13
134	14
134	15
136	16
135	16
135	23
135	11
135	34
136	23
136	12

ProfileLineHasSurveyKeys

SurveyHasSurveyKeys

ProfileLine

FeatureID	FeatureCode	Orientation	RecordedTime	TransectType	TransectSource
21	Trans03	187.69	29:04:2004	1	
28	Trans47	199.44	29:04:2004	1	
14	Trans63	191.11	11:12:2000	1	
11	Trans88	21.5	24:05:2004	1	
35	Trans44	89.48	21:01:1999	1	

SurveyInfo

SurveyID	StartDate	EndDate	Description	DeviceID	TrackID
100	30:03:98 12:00:00	30:03:98 22:00:00		1	1001
121	31:03:98 10:30:00	31:03:98 22:30:00		1	1001
132	01:04:98 16:30:00	01:04:98 23:30:00		1	1002
131	03:03:98 18:00:00	04:03:98 01:00:00		1	1004

SurveyInfoHasPoints

InstantaneousPoint

FeatureID	FeatureCode	TimeValue	ZValue	SurveyID	SeriesID	PointType
691	CS-103a	30:03:98 18:30:00	56.34	121	0	3
673	CS-103a	30:03:98 18:30:00	55.89	121	0	3
687	CS-103a	30:03:98 18:30:00	56.12	121	0	3
561	CS-103a	30:03:98 18:30:00	55.62	136	0	3
564	CS-103a	30:03:98 18:30:00	56.28	136	0	3

Survey, will repeat for each instance of a ProfileLine. Consequently, a relationship class, termed ProfileLineHasSurveyKeys, links the ProfileLine feature class with the SurveyKey table. A second relationship class, SurveyHasSurveyKeys, links the SurveyInfo table to the SurveyKey table (figure 6.6). Chapter 3 introduced the SurveyInfo table, which describes how the SurveyID attribute distinguishes one survey from another and then correlates to a collection of points stored in the InstantaneousPoint feature class.

Linear surveys of west Hawaiian reef fish

The western Hawai'i reef fish case study makes significant use of SurveyInfo, as linked to the Survey subtype of the InstantaneousPoint feature class, in dealing with observations along linear SCUBA transects. Fish observation datasets from all of the main Hawaiian Islands were obtained from various federal, local, and academic institutions through the Hawai'i Natural Heritage Program (HNHP), which included SCUBA surveys conducted by the Western Hawai'i Aquarium Project (WHAP), the Coral Reef Assessment and Monitoring Program (CRAMP), the state of Hawai'i's Division of Aquatic Resources (DAR), the Saving Maui's Reefs project, and individual peer-reviewed journal articles input into a database for the HNHP. The datasets obtained through the HNHP contain information on 121 sites located throughout the main Hawaiian Islands (figure 6.2).

The study area for habitat use analysis on the west coast of Hawai'i extends from Lapakahi to Manuka (figure 6.3) and represents approximately 212 sq km of shoreline, 15 different habitat types, 5 reef zones, and varying levels of protected status (NOAA Biogeography Team, http://ccma.nos.noaa.gov/ecosystems/coralreef/main8hi_mapping.html). The availability of fish survey data and habitat information led researchers to choose this area from among the eight Hawaiian Islands.

They combined all datasets into a single Microsoft Access database consisting of four primary tables: (1) survey location information, (2) Divemaster, (3) Run Detail, and (4) species information. All tables used a key field to relate one table to another, allowing users to perform queries involving variables of space, time, and fish species.

Researchers used the Survey subtype of the InstantaneousPoint feature class to store the x-, y-, and z-locations of an observation along a linear fish survey. Many survey point locations in this case study represent only an approximation of the location where the fish survey was conducted, as the exact latitude and longitude coordinates are unknown. The information recorded in the geodatabase reflects the best possible estimate.

Researchers established the spatial extent and project of the feature classes before adding any datasets to the geodatabase. They imported the NAD83 UTM Zone 4 projection information and spatial extent from a polygon shapefile of the main Hawaiian Islands (DBEDT 2004) into the Arc Marine data model. Accordingly, all subsequent shapefiles imported into the geodatabase would need to be in the same projection (i.e., NAD83 UTM Zone 4) and fall within maximum x,y spatial extent.

Researchers then used the CREATEXY function to import the Microsoft Access table containing the survey latitude and longitude coordinates into ArcGIS to generate a point shapefile. This two-dimensional (2D) shapefile was converted into a three-dimensional (3D) shapefile using the z-values (depth) in the attribute table. This was necessary because all shapefiles imported into the Survey subtype must be 3D in accordance with the established data model parameters, even if the 3D values do not exist.

It was initially thought that Survey could be further defined with information stored in the SurveyInfo object class. However, this was not possible due to the large amount of data. With more than 250,000 entries, it took too long to perform one query if all of the data were combined into one table representing the main Hawaiian Islands. But by separating data by island, queries took less than one minute, and multiple queries could be conducted if information on more than one island was needed. As a result, Arc Marine was customized by adding additional field names and tables to the geodatabase: Divemaster, Run Detail, and Integrated Species, which were specific to each island (e.g., Oahu Divemaster, Hawai'i Run Detail). These tables further describe Survey by providing information such as survey dates, who conducted the survey, and which species were observed along the way.

When all the data was entered into the geodatabase, relationships were established between the feature classes (spatial) and the tables (nonspatial) (figure 6.7). These relationships consisted of one-to-one and one-to-many relationships. A one-to-one relationship matches one entry to an identical entry in a separate column/table. A one-to-many relationship matches one entry to multiple identical entries in a separate column or table. Additionally, due to the nature of the geodatabase, these relationships are permanent. And unlike joins, the relationships will not have to be reestablished in each new project.

Researchers used Arc Marine in the habitat utilization analysis in large part because the resulting geodatabase could be easily and efficiently queried for space, time, and fish species. This allowed researchers to determine where a specific fish species was observed (figure 6.8). These sites could then be overlain on large-scale habitat types to determine what species were found in what habitat types.

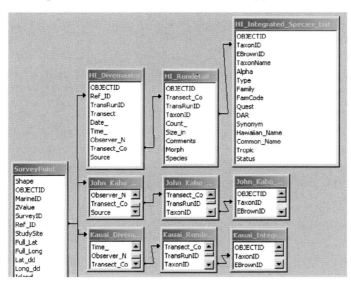

Figure 6.7 The relationships established between the Survey subtype (renamed SurveyPoint) and the various attribute tables in the western Hawai'i reef fish case study, as seen in Microsoft Access.

Courtesy of Alyssa Aaby, University of Hawai'i and the National Park Services (NPS).

117

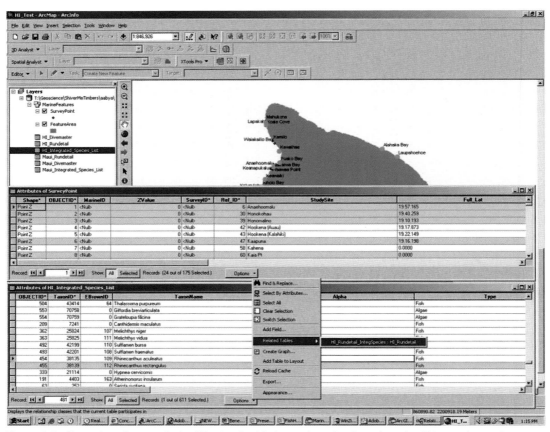

Figure 6.8   Illustration of a query in ArcGIS using Arc Marine to show the sites where the *Rhinecanthus aculeatus* (Blackbar triggerfish) was observed during fish surveys by SCUBA. This information was then used in the regional habitat analysis.

Courtesy of Alyssa Aaby, University of Hawai'i and the National Park Services (NPS).

Researchers examined the spatial habitat utilization patterns of reef fish along the western Hawai'i coast after importing the fish datasets into Arc Marine. They used three spatial datasets to determine these patterns: (1) the WHAP fish survey dataset stored in Arc Marine, (2) the NOAA Biogeography Team's large-scale habitat delineations (Coyne et al. 2001) stored in Arc Marine, and (3) the WHAP substrate dataset. Researchers investigated three questions to answer the question of habitat utilization: (1) How do specific fish species use certain habitat types? (2) Does depth play a significant role in the classification of these habitat types? (3) Does small-scale substrate information correlate with large-scale NOAA habitat information?

Researchers used the WHAP dataset because it is one of the most comprehensive and statistically significant Hawaiian reef fish datasets. Additionally, it covers 23 sites along the

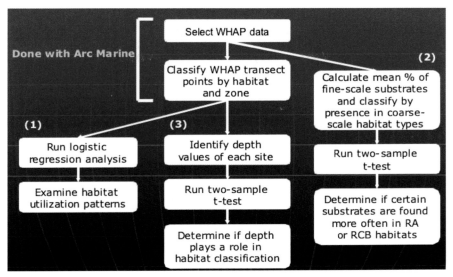

Figure 6.9   Flowchart of the specific steps taken in the fish analysis portion of western Hawai'i reef fish case study.

west coast and spans a multiyear time period. The detailed steps taken to answer each of the three subquestions are outlined below (figure 6.9).

To analyze this WHAP dataset, researchers used Arc Marine to query and separate the WHAP data from the other data in the geodatabase. This required isolating data specific to WHAP to avoid confusing a fish species observed on a DAR survey at the same site as fish species observed on a WHAP survey. Moreover, it was important to separate the WHAP data because survey methodologies differed between datasets. Separating the data created a new feature class called WHAP Location, along with three tables: WHAP Divemaster, WHAP Run Detail, and WHAP Species. This data remained in Arc Marine, and new relationships formed between the tables and feature class, following the initial Arc Marine schema.

To determine the habitat type and zone for each of the WHAP sites, the WHAP Location feature class was overlain on a NOAA large-scale benthic habitat layer, derived from hyperspectral and IKONOS satellite imagery for the Island of Hawai'i (NOAA Biogeography Team, http://ccma.nos.noaa.gov/ecosystems/coralreef/main8hi_mapping.html). Based on this imagery, a hierarchical classification scheme was created to define and delineate habitats zones (NOAA Biogeography Team, http://ccma.nos.noaa.gov/ecosystems/coralreef/main8hi_mapping.html). This classification shows only continuous habitats greater than 1 acre in size (Coyne et al. 2001). Using the Select by Location function in ArcGIS, the habitat types and benthic habitat zones for each of the WHAP sites were determined.

After classifying each WHAP site according to habitat type and zone, researchers used a logistic regression analysis to determine the pattern of habitat utilization of six aquarium and seven nonaquarium fish species (figure 6.10) between the different habitat types. These fish species were selected because they represent commonly collected aquarium and reef fish observed during WHAP surveys. Following the methodology outlined by

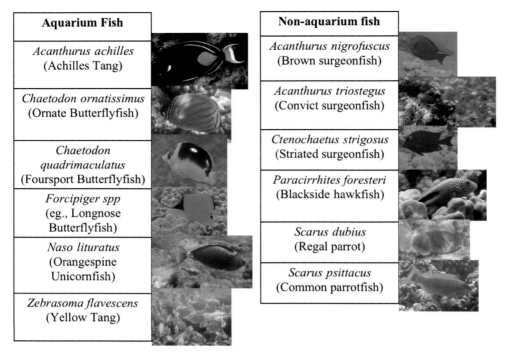

Aquarium Fish	Non-aquarium fish
Acanthurus achilles (Achilles Tang)	*Acanthurus nigrofuscus* (Brown surgeonfish)
Chaetodon ornatissimus (Ornate Butterflyfish)	*Acanthurus triostegus* (Convict surgeonfish)
Chaetodon quadrimaculatus (Foursport Butterflyfish)	*Ctenochaetus strigosus* (Striated surgeonfish)
Forcipiger spp (eg., Longnose Butterflyfish)	*Paracirrhites foresteri* (Blackside hawkfish)
Naso lituratus (Orangespine Unicornfish)	*Scarus dubius* (Regal parrot)
Zebrasoma flavescens (Yellow Tang)	*Scarus psittacus* (Common parrotfish)

Figure 6.10 Aquarium and nonaquarium fishes examined in the western Hawai'i reef fish case study.

Photos courtesy of Larry Basch, NPS. Reprinted by permission.

Christensen et al. (2003), a binary response (y=1 if present or 0 if not present) was fit to the independent variable (x=habitat type). This meant that for each column, there was either a probability of being present (p) or of not being present (p-1). Arc Marine was then used to query the location of each specific fish to determine its presence or absence at each WHAP site.

Researchers conducted further analysis into the habitat utilization of specific fish species to determine possible correlations between the small-scale substrate information gathered in 1999 by the WHAP researchers (Tissot et al. 2004) and the large-scale habitat information delineated by NOAA (NOAA Biogeography Team, http://ccma.nos.noaa.gov/ecosystems/coralreef/main8hi_mapping.html). To do this, they calculated mean percentages of each small-scale substrate type found at each WHAP site. The WHAP sites were then categorized according to habitat type, and the information was compared using a two-sample t-test.

Researchers determined the depth values of each WHAP site to learn if depth values played a role in the classification of NOAA's large-scale habitat types. The WHAP sites were then categorized by habitat type, and the information was compared using a two-sample t-test.

For the 23 WHAP fish sites, the benthic habitat type of each WHAP survey site was determined by overlaying the WHAP location feature class on NOAA's benthic habitat shapefile (table 6.1).

Habitat type	Reef/Aggregate Coral (RA)	Reef/Colonized Volcanic Rock/Boulder (RCB)	No data
Location	Aneehoomalu	Kalahiki Beach	Honokohau
	Keawaiki	Kamilo Gulch	Hookena (Auau)
	Keei	Kaupulehu	Makalawena
	N. Keahuhou	Kealakekua Bay	Manuka
	S. Oneo Bay	Keopuka	Omakaa
	Red Hill	Kualanui Point	Wawaloli
	Waiakailio Bay	Lapakahi	Wawaloli Beach
		Papawai	
		Puako	

Table 6.1 WHAP study sites (figure 6.3) categorized by habitat type, western Hawai'i reef fish case study.

Once the WHAP sites were categorized by habitat type, a logistic regression was used to determine the habitat utilization patterns of the selected reef fishes. Researchers found some habitat utilization preference between the RA and RCB habitat types for these selected species (table 6.1). A slight preference for the RCB habitat type was observed, but further studies are needed to verify these results. Complete results are presented and discussed in Aaby (2004).

More surveys: National Park Service coral reef monitoring

The Hawaiian NPS case study started with a large number of data tables, lookup tables, and cross-reference tables of fish observations from a visual census during SCUBA transects or free swims (figure 6.11), invertebrate recruitment data and classifications (figures 6.12 and 6.13), taxonomies and descriptions of life histories for invertebrates, sampling events, cross-reference tables between events and contacts, and more. These were initially stored in Microsoft Access with relationships drawn between fields similar to figure 6.7 for the western Hawai'i reef fish case study. Next, shapefiles were created and organized according to the NPS standard file structure (Park Name ‡ Data, Images [and within that digital raster graphics or photos], Tools [and within that extensions or legends], and Workspace [and within that documents and metadata]). Organizing shapefiles this way streamlined the process of exporting them to the geodatabase. The four main shapefile directories eventually became the four feature datasets created in the geodatabase: (1) Hawai'i Island, (2) KAHO (Kaloko-Honokohau NHP), (3) PUHO (Pu`uhonua o Honaunau NHP), and (4) PUHE (Pu`ukohola Heiau NHS). The Hawai'i Island folder contained marine datasets obtained from NPS and partners that were clipped to the boundary of Hawai'i. The KAHO, PUHE, and PUHO folders contained appropriate terrestrial datasets that were all clipped to the watershed boundary. All datasets are projected in UTM Zone 5 NAD 1983.

Figure 6.11 Example of fishes observed (mostly convict surgeonfish) during SCUBA or free swim surveys for the Hawaiian NPS case study.

Photo courtesy of Jennifer Smith, University of California, Santa Barbara. Reprinted by permission.

Figure 6.12 An invertebrate recruitment settlement plate as a primary data collecting device, Hawaiian NPS case study.

Photo courtesy of Larry Basch, NPS. Reprinted by permission.

Figure 6.13 Examples of the invertebrate recruits commonly collected by settlement plates as shown in Figure 6.12, Hawaiian NPS case study.

Photos courtesy of Larry Basch, NPS. Reprinted by permission.

As with the western Hawai'i reef fish case study, the Survey subtype of the Instantaneous-Point feature class was used to store the x-, y-, and z-locations in all the data tables. The lookup and cross-reference tables were imported from the Microsoft Access database and all relationships were established. The spatial reference was set to the main Hawaiian Islands, and the projection used was UTM Zone 5 because the dataset was almost entirely located around the perimeter of the island of Hawai'i.

Shapefiles were imported as feature classes and organized within feature datasets according to the NPS standard file structure. All shapefiles were batch exported to the feature datasets according to park unit or island. The marine datasets were not limited to individual park units, as most were from coastal locations along the west coast of Hawai'i. This was done with the understanding that marine ecosystems are open systems and do not lend themselves as well as terrestrial datasets to clipping based on boundaries such as watersheds.

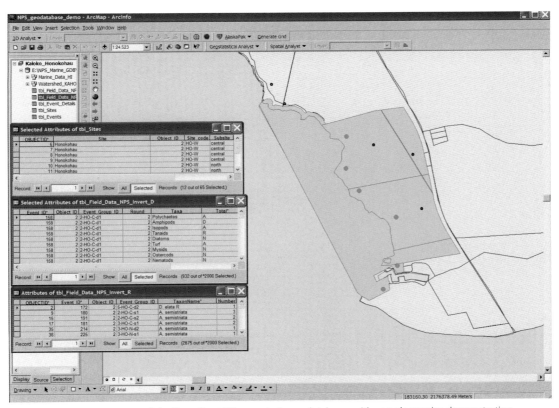

Figure 6.14 Screen capture of the Hawaiian NPS case study geodatabase, with sample queries demonstrating how users can extract useful information to aid management decisions at Pacific Islands National Parks. More examples are available on the book's accompanying Web site, http://dusk.geo.orst.edu/djl/arcgis.

Courtesy of Lisa Wedding, University of Hawai'i, NPS. Reprinted by permission.

With the geodatabase fully populated with data, researchers test it with a series of initial queries. Two scenarios discussed by Wedding et al. (2005) are (1) a resource manager at KAHO wants to generate a species list of all marine organisms in the park unit based on data from several research sites in the area, and (2) a resource manager at PUHO is planning a marine monitoring program and wants to review the monitoring protocols used in recent research projects near the park. Figure 6.14 shows one of many possible examples of queries that may be performed to fulfill these needs. The Microsoft PowerPoint file associated with this chapter on the book's accompanying Web site, http://dusk.geo.orst. edu/djl/arcgis/, includes many more screen captures of successful queries.

Arc Marine contains feature classes and tables that do not entirely match the NPS logical model, but these are being kept because the PICRP is continuing to obtain and create new datasets that will take advantage of these feature classes in the future. These will include time series points from marine species inventories, water quality instrumentation data (figure 6.15), digital underwater video, benthic fisheries harvest monitoring, more invertebrate recruitment monitoring, and locations series from sea turtle tracking data (figure 6.16). As a result, the use of Arc Marine allows NPS to include future datasets with ease while managing existing data to support management decisions.

Figure 6.15 Installation of a joint NPS/USGS/State of Hawai'i oceanographic instruments (e.g., current meters, water clarity/quality sensors) representing new marine and coastal datasets that will be incorporated into the Hawai'i NPS case study geodatabase in the near future.

Photo courtesy of Larry Basch, NPS. Reprinted by permission.

Figure 6.16   Sea turtle and turtle tracking device that will provide future datasets anticipated for the Hawaiian NPS case study.

Photos courtesy of Jennifer Smith, University of California, Santa Barbara, and Sallie Beavers, NPS. Reprinted by permission.

Shorelines, FeatureLines, and FeatureAreas in Martin County, Florida

The Martin County, Florida, case study aimed to integrate disparate datasets to streamline the management of its coastal programs. This is part of a phased strategy to implement a coastal GIS infrastructure (Phase I, a scoping exercise in 2003; Phase II, assessment, refinement, and the creation of a coastal GIS implementation framework in 2004; Phase III, the prototype implementation itself to build a first generation Coastal GIS Geodatabase in 2005; Phase IV, migration to a production system in 2006; and Phase V, maintenance and ongoing enhancements). The Arc Marine case study largely comprised Phase III.

First, researchers conducted an inventory of potential data for inclusion in the coastal GIS. The inventory included nearly 250 datasets associated with Martin County field projects, Florida Department of Environmental Protection (FDEP) datasets (hurricane tracklines, point locations of photography, and videography), and basemap or framework data as defined by the Federal Geographic Data Committee (FGDC). Researchers obtained the framework data from sources such as the NOAA Coastal Services Center, Florida Marine Research Institute, Florida Inland Navigation District, Florida Geographic Data Library, Florida Land Boundary Information System, the USGS, and NorthStar Geomatics. Table 6.2 summarizes the wide variety of imagery and raster grids gathered or generated for input to the geodatabase.

The datasets were further cataloged based on thematic groupings and Arc Marine feature classes, using primarily the Shoreline, FeatureLine, and FeatureArea feature classes where appropriate; and with the determination and specification of customized subtypes such as ArtificialReefs, BeachManagement, NavigationManagement, HabitatManagement, and

125

CoastalMonitoring. A FeatureID and a ProjectID were created and can be traced throughout the entire geodatabase. Any additional GIS layers associated with that project will contain the same MarineID. Additional tables (some for customized Arc Marine object classes) were created to store project fieldwork information such as benthic species lists, artificial reef site attributes, and nearshore cruise information, and administrative details such as organizations involved, permitting information, grant agency details for proposals info, and Martin County program information. Relationships were then created between spatial and nonspatial data, and between spatial data and topological rules. Finally, researchers established procedures for the efficient creation and population of FGDC-compliant metadata on all datasets, as necessary.

Next, the geodatabase was fully populated, with priority GIS layers and related tables loaded into ArcSDE. This effort included adherence to several protocols and procedures developed in Phase II:

- Specifications for conversion to geodatabase format of coastal related GIS data to be stored in Oracle and ArcSDE. This included vector data, raster data, and related stand-alone tables.
- Procedures related to the implementation of the Arc Marine UML for the creation of a coastal geodatabase schema in ArcSDE.
- Procedures to populate the coastal geodatabase with Martin County coastal data, including vector data and related tables, and as raster layers.
- Creation and QA/QC (quality assurance/quality control) procedures on all relationships for GIS layers and related business tables. QA/QC procedures for all ArcSDE coastal layers, rules, and behaviors.
- Procedures for implementation of FGDC compliant metadata on all relevant layers.
- Procedures for the connection of the county's existing financial database to Florida's Critical Infrastructure Management System (for, among other things, emergency planning and response in the wake of natural hazards).

Fitzpatrick et al. (2006) discuss ways in which coastal engineers and resource managers would need to use the coastal geodatabase, such as management of Martin County's habitat, beach, inlet, and artificial reef resources through the effective implementation of engineering and restoration projects; monitoring and analyzing the effectiveness of the Coastal Program's engineering and restoration projects; and tracking permit requirements and automating the required permit submittals. Queries (selections, reselections, and relates) and retrieval from the geodatabase can fulfill many initial needs, as shown by the example in figure 6.17.

The county also used the FDEP ArcIMS site (http://www.dep.state.fl.us/beaches/) to obtain additional datasets for the coastal geodatabase. The Martin County team downloaded and then stored in Arc Marine the FDEP hurricane tracks, satellite imagery, and aerial photography (pre- and post-hurricane). The team created hyperlinks from point layers to allow point-and-click viewing of digital photos and videography at selected locations (figures 6.18 and 6.19). The team stored photo and video files outside the geodatabase as flat files. In similar applications involving artificial reef data, point locations were hyperlinked to associated PDF files.

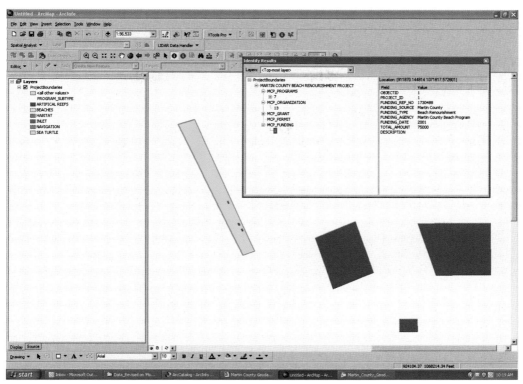

Figure 6.17   Screen capture of the Martin County case study geodatabase with a sample query and selection of beach nourishment FeatureAreas. More examples are available on the book's accompanying Web site, http://dusk.geo.orst.edu/djl/arcgis.

Data provided by Martin County and Photo Science, Inc.

Figure 6.18   Screen capture from the FDEP ArcIMS site provides some of the data for the Martin County, Florida, case study. Landsat Thematic Mapper imagery is the underlay, blue dots show impact monitoring points for Hurricanes Frances or Jeanne, and red dots are hyperlinked points for video files.

Data provided by Martin County and Photo Science, Inc.

Data Type	Description	Thumbnail Example
DOQQ—Digital Orthophoto Quarter Quadrangles	DOQQs were obtained from FDEP on DVD. The images were mosaicked and made available for loading into ArcSDE. Since NorthStar currently has aerial photos loaded in the Martin County production geodatabase, duplication of the aerial photographs into the Martin County coastal geodatabase was not necessary.	
ETOPO	ETOPO 2 layer was obtained by NOAA Coastal Services Center. The image shows both bathymetry and topography for the southern United States, and may be clipped to Martin County to provide an additional basemap layers.	
Nautical Charts	NOAA Nautical Charts were downloaded and mosaicked in order to form a seamless layer in the Martin County coastal geodatabase.	

Sidescan Sonar	Sidescan sonar datasets were provided by Martin County. Photos do not contain georeferenced information. Additional rectifying and/or registering of the images will allow for GIS overlays. The layers can then be stored in the geodatabase.	
Land Use	Land-use raster layer was downloaded from the Florida Cooperative Fish & Wildlife Research Unit. The layer was clipped to Martin County.	
Surfaces	Surfaces were created from point data layers as appropriate. These surfaces allow for detailed viewing and analysis of static tabular information.	
TM Imagery	Thematic Mapper (TM) imagery was downloaded from the USGS. The sensor is a multispectral scanning radiometer that was carried on board Landsats 4 and 5 and has provided nearly continuous coverage from July 1982 to present, with a 16-day repeat cycle. The layer was clipped to Martin County.	

Table 6.2   Raster grids and images and associated procedures of the Martin County, Florida, case study (from Fitzpatrick et al. 2006).

Data provided by Martin County and Photo Science, Inc.

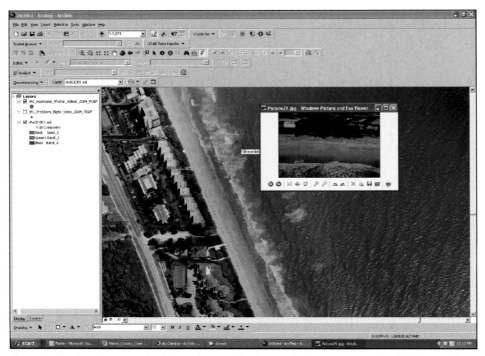

Figure 6.19 Another example of FDEP data used in the Martin County case study; this time aerial photography, with a red dot serving as a hyperlink, points to a 2004 hurricane photo snapped at that location.

Data provided by Martin County and Photo Science, Inc.

The case study generated five main products (the nonproprietary items are available on the book's accompanying Web site at http://dusk.geo.orst.edu/djl/arcgis):

- A data inventory spreadsheet in Microsoft Excel
- A UML diagram of the modified Arc Marine data model, using Microsoft Visio and ESRI Geodatabase Designer
- A geodatabase report describing GIS layers, relationships, tables, and raster datasets
- A populated Martin County coastal geodatabase with vector data, raster data, stand-alone tables, spatial and nonspatial relationships, and rules stored in Oracle and ArcSDE according to Arc Marine schema
- Martin County coastal geodatabase documentation

The next steps include the building of associated tools and portals.

Extending ProfileLine to transects and baselines

The objective of the ProfileLine feature class is to assign values at locations along the feature based on values associated with the points of a survey. In earlier examples, points marked locations of observations or samples along a FeatureLine or Shoreline. But this case study shows that points may be graphed using the distance along the ProfileLine feature as the x-axis and the values associated with the survey points (logically selected within a specified distance from the ProfileLine feature) as the y-axis (figure 6.20).

At DHI Water & Environment, the customized version of the Arc Marine data model uses ProfileLine features for implementing transects and baselines. Transects derive profile data from a survey, and baselines are used to measure the changes in accretion and erosion along the shoreline. Although both features derive data from a survey, they are used in different applications with different attributes. Consequently, they were added as two new feature classes. In other words, ProfileLine was changed to an abstract class for this case study, and two new subclasses, Transect and Baseline, were added. Transect can be used to create a bathymetric profile along a Transect feature. A bathymetric profile is

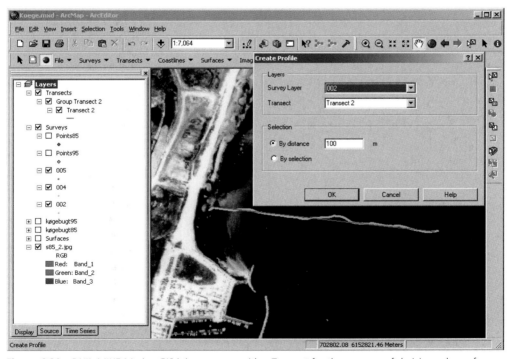

Figure 6.20   DHI's MIKE Marine GIS joins a survey with a Transect for the purpose of deriving values of a profile along the Transect feature.

Courtesy of Uwe Jacobs, Køge Kommune.

often imported into a numeric model for defining the shape of the seafloor, which in turn influences the transport area for sediment. In the Transect feature class, four additional attributes exist: Orientation, for storing the orientation of a Transect; RecordedTime, the time stamp when the Transect was created; TransectType, for determining if the Transect feature was digitized or imported from a numeric model; and TransectSource, the input file of a model-generated Transect. Within DHI's MIKE Marine GIS, software tools are available for either digitizing a Transect or importing data from DHI's modeling software (figure 6.21). In either case, once a Transect has been added, users can create a bathymetric Profile by collecting the ZValues from the points of a selected survey that are within a specified distance of the Transect feature (figure 6.22).

Figure 6.21 The value of a point in a survey is assigned to a location along the transect. This is done by constructing perpendicular lines between the survey points and the transect.

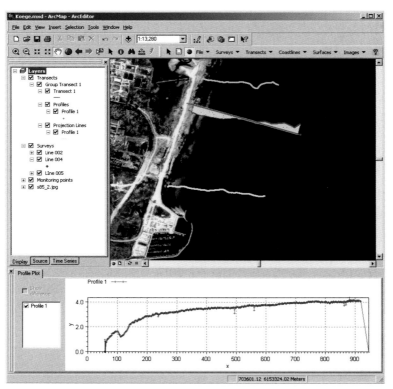

Figure 6.22 A profile is drawn using MIKE Marine GIS where the x-axis is based on the length of the transect feature and the y-axis is determined from the values of the survey points as positioned along the transect.

Survey data provided by Køge municipality. Background image provided by Geographic Institute of Denmark.

When deriving a profile, the survey points should be projected to a location that is determined along the transect by constructing a perpendicular line from the survey point to the transect (figure 6.21). The points may then be stored as point events in a new object class called TransectPoints, where the position along the Transect feature is stored and has been assigned with a ZValue of the original survey point. Additional attributes for describing sediment transport, such as Roughness, d50, and Spreading, may be stored in the TransectPoints table.

The second subclass of ProfileLine implemented in the DHI data model is termed Baseline. This feature class is used similarly to Transect except that rather than assigning the depth (ZValue) of the points to the transect feature, the distance from the survey point is projected to a perpendicular location along the Baseline feature. This allows for measuring the changes in one shoreline survey to another based on an established feature—the Baseline. By storing a Baseline feature in a geodatabase when new surveys are available, the original Baseline would be used for deriving changes in the shoreline. Similar to the TransectPoints object class, an additional object class called CoastlinePoints is added for storing the point events along the baseline and the distance from the point to Baseline. Additionally, a line is drawn through the survey points that have been selected and projected to Baseline. This line is added as a Shoreline feature. The combination of a Shoreline and a Baseline constitute what is termed a Coastline. The Coastline feature can then be plotted as a graphic using MIKE Marine GIS where further volumetric differences can be calculated and plotted in conjunction with Coastline.

The final subclass of MarineLine is the TimeDurationLine feature class. The TimeDurationLine feature class is discussed in great detail in chapter 4. Please refer to this chapter for a complete description.

Sediment transport

In the DHI case study of sediment transport simulation, a combination of recent bathymetric surveys along the coast of Køge is used together with Transect features for generating profiles. These profiles can then be used as input to the numerical model known as LITPACK. Tools are available in MIKE Marine GIS for exporting the profile data into a format that LITPACK recognizes. With knowledge of local wave conditions and sediment properties, the profile can be used to simulate the littoral drift along the coastline. Figure 6.23 shows the simulated littoral drift for typical eastern wave conditions. Notice that the resulting transport direction for this wave direction is southward. In the present situation, sand is transported along the coast toward the north when waves arrive from southern directions and toward the south when waves arrive from northern directions. The annual net transport is defined as the difference between the total northward transport and the total southward transport. The net transport determines the shoreline evolution at both sides of the port. Using nearshore wave conditions, calculated by DHI for the purpose of this study, and sampled sediment data, the profile formed the basis of the calculation of annual sediment drift.

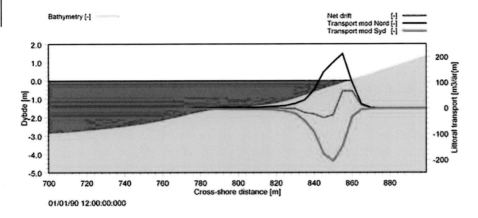

Figure 6.23   The result from the LITDRIFT module of LITPACK showing the calculated transport rates north of the port based on the bathymetric profile derived in MIKE Marine GIS. The black and green curves indicate the total northward and southward transport, respectively. The red curve represents the net annual transport.

Data provided by Ann Skou, DHI Water & Environment.

Shoreline evolution

In addition to the sediment transport, the DHI case study also looked at the Shoreline evolution. Using the tools in MIKE Marine GIS, a straight baseline feature was drawn and positioned parallel to the coastline. The measured coastline data, derived from aerial photographs and stored as two separate surveys from 1985 and 1995, was used to create a shoreline by projecting the respective positions and distances of the survey points to the common baseline. From this, the coastlines could be plotted along with the calculated volumetric differences. The analysis in this case showed the volume difference to be approximately 7,200 m^3/m for the 10-year interval (figure 6.24). The total volume in cubic meters can be found by multiplying the length and width of the coastline with the depth of the active layer. Assuming the active layer thickness is about 3 m, the net sediment transport rate in the area can be estimated as 22,160 m^3 in 10 years. This corresponds to an annual accumulation of 21,60 m^3/year, a relatively small amount, which supports the general perception about the coastline in this area being stable.

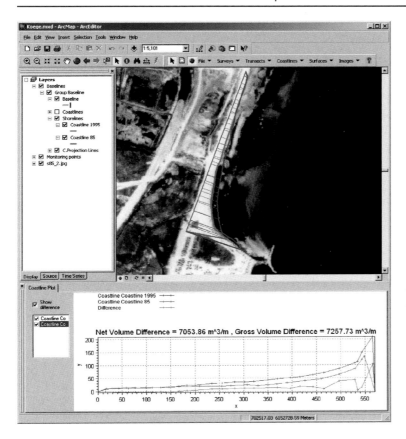

Figure 6.24   Coastline plots and shoreline processing of the net volume difference and the gross volume difference from MIKE Marine GIS. The image shows a baseline in purple, a 1985 shoreline in green, and a 1995 shoreline in blue.

Image courtesy of Niels Nielsen, Institute of Geography, Denmark, and Uwe Jacobs, Køge Kommune.

Conclusion

This chapter and the case studies it revolves around amply illustrate the flexibility of the Arc Marine data model. In each of these case studies, the data model was highly customized and extended to accommodate the application and the data used. The researchers preserved the core classes, while also adding their own feature classes or object classes where they saw fit. This illustrates a fundamental concept that the Arc Marine data model is not meant to be the solution, but rather the foundation from which a solution can be built.

Linear features play an important role in marine applications, even without the networks of linear infrastructure that are so typical of terrestrial applications. In marine applications, linear features often delineate a path or track along which measurements, observations, or samples have been made. So this chapter is less about describing the linear features than it is about describing how the lines are used as part of the process of determining where or what happens along the line. The lines are mapped using GIS not because they represent a physical feature but because something has happened, has been measured, or has been derived along that line.

Arc Marine class definitions featured in this chapter

FEATURE CLASSES	**InstantaneousPoint** is a feature class representing features that are single observations in time and space. The x- and y-coordinates, plus a time stamp, create the unique feature. An InstantaneousPoint can have multiple ZValues by implementing a relationship to the Measurement object class.		
	Subtype	Survey	
	Notes	InstantaneousPoint is a subclass of the superclass MeasurementPoint.	
	Properties	None apply	
	Fields	FeatureID	A geodatabase-wide unique identifier and key field for participating in relationships
		FeatureCode	A user-defined code used for identifying a feature
		CruiseID	A key field for relating this feature class to a Cruise
		TimeValue	The time stamp for the point
		ZValue	A single depth value for the point
		SurveyID	A foreign key to the SurveyInfo object class
		SeriesID	A foreign key to the Series object class
		PointType	Defines the subtype to be one of the following: 1 = Instant (default value) 2 = Sounding 3 = Survey 4 = LocationSeries
	ProfileLine is a feature class representing linear features that are not physical features themselves but rather features that are interpolated, along the line, from another source—for example, a profile interpolated from a bathymetry survey.		
	Subtype	None apply	
	Properties	HasM = True HasZ = True	
	Notes		
	Fields	FeatureID	A geodatabase-wide unique identifier and key field for participating in relationships
		FeatureCode	A user-defined code used for identifying a feature
		CruiseID	A key field for relating this feature class to a Cruise
	ShoreLine is a feature class representing the measured intersection between the shore and mean high waterline.		
	Subtype	None apply	
	Properties	HasM = True HasZ = True	
	Notes		
	Fields	FeatureID	A geodatabase-wide unique identifier and key for participating in relationships
		FeatureCode	A user-defined code used for identifying a feature
		CruiseID	A key field for relating this feature class to a Cruise
		VDatum	Defines the vertical datum for the Shoreline feature

FEATURE CLASSES (cont'd)	**FeatureArea** is a feature class representing homogeneous areas.		
	Subtype	None apply	
	Properties	None	
	Notes		
	Fields	FeatureID	A geodatabase-wide unique identifier and key field for participating in relationships
		FeatureCode	A user-defined code used for identifying a feature
		CruiseID	A key field for relating this feature class to a Cruise
OBJECT CLASSES	**SurveyInfo** is an object class designed for storing information about a specific survey.		
	Notes		
	Fields	SurveyID	A key field for relating this table to a feature class
		StartDate	The beginning date of the survey
		EndDate	The ending date of the survey
		Description	A general description of the survey
		DeviceID	A key field for relating a survey with a Measuring device
		TrackID	A key field for relating a survey with a Track
	SurveyKey is an object class designed as an intermediate key table with one-to-many relationships on both sides of it for modeling a many-to-many relationship between the ProfileLine and SurveyInfo tables.		
	Notes	The two fields, SurveyID and FeatureID, can be repeated any number of times forming unique combinations of relationships between features and survey	
	Fields	SurveyID	A key field for relating this table to the SurveyInfo table
		FeatureID	A key field for relating this table to a feature class
	Cruise is an object class that defines the characteristics of a ship for the duration of an expedition.		
	Notes		
	Fields	CruiseID	An identifier for a given cruise
		Code	An user-defined code for a given cruise
		Name	The name of the cruise
		Purpose	The purpose of the cruise
		Status	Defines the status of the cruise
		Description	A general description of the cruise
		StartDate	The beginning time stamp for the cruise
		EndDate	The ending time stamp for the cruise
		ShipName	The name of the ship participating in the cruise

RELATIONSHIPS	**SurveyInfoHasPoints**	1 : *	One Survey can have zero or many points
	ProfileLineHasSurveyKeys	1 : *	One ProfileLine can have zero or many SurveyKeys
	SurveyHasSurveyKeys	1 : *	One Survey can have zero or many SurveyKeys
	CruiseHasTracks	1 : *	One Cruise can have zero or many Tracks

References

Aaby, A. 2004. *Testing the ArcGIS Marine data model: Using spatial information to examine habitat utilization patterns of reef fish along the west coast of Hawai'i.* M.S. thesis, Corvallis, Ore.: Oregon State University.

Bartlett, D. J. 2000. Working on the frontiers of science: Applying GIS to the coastal zone. In *Marine and coastal geographical information systems,* ed. D. J. Wright and D. J. Bartlett, 11–24. London: Taylor & Francis.

Byrnes, M. R., R. A. McBride, and M. W. Hiland. 1991. Accuracy standards and development of a national shoreline change database. In *Proceedings of a specialty conference on quantitative approaches to coastal sediment processes (Coastal Sediments '91),* ed. N. C. Kraus, K. J. Gingerich, and D. L. Kriebel, 1027–42. Seattle, Wash.: American Society of Civil Engineers.

Carr, M., J. Neigel, J. Estes, S. Andelman, R. Warner, and J. Largier. 2003. Comparing marine and terrestrial ecosystems: Implications for the design of coastal marine reserves. *Ecological Applications* 13(1) Supplement: S90–S107.

Christensen, J. D., C. F. G. Jeffery, C. Caldow, M. E. Monaco, M. S. Kendall, and R. S. Appeldorn. 2003. Cross shelf habitat utilization patterns of reef fishes in southwestern Puerto Rico. *Gulf and Caribbean Research* 4(2): 9–27.

Coyne, M. S., M. E. Monaco, M. Anderson, W. Smith, and P. Jokiel. 2001. *Classification scheme for benthic habitats: Main eight Hawai'ian Islands.* NOAA technical report. Silver Spring, Md.: NOAA Center for Coastal Monitoring and Assessment, Biogeography Team. http://ccma. nos.noaa.gov/products/biogeography/Hawaii_cd/.

Department of Business, Economic Development and Tourism (DBEDT). 2004. Overview of the Hawai'i Statewide Planning and Geographic Information System. http://www.state.hi.us/ dbedt/gis/organiz.htm. Honolulu, Hawai'i: State of Hawai'i Office of Planning.

Fitzpatrick, K., A. Carvalho, and R. Hudson. 2004. Advancement of an enterprise coastal GIS in Martin County, Florida. *Proceedings of the ESRI International User Conference* 24, Paper 1418. http://gis.esri.com/library/userconf/index.html.

Fitzpatrick, K., H. Mounts, and R. Hudson. 2006. *Building a coastal GIS at the county level using the Marine data model: The Martin County, Florida case study.* Internal project report. Stuart, Fla.: Martin County Engineering Department.

Friedlander, A., and E. Brown. 2003. *Fish habitat utilization patterns and evaluation of the efficacy of marine protected areas in Hawaii: Integration of NOS digital benthic habitat maps and reef fish monitoring studies.* NOAA technical report. Silver Spring, Md.: NOAA Center for Coastal Monitoring and Assessment, Biogeography Team.

Leslie, H., M. Ruckelshaus, I. Ball, S. Andelman, and H. Possingham. 2003. Using siting algorithms in the design of marine networks. *Ecological Applications,* 13(1) Supplement: S185–S198.

Palmer, H. and L. Pruett. 2000. GIS applications to maritime boundary delimitation. In *Marine and coastal geographical information systems,* ed. D. J. Wright and D. J. Bartlett, 279–94. London: Taylor & Francis.

Sherin, A. 2000. Linear reference data models and dynamic segmentation: Application to coastal and marine data. In *Marine and coastal geographical information systems,* ed. D. J. Wright and D. J. Bartlett, 95–116. London: Taylor & Francis.

Tissot, B., W. Walsh, and L. Hallacher. 2004. Evaluating the effectiveness of a marine reserve in west Hawai'i to improve management of the aquarium fishery. *Pacific Science,* 58(2): 175–88.

Wedding, L., and L. Basch. 2006. *Marine geodatabase report.* Internal technical report. Honolulu, Hawaii: Pacific Islands Coral Reef Program, U.S. Department of the Interior National Park Service, Hawaii-Pacific Islands Cooperative Ecosystem Studies Unit, University of Hawai'i at Manoa.

Wedding, L., M. Lane-Kamahele, S. Margriter, L. Basch, and G. Dicus. 2005. Preliminary results of the NPS PICRP marine geodatabase efforts. *Proceedings of the ESRI International User Conference* 25, Abstract 2390. http://gis.esri.com/library/userconf/index.html.

Chapter acknowledgments

Dawn Wright, Oregon State University

Michael Blongewicz, DHI Water & Environment

Ann Skou, DHI Water & Environment

Lisa Wedding, Larry Basch, Melia Lane-Kamahele, Sandy Margriter and **Gordon Dicus,** U.S. National Park Service, Pacific Islands Coral Reef Program and Pacific Islands Network Inventory and Monitoring Program, Honolulu, Hawai'i-Hawaiian NPS Case Study

Alyssa Aaby, University of Hawai'i at Manoa, Honolulu, Hawai'i-Western Hawai'i Reef Fish Case Study

Rob Hudson and **Heather Mounts,** Photo Science, Inc., St. Petersburg, Florida-Martin County, Florida, Case Study

Kathy Fitzpatrick, Martin County Engineering Dept., Stuart, Florida-Martin County, Florida, Case Study

Model meshes

The Model Mesh dataset was added to the Arc Marine data model to support numeric modeling and modeling applications within the ArcGIS environment. While this book includes other case studies that illustrate the use of model data, they generally focus on storing and accessing model input data. This chapter focuses on storing and accessing model results, specifically 2D model data and 2D data with multiple values that vary over time. It also further examines data three dimensionally by stacking 2D data at different depths so that each layer represents a unique slice in space. This layered representation allows one to drill down through space to retrieve a single value or multiple values from any number of depths (layers) at a given time step.

This chapter revolves around the case study of the Federal Maritime and Hydrographic Agency of Germany, where Arc Marine has become an important component in its geodata infrastructure and warehouse, which is currently increasing from 80,000,000 scalar values to approximately 3,000,000,000 scalar values.

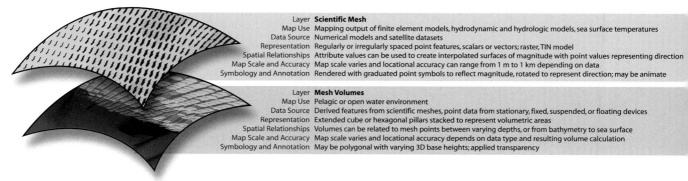

Layer **Scientific Mesh**
Map Use Mapping output of finite element models, hydrodynamic and hydrologic models, sea surface temperatures
Data Source Numerical models and satellite datasets
Representation Regularly or irregularly spaced point features, scalars or vectors; raster, TIN model
Spatial Relationships Attribute values can be used to create interpolated surfaces of magnitude with point values representing direction
Map Scale and Accuracy Map scale varies and locational accuracy can range from 1 m to 1 km depending on data
Symbology and Annotation Rendered with graduated point symbols to reflect magnitude, rotated to represent direction; may be animate

Layer **Mesh Volumes**
Map Use Pelagic or open water environment
Data Source Derived features from scientific meshes, point data from stationary, fixed, suspended, or floating devices
Representation Extended cube or hexagonal pillars stacked to represent volumetric areas
Spatial Relationships Volumes can be related to mesh points between varying depths, or from bathymetry to sea surface
Map Scale and Accuracy Map scale varies and locational accuracy depends on data type and resulting volume calculation
Symbology and Annotation May be polygonal with varying 3D base heights; applied transparency

Introduction

Ocean numerical modeling is a main pillar of marine sciences and services, along with data collected during surveys. The marine community uses operational numerical models to predict currents, sea water temperatures, salinity, water levels, sea state, and other parameters in real or near real time. These important tools support storm surge warning, rescue operations, abatement of marine pollution, ship routing, integrated coastal zone management, and approval processes of offshore facilities. Numerical models are often used for supporting marine survey planning and marine data processing.

The integration of numerical modeling and GIS recently evolved from a relationship of mere exchanging of files to more intimate integration. This integration might consist of either having GIS capabilities embedded into the modeling software or having models executed from within a GIS using GIS-based data sources as the input. One of the principle reasons for this evolution is the ability to integrate or otherwise share the same data sources. GIS has long been able to preprocess and post-process model data and in some cases provide limited display capabilities of model results in conjunction with other spatial features. Historically, this was generally accomplished through an export/convert/import processing of the data by both GIS and modeling software. Now, this requirement of greater integration is more obvious as more input data for models is being collected and stored in large enterprise databases and is being generated and accessed in a client/server environment by multiple users with varying applications. Data sharing is the most basic and essential means of integration between GIS and numerical modeling software. If the software can operate on a common dataset, including model results, then integration advances and user efficiency greatly increases. Geodatabases offer data-sharing capabilities unavailable from earlier file-based data structures. For these reasons, Arc Marine aids the integration between the two by including the needed feature classes and object classes to support the storage of model data.

Numerical modeling

Numerical modeling is the use of sophisticated numerical algorithms with the aid of computers to solve differential equations simulating physical, chemical, and biological processes that occur in nature. For the purpose of this book, the examples are limited to the use of physical models. The accuracy of the numerical model results is dependent on the accuracy of the boundary and initial conditions used to provide the input and the modeler's ability to calibrate and validate the model. It is also dependent on the modeler's ability to determine the appropriate parameters for the model. Numerical modeling relies on different dimensionality—one dimension (1D), two dimensions (2D), and three dimensions (3D)—to accurately portray the physical world. Numerical modeling is generally grouped into categories of either steady state or dynamic.

Numerical models in 1D attempt to simulate or solve the flow along a line (e.g., rivers) with basic fluid mechanics algorithms. Points along that line and data associated with it are used to describe the state of the flow at that location and to interpolate to the next point down the line.

Two-dimensional modeling simulates flow through an area or surface (e.g., floods or statistical surfaces temperature of the water at a given depth). The geometry of a 2D model can be represented by either raster or vector data in the form of nodes and faces. Vector nodes can be used to build either a finite element mesh of irregularly shaped faces defined by three or four nodes, or a regularly spaced mesh of rectangular faces referenced by a linear or even curvilinear 2D coordinate system independent of the underlying projected or geographic coordinate system. The geometry of 3D model is volumetric in nature and is either regularly subdivided into cuboids referring to some linear or curvilinear 3D coordinate system or is a 3D mesh of finite elements (tetrahedrons) representing the volume of interest.

Numerical modeling additionally relies heavily on the element of time. The temporal capability of numerical modeling is the ability to replicate or otherwise forecast a certain phenomenon over time. Whether the model data is collected with recorders or calculated through an interpolation, how the values change or move over time is what modelers find most revealing.

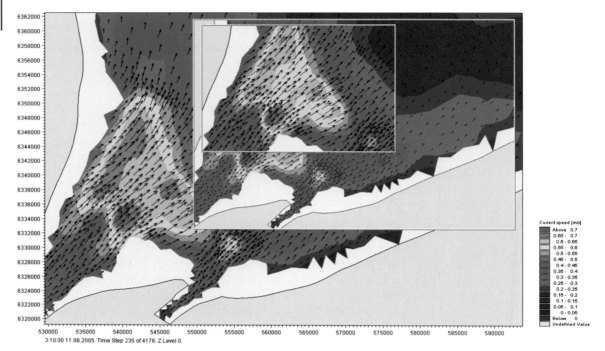

Figure 7.1 This diagram illustrates an example of 2D results from a numeric mesh model developed by Manitoba Hydro using DHI's MIKE 21 software.

Featured case study

The Bundesamt für Seeschifffahrt und Hydrographie (BSH, Federal Maritime and Hydrographic Agency) is a federal authority in Germany under the jurisdiction of the Federal Ministry of Transport, Building, and Urban Development. As a maritime partner to industry, science, and environmental organizations, the BSH provides a wide range of services in the fields of navigation and maritime transportation and the marine environment. BSH has used numerical models for many years to support the services of routine daily simulations and predictions of the North Sea and Baltic Sea dynamics, including current, water level, temperature, salinity, and dispersion of substances. The model system comprises several interacting computer programs that produce output data automatically without intervention. The model is 3D, consisting of two nested 3D models established in spherical coordinates with a horizontal regularly spaced square grid cell size of approximately 6 nautical miles and 1 nautical mile, extending to nine and five vertical depth levels, respectively. The coarser model covers the entire North Sea and Baltic Sea with a total number of 36,703 grid cells. The fine-resolution grid consists of 72,636 cells covering the German coastal areas. In addition, external surges entering the North Sea are computed by a 2D model having a regular grid spacing of approximately 24 nautical miles. A detailed description of the BSH numerical model system can be found in Dick (2001) or Dick et al. (2001). The case study featured in this chapter uses data of the BSH fine-resolution 3D model grid.

Multiple dimensions

Model data and model results in 2D and 3D generally are represented as a raster or a stack of rasters. Arc Marine can support a vector representation for each of these dimensions, inclusive of a time element. The ProfileLine feature class, explained in detail in chapter 6, can support 1D numerical models. In Arc Marine, MeshFeature provides the feature and object classes necessary for storing data generated by 2D and 3D numerical models. Although not yet possible to define in UML, 2D rasters representing modeled surfaces can be included as part of the data model and subsequent geodatabases. This chapter focuses on the data model's vector representation of 2D and 3D data, the ability and means of accessing the data, and how to render the model data for analytical or presentational purposes.

Meshes and mesh features

MeshPoint features are points that describe data from a 2D or 3D numerical model as either a regularly spaced grid point or as an irregularly spaced node of a finite element mesh or other mesh type. MeshPoint features represent either the center of the cell of a regular 2D or 3D raster (GridPoint subtype), or they define the nodes (NodePoint subtype) of the finite element faces. The MeshPoint feature class is a subclass of MarineFeature and consequently inherits the FeatureID and FeatureCode attributes, which are used by several relationship classes. The MeshPoint feature class also adds attributes such as IPosition, JPosition, and KPosition that are traditionally used in modeling to describe the row, column, and depth location of a point within a mesh. The MeshID attribute is used as a key field for identifying in which Mesh a point participates. The PointType field is a subtype field for determining if the point is a GridPoint and used in a regular mesh or a NodePoint and used in an irregular mesh.

The MeshElement feature class is a polygonal feature class that inherits from Marine-Feature for representing the face of an irregular mesh. At least three MeshPoint features must define a MeshElement, but it might also be defined by four MeshPoints. This feature class has four attributes in addition to those inherited from MarineFeature—Node1ID, Node2ID, Node3ID, and Node4ID. These attributes are used as key fields for identifying the FeatureID of the MeshPoint that marks the corners of the MeshElement. In this case, the PointType attribute of MeshPoint should be set to 2, identifying that the MeshPoint is subtyped as a NodePoint as opposed to a GridPoint.

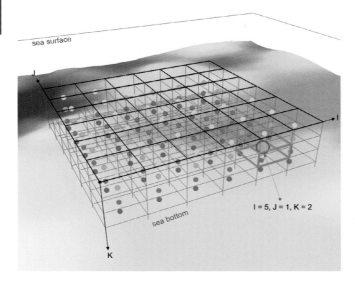

Figure 7.2 This diagram illustrates the 3D location of points of the MeshPoint feature class within a Mesh, where the points are symbolized based on their KPosition (depth layer) in the Mesh.

Provided by Jürgen Schulz-Ohlberg, Federal Maritime and Hydrographic Agency, Germany. Used with permission.

MeshPoint features can participate in one or more meshes and meshes of different dimensionality, and can be referenced by either the coordinate property of their shape or their 3D location within a Mesh. The points, however, have no attributes that reflect information about the mesh itself. It is the Mesh object class that defines the Mesh and which points are used.

The Mesh object class defines the size, shape, and dimensionality of the mesh. The MeshID serves as a key field to uniquely identify the mesh. The relationship class named MeshHasPoints is used to link the mesh with the points in the MeshPoint feature class.

The MeshID is a user-defined identifier and is not an auto-generated value. The MeshHasPoints relationship class is a one-to-many relationship, allowing for one mesh to have many points. Furthermore, features from the MeshPoint feature class can participate in more than one Mesh, and Meshes of varying dimensionality can be created from the same feature class of MeshPoints. The TotalPoints attribute is simply the total number of points actually participating in the Mesh, while the attributes NoOfPointsI, NoOfPointsJ, and NoOfPointsK store the possible number of points in the respective three directions. The Dimension field is defined by a CodedValueDomain called MeshType to determine the dimensionality of the mesh as linear and 1D, a 2D area, or a 3D volume.

The TotalPoints is not necessarily the product of NoOfPointsJ by the NoOfPointsI by the NoOfPointsK, spanning the 3D mesh space. It is not necessarily true that the same number of points populates each depth layer defined by the mesh. In a simple example, a mesh could have a value of three for the NoOfPointsK, indicating that this volumetric mesh has three depth layers. The TotalPoints might be set to 22, where the first and second layers each have nine points and the third layer has only four points. In ocean numerical modeling, TotalPoints is often referred to as the number of wet grid points.

Vector and scalar quantities

Numerical models generally produce time-varying quantities of scalar or vector values. The VectorQuantity or the ScalarQuantity tables further define the Mesh Points so that data will be stored depending on its scalar or vector nature, respectively. The table entries also carry a time stamp so that the values of a particular quantity for a single location can vary over time. Points can have values in both tables, and these are managed through the MeshPointHasVectors and MeshPointHasScalars relationship classes. These relationships are one-to-many relationships, so a point can have one or more Vector Quantities and one or more Scalar Quantities.

The VectorQuantity table uses the FeatureID attribute as a key field for participating in the relationship associating vector values to specific points of the MeshPoints feature class and the ParameterID as a key field for participating in the relationship to the Parameter object class. The attributes, XComponent, YComponent, and ZComponent are used to define the three quantities of a vector. It will then be up to the user or a specific application to calculate the direction and magnitude of the vector (e.g., current direction and current speed). For storing the calculated magnitude and direction explicitly, users are free to add the necessary attributes to the VectorQuantity table. TimeValue is the attribute storing the associated time step of these values. The x, y, and z components could vary for every time step, indicating a FeatureID for a given point and a ParameterID for a given parameter.

The Scalar Quantities table also uses the FeatureID as the key field for participating in a similar relationship class with the MeshPoint feature class called MeshPointHasScalars. This table also has the ParameterID attribute used as the key field for the relationship class connecting the Parameter table. The DataValue attribute is used to store the actual value of the scalar, and the TimeValue attribute is used to store the time stamp of the data value.

Having vector and scalar data as attributes associated with the same set points, the same mesh can be rendered differently for each parameter type. Rendering vector data together with scalar data of the same mesh provides the ability to illustrate attributes in relation to each other. The BSH will often choose to look at current speed and direction in relation to sea temperature at varying depths and different time steps.

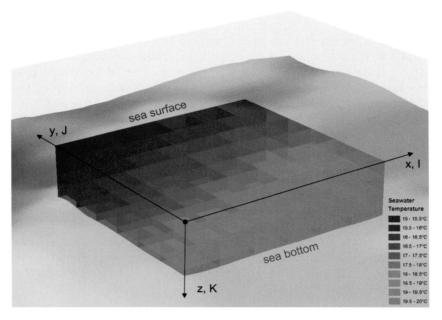

Figure 7.3 The capabilities of rendering a Mesh based on the scalar quantities of the Mesh Points.

Provided by Jürgen Schulz-Ohlberg, Federal Maritime and Hydrographic Agency, Germany. Used with permission.

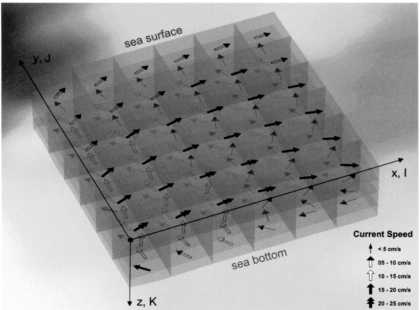

Figure 7.4 The capabilities of rendering a Mesh based on the vector quantities of the Mesh Points.

Provided by Jürgen Schulz-Ohlberg, Federal Maritime and Hydrographic Agency, Germany. Used with permission.

Parameters

The Parameter object class is designed as a lookup table for all parameters for which the user has data in the geodatabase. The Parameter table stores basic attributes describing the parameters. Users can easily add attributes to this table to support other specific data types and applications. The Parameter table uses the ParameterID as the unique identifier for each parameter. The Name, Description, Unit, and SignificantDigits are then used to define the parameter. The Quantity attribute uses a coded value domain for defining whether it is a Scalar, Vector, or some other quantity.

This table can be approached in various ways. When users query the table for a specific parameter, access is provided through the relationship classes to the actual data values and ultimately the associated features. Likewise, when investigating specific features and data values, the same set of relationship classes provides access to the Parameter table and to information describing the data values.

Figure 7.5 illustrates the structure of the Mesh Features dataset. Its feature classes, object classes, and their relationships provide several access routes to the data. From the spatial perspective, starting with a Mesh (MeshID = 3) and going through the MeshHasPoints relationship class, all participating point features (e.g., FeatureID = 3004360, 3004227, 3004087)

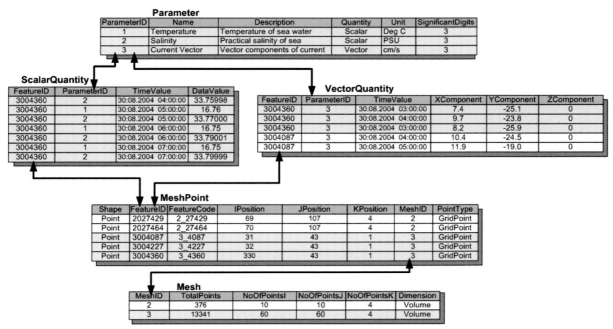

Figure 7.5 This diagram illustrates the connectivity of the data. The structure allows users to approach the data from several directions, either spatially by querying a Mesh for points and then determining the data available, or to find all points of a certain parameter type.

149

form the selected dataset of the MeshPoint feature class. Within the feature class, the points can be further queried based on their depth position within the Mesh (KPosition = 1). All scalar data values associated with the selected points at this depth can be found, proceeding from the MeshPoint feature class through the MeshPointHasScalars relationship to the ScalarQuantities table. In the example, the point with the FeatureID = 3004360 has scalar values for two different Parameters (ParameterID = 2 and ParameterID = 1, Salinity and Temperature, respectively). Additionally, through the MeshPointHasVectors relationship class, the same set of points at this depth has vector quantities. Furthermore, for the scalar quantities and the vector quantities, each value for each of the points changes for each time step. This adds the fourth dimension to the data and another means of organizing specific values. That is, the values for these select points (or this mesh) for a specific parameter (Temperature) will change and can be rendered differently on a time-step-by-time-step basis. This allows for comparison of the data from one point in time to another. The results could be further narrowed by querying for a particular time period. The ParameterID is the key field by which the particular parameter (e.g., Salinity, Temperature) in the Parameter table can be identified.

Conversely, the path through the relationships and tables are in reverse of the previous example if the approach is to query by parameter type and to locate the mesh features or an entire mesh that represents a particular parameter. To find the type of quantity data present, the Parameter table can be viewed for all available types, either scalar or vector. If Current is selected, for example, through the ParameterHasVectors relationship class, all of the records in the VectorQuantity table are selected with the corresponding ParameterIDs. In this table, the FeatureIDs and their corresponding data values (XComponent, YComponent, and ZComponent) for the varying time steps can be seen. This data can be further queried for a particular range of values or time period. Through the MeshPointHasVectors relationship class, the actual point features that meet the criteria can be highlighted in the MeshPoint feature class. Finally, ArcMap can render and symbolize the entire mesh or the subset of the mesh that these points represent, based on one or more of these values.

Rendering mesh features

At the Marine Sciences department of the Federal Maritime and Hydrographic Agency (BSH) of Germany in Hamburg, Dr. Jürgen Schulz-Ohlberg and Kai Jancke are working with a team on the development of a customized, GIS-based marine data management, information, and analysis system. The system aims to achieve a more homogeneous and efficient treatment of disparate marine datasets comprising mainly oceanographic and marine chemical measurements as well as numerical model results. The BSH has contributed extensively to the design of the Mesh Features dataset and is using an extended version of Arc Marine. The BSH is implementing a centralized large-scale ArcSDE/Oracle geodatabase storing several hundred million objects, the majority of them in data resulting from daily numerical model predictions. In detail, holding 30 days of hourly BSH mesh data makes for approximately 72 million rows per parameter in the ScalarQuantity and

VectorQuantity tables, for the parameters Temperature, Salinity, and Current. Everyday after the forecast calculation is complete, three days worth of data are replaced in the geodatabase. Given that the forecast extends for three days into the future, two days are updated, one is added, and the oldest day is dropped.

Users access data through the Parameter table for the GIS application based on the Arc Marine data model being developed at the BSH. This application is an ArcGIS tool that extracts mesh data based on user-specified values. It uses the Parameter table and its relationship classes to populate the content of the dialog elements, for example, selection lists, with the available data. In the example illustrated in figures 7.6 and 7.7, the application presents available data in the existing geodatabase associated with the two meshes described previously. From these two meshes, the user can query and create a new point feature class representing either a particular scalar or vector parameter at a specified depth and for a specific time step. In figure 7.6, a MeshPoint feature class is created from the points at the second depth layer of a selected Mesh (MeshID = 3) and at a specified time step for the parameter of Current Vector. Likewise in figure 7.7, the same Mesh (MeshID = 3) is being queried for all temperature values at depth layer 3 for a particular moment in time.

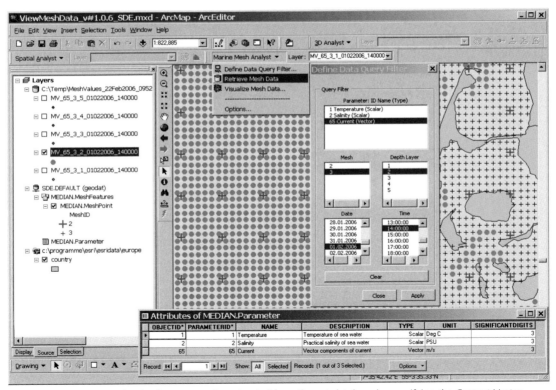

Figure 7.6   At BSH, MeshPoint features can be extracted from the geodatabase by specifying the Current Vector parameter, the second depth layer (Kposition = 2), and a specific date and time.

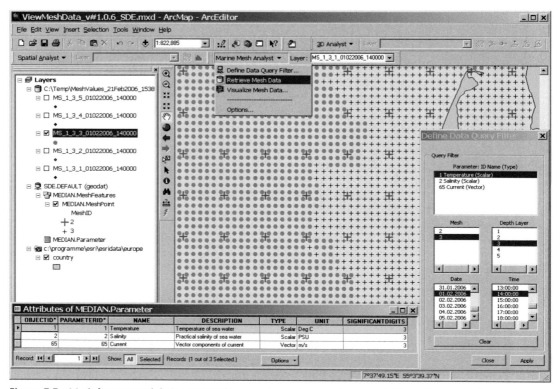

Figure 7.7   Mesh features and their associated temperature values may be extracted from the geodatabase using the BSH application by specifying the Temperature parameter and the values from the third depth layer (KPosition = 3) and a specific data and time (time step) and an existing mesh (MeshID = 3).

Provided by Jürgen Schulz-Ohlberg, Federal Maritime and Hydrographic Agency, Germany. Used with permission.

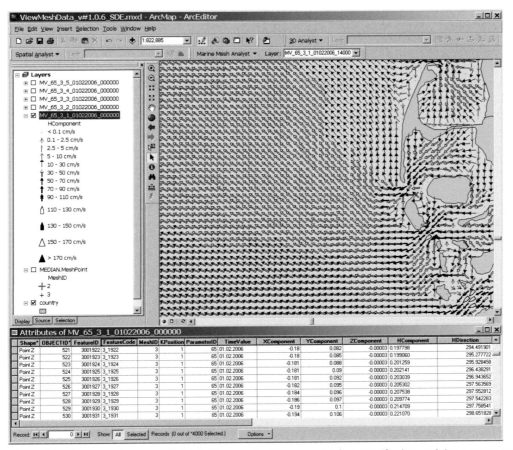

Figure 7.8   The sea surface current distribution near the German coast for a specific date and time uses vector data extracted from the geodatabase. The speed and the direction of the current are rendered as graduated and rotated symbols.

Provided by Jürgen Schulz-Ohlberg, Federal Maritime and Hydrographic Agency, Germany. Used with permission.

153

These feature classes can then be further rendered in various ways to visualize and present the model values. In the example illustrated in figure 7.8, the data from the first query is rendered using the vector values of the parameter Current. The newly created MeshPoint feature class holds the XComponent, YComponent, and ZComponent and is joined with selected attributes of the VectorQuantity object class. Using the BSH application, the vector properties of magnitude and direction are automatically calculated from the x-, y-, and z-components and stored in the attributes HComponent and HDirection. The magnitude (speed) and the direction values determine the graduated size and the angle of each symbol. If this process repeats for each possible time step, the user can see how the data evolves over time at the specified depth. And if the complete procedure repeats for each depth layer, then the user can visualize the variation in the values over time and over varying depths.

Furthermore, statistical surfaces, which might be more revealing and intuitive than rows and columns of points, can be interpolated from mesh points associated with scalar values. Users can interpolate these values to a raster resulting in a distribution of values across the

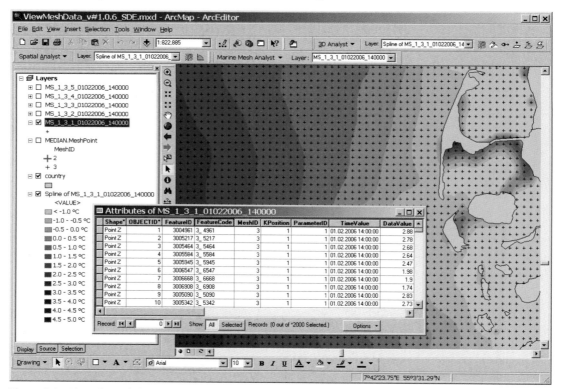

Figure 7.9   The color-coded sea surface temperature distribution near the German coast represents a specific date and time. The underlying raster layer is an interpolated surface of temperature data values extracted from the MeshPoints feature class using the BSH application.

surface. Continuing the example of the second query using temperature data in figure 7.7, the temperature values associated with the points are used in a spline interpolation showing the temperature distribution at a given depth and at a specified date and time. This effect is illustrated in figure 7.9.

Because the mesh points generating the temperature surface also have vector values for the Current, the two data types can be graphically overlaid in ArcMap. The resulting map displays the color-coded temperature distribution and the speed and direction of the current rendered as rotated graduated point symbols.

This data becomes even more informative when rendered in 3D. This can be achieved in different ways. In one approach taken at the BSH, a scalar mesh quantity (temperature) may be interpolated to a raster (as shown in figure 7.9 and described above) repeatedly for all depth layers of a single mesh. ArcScene can display the resulting set of raster layers, one stacked on the other with the base height of each raster layer set to the depth value of the corresponding model layer. Controlling the transparent display property of the rasters gives a pseudo 3D impression of the horizontal and vertical temperature distribution.

Another approach produces a similar looking result but avoids the intermediate steps of the raster interpolation. This approach works when the cuboid cells of a model mesh have already been built as a regular 3D raster, which may be regarded as a vertical stack of 2D rasters (compare to figure 7.2). Instead of using a representation by a number of points stored in the MeshPoint feature class, each of these 2D rasters can be represented by an identical number of conjoined regular rectangles describing the upper horizontal faces of the cuboid cells in the numerical model. Like the points in the MeshPoint feature class, these rectangles need to be created only once in advance and may be retained in an additional polygonal feature class (referred to as MeshFace below). In this feature class, the FeatureID is obtained from the ID of the point coincident with the center of the polygon. The depth of each rectangle should be stored as the z-coordinate property of the feature's geometry enabling rendering in 3D. Using the temperature data as an example again, the temperature values associated with the points for a single mesh for all depth levels at a specified date and time can easily be joined to the MeshFace feature class via the FeatureID attribute. ArcScene can then render the MeshFace feature class using graduated colors and transparent display for the temperature values (figure 7.10). As with interpolated rasters, this type of representation reveals—while not fully 3D—the horizontal and the vertical distribution of the mesh values.

To allow for a combined analysis or comparison of temperature and current values in 3D as represented in figure 7.11, the current vector data values are extracted from the geodatabase for each of the depth layers represented by the NoOfPointsK attribute. These new MeshPoint values are joined to the points coincident to the polygons of the MeshFace feature class and graphically overlaid with the stacked temperature layers in ArcScene. The current data is rendered using graduated arrow symbols as illustrated in figure 7.11. The rotation angle of the arrows indicates the ocean current's direction, and the size of the arrows is scaled according to the ocean current's speed. This results in a true rendering of scalar and vector values for the same mesh point at each of the depth layers. By adding the fourth dimension of time, the scene can be animated to show the change in values of depth over time.

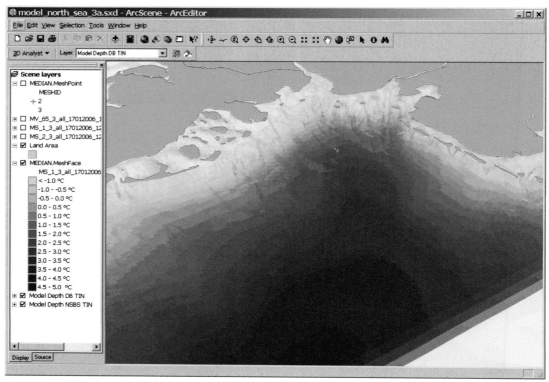

Figure 7.10 This 3D view of vertically stacked polygonal layers simulates the raster layers, color coded by temperature value in the German Bight for a specific date and time (for further explanation, see text).

This data can be furthered queried or accessed and then presented using standard ArcGIS tools. Figure 7.12 shows that once the raster data layers for temperature are created for each depth layer in a Mesh, the graphing tools from the ArcGIS 3D Analyst extension can be applied for extracting data. In this example, the tools extract data along a line for a certain depth layer. The data is graphed to display the change in temperature along that line. Additionally, the tools create a drilling effect through the various raster layers to see the varying temperatures for the existing depths at a given location.

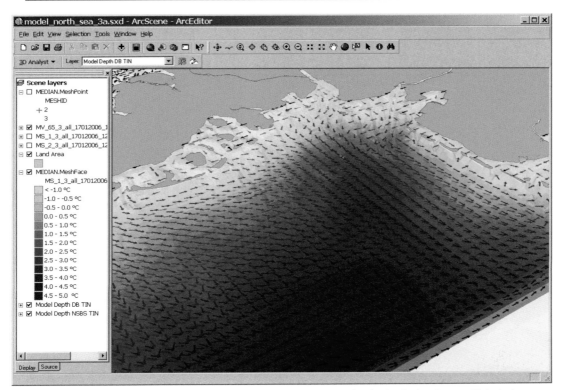

Figure 7.11   The combined 3D view of stacked temperature and current distribution in the German Bight is shown for a specific date and time, with the current data being rendered at all model depth levels using graduated and rotated arrow symbols.

Provided by Jürgen Schulz-Ohlberg, Federal Maritime and Hydrographic Agency, Germany. Used with permission.

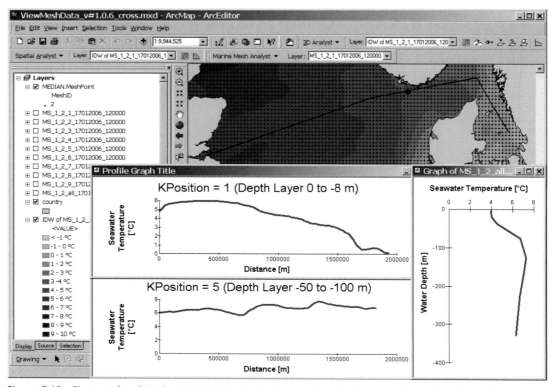

Figure 7.12 The use of tools in the ArcGIS 3D Analyst extension allow for data extraction, either along a line or at a given point from the raster layers interpolated from various depth layers of a Mesh.

Conclusion

Debate continues over the logic of storing model results, which can be voluminous, in a database. However, no one argues about the querying capabilities of a relational database. Users can apply the same capabilities to model results by storing the data as a normalized vector structure in a database, especially a spatially enabled database such as the geodatabase. As seen in the case study provided by the BSH, the Mesh Features dataset of Arc Marine provides a good means for storing the data so that it can be queried and accessed from varied perspectives for different applications.

Arc Marine class definitions featured in this chapter

FEATURE CLASSES	**MeshPoint** is a feature class representing point features from a 1D, 2D, or 3D numerical model as either an equally spaced mesh or irregularly spaced mesh, where the values of each point will change over time.		
	Subtype	GridPoint NodePoint	
	Notes		
	Properties	HasZ = True	
	Fields	FeatureID	Integer	A geodatabase-wide unique identifier and key field for participating in relationships
		FeatureCode	String	A user-defined code used for identifying a feature
		IPosition	Integer	A feature's location in the I direction for a given mesh
		JPosition	DateTime	A feature's location in the J direction for a given mesh
		KPosition	Double	A feature's location in the K direction for a given mesh
		MeshID	Integer	A user-defined identifier for a given mesh
		PointType	Coded Value Domain	A coded value domain defining the subtype to be one of the following: 1 = GridPoint 2 = NodePoint
	MeshElement is a polygonal feature class representing a face of a finite element.		
	Subtype	None apply	
	Properties	None apply	
	Notes	MeshElements are polygonal features composed of a combination of either three or four nodes.	
	Fields	FeatureID	Integer	A geodatabase-wide unique identifier and key for participating in relationships
		FeatureCode	String	A user-defined code used for identifying a feature
		Node1ID	Integer	A key field for identifying the FeatureID of a MeshPoint that represents a corner of the MeshElement
		Node2ID	Integer	A key field for identifying the FeatureID of a MeshPoint that represents a corner of the MeshElement
		Node3ID	Integer	A key field for identifying the FeatureID of a MeshPoint that represents a corner of the MeshElement
		Node4ID	Integer	A key field for identifying the FeatureID of a MeshPoint that represents a corner of the MeshElement

OBJECT CLASSES	**Mesh** is an object class that stores necessary information for defining the dimension and structure of a Mesh grid.			
	Notes	A Mesh is a collection of points forming either a line, area, or volume features in nature.		
	Fields	MeshID	Integer	The unique identifier for a mesh
		TotalPoints	Integer	Total number of points participating in the Mesh
		NoOfPointsI	Integer	Total number of points available in the I direction within a Mesh
		NoOfPointsJ	Integer	Total number of points available in the J direction within a Mesh
		NoOfPointsK	Integer	Total number of points available in the K direction within a Mesh
		Dimension	Coded Value Domain	A coded value domain defining the subtype to be one of the following: 1 = Linear 2 = Area 3 = Volume
	VectorQuantity is a table that stores the vector values associated with a MeshPoint.			
	Notes			
	Fields	FeatureID	Integer	A key field for relating this table to a feature class
		ParameterID	Integer	A key field for relating this table to the Parameter table
		XComponent	Double	The Vector x component value
		YComponent	Double	The Vector y component value
		ZComponent	Double	The Vector z component value
		TimeValue	DateTime	The time stamp assigned to the vector value
	ScalarQuantity is a table that stores the scalar values associated with a MeshPoint.			
	Notes			
	Fields	FeatureID	Integer	A key field for relating this table to a feature class
		ParameterID	Integer	A key field for relating this table to the Parameter table
		DataValue	Double	The measured scalar value
		TimeValue	DateTime	The time stamp assigned to the scalar value

OBJECT CLASSES (cont'd)	**Parameter** is an object class that stores some basic information about the represented parameters.			
	Notes	This table is designed to be a lookup table of parameter types. It can be used as a mechanism for querying a geodatabase for a specific parameter and then finding values of a particular type in related tables. Alternatively, it can be used as a lookup table of parameter types for a particular value.		
	Fields	ParameterID	Integer	The unique identifier of a specific parameter
		Name	String	The name of a parameter
		Description	String	The description of a parameter
		Quantity	Double	The quantity type for a parameter. A coded value domain defining the subtype to be one of the following: 1 = Other 2 = Scalar 3 = Vector
		Unit	String	The unit of measure for a parameter
		Significant Digits	Integer	The number of significant digits defining the precision of this parameter

RELATIONSHIPS	**MeshHasPoints**	1 : *	One Mesh has one or more MeshPoints
	MeshPointHasScalars	1 : *	One MeshPoint can have zero or many Scalar values
	MeshPointHasVectors	1 : *	One MeshPoint can have zero or many Vector values
	ParameterHasScalars	1 : *	One Parameter can have zero or many Scalar values
	ParameterHasVectors	1 : *	One Parameter can have zero or many Vector values

References

Dick, S. 2001. Operational ocean modeling forecasting and applications. In *Operational Oceanography, Scientific Lectures at JCOMM-I.* Akureyri, Iceland: WMO/TD-No. 1086, JCOMM Technical Report No. 14.

Dick S., E. Kleine, S. H. Müller-Navarra, and H. Komo. 2001. The Operational Circulation Model of BSH (BSHcmod), model description and validation. Berichte des BSH Nr. 29/2001. Hamburg, Germany: Bundesamt für Seeschifffahrt und Hydrographie (BSH, Federal Maritime and Hydrographic Agency).

Chapter acknowledgments

Michael Blongewicz, DHI Water & Environment

Jürgen Schulz-Ohlberg, Bundesamt für Seeschifffahrt und Hydrographie (BSH)

Kai Jancke, Bundesamt für Seeschifffahrt und Hydrographie (BSH)

Multidimensional GIS

GIS has improved its ability in recent years to visualize and analyze three-dimensional (3D) and four-dimensional (4D) spatial relationships and problems. Many of the recent ArcGIS data models in turn have focused on questions related to these multidimensional datasets. This has resulted in different approaches to finding the best way to store, query, and display these data types in a GIS. While the work is oriented toward research and development, the results and findings are extending the limits of using GIS and contributing to choices in software development. While the issues of vertical representation, volumetrics, and temporal query and analysis are important to the marine user community, this interest transcends to other industries and disciplines, including atmospheric, groundwater, geology, archaeology, and petroleum. Collaboration with industry and academia in these areas has provided useful insights regarding new ways to approach the many challenges of implementing GIS using multidimensional datasets. This chapter reviews some of these insights, poses some solutions as they relate to Arc Marine, and discusses similarities and possible linkages to the Climate and Weather, and Groundwater data models.

Introduction

Advances in remote sensing technology during the past 20 years have enabled marine scientists and resource managers to apply high-resolution acoustic and optical imaging techniques spanning the range of mapping scales from kilometers to centimeters. A critical requirement in the success of these efforts is the generation and study of multidimensional datasets. In this chapter, the term "multidimensional" refers to the combined use of the first two dimensions of longitude (x) and latitude (y), with a third dimension of elevation or depth (z, or -z), a fourth dimension of time (t), and a fifth dimension, consisting of measurements from an instrument in the field or the iterative results of models that may go forward or backward in time. Multidimensionality is also discussed at length in chapter 7, which describes Arc Marine's representation of multidimensional data for finite element numerical modeling. Chapter 5 looks at the multidimensionality of a point and the application of multiple variables being recorded at multiple depths for a given location. This is furthered with the additional dimension of values recorded over time. Multidimensionality is a focus in the marine context because it is critical for mapping, monitoring, and understanding currents, tides, shorelines, ice movements, El Niño/La Niña effects, biotic distributions and their associated habitats, navigational obstacles that appear and disappear, and many more. Simulation and continual updating of marine parameters based on location have become important in predicting these changes over time. Space does not permit a full review of the recent progress made in dealing with problems of multidimensionality for the marine environment, but the reader is referred to the suggested reading list at the end of the chapter.

The industry-specific ArcGIS data models have much in common in structuring tabular data, features (points, lines, and polygons), and rasters in ways that intuitively represent multidimensional phenomena in the real world. Common data structures for representing elevation or depth include digital elevation models (DEMs), bathymetric grids, triangulated irregular networks (TINs and terrains), or combinations thereof (figure 8.1). Also common is the use of interpolation methods such as kriging or inverse distance weighting

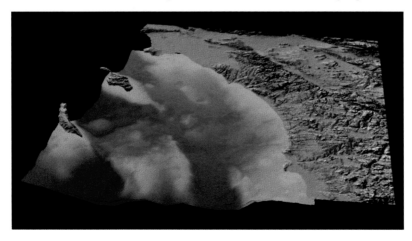

Figure 8.1 A digital elevation model (DEM) represents the land layer and has been integrated with a seafloor layer, which was created from the interpolation of scattered underwater soundings.

Courtesy of National Ocean Service Hydrographic Surveys, U.S. Geological Survey Coastal and Marine Geology Team, and the State of California.

(IDW). These methods provide what has been called a two-and-a-half dimensional surface (figure 8.1), because elevation or depth are treated as an attribute of a 2D point or line rather than as an independent variable that is part of the locational coordinate of the object. This potential limitation is an area of important research in geographic information science (e.g., Buckley et al. 2004; Hobona et al. 2006; Raper 2000) and in related areas of applied oceanography (e.g., Fonseca et al. 2002; Mayer 2006).

Thinking creatively, we can use GIS to implement multidimensional display, query, and analysis as never before. We often start with a set of 3D points and some research questions. For instance, an oceanographer may ask, "Where does the temperature in the water column drop to below 20°C?" A marine geophysicist may consider the question, "Where is the next most likely place to encounter oil within a certain subsurface stratigraphy?" A physical oceanographer may want to trace the extent of a hydrothermal plume near the seafloor or a nutrient layer higher in the water column. A fisheries manager may ask, "What seasonal abiotic conditions in the water column relate most to the density of a target species?" To answer these questions, advanced users may desire the ability to create "cubes" of data, slice through them in any direction, perform volumetric analysis based on any variable, and calculate new variables such as mixed-layer depth, geostrophic velocity, or dynamic height (e.g., Vance et al. 2006). Others may want to work with stacks of rasters while also capturing, querying, and displaying meaningful data between the layers. Users may also need to interpolate in the z-direction between these layers. To accomplish these tasks and analyses, users often need new tools to complement the data model. In turn, a data model design that has already considered aspects of multidimensionality (such as how additional dimension values will be assigned and how they will be used in different applications), allows developers to code proper functions into the complementary tools, or users to take better advantage of existing tools. While some tools build on the additional dimension as it exists in the feature's attribute table, others use the dimension as it is stored in the value of the shape or geometry of the feature (meaning the features added to the data model will need to be "Z-aware" or "M-aware," where M is a linear measurement of GIS geometry). Data preparation, including its constructs, naming conventions for storage, and elements for eventual visualization and display, is an important consideration in tool design. As we try to further define space in more dimensions for a more precise representation of natural phenomena, the interpolation of a z (between the layers) of a volume still has limitations similar to those of interpolating planar surfaces, either physical or statistical.

3D interpolator tool

As an example of a tool conceived in tandem with data model development, this section describes the 3D interpolator tool, which was created as a prototype to facilitate analyses with the ArcGIS Groundwater data model and Arc Marine, and may be used with other data models routinely dealing with multidimensional data. The tool is freely available on the companion Web sites for this book. A test case for Arc Marine was created using 3D points generated from the California Cooperative Oceanic Fisheries Investigations (CalCOFI) database. This database is hosted online (http://www.calcofi.org/data/data.html) and represents a longstanding partnership of the California Department of Fish and Game, Scripps Institution of Oceanography, and the NOAA Fisheries Service. The following section presents an example of how the interpolator can be used to solve a problem related to temperature values in the water column.

The CalCOFI database previously mentioned was spatially enabled by creating 3D InstantaneousPoints from the sensor values. Using this point feature class as the primary analysis layer with the 3D interpolator tool, one can begin to make some generalizations about temperature values in the water column where no data exists. The 3D points as shown in figure 8.2 are symbolized based on their temperature properties. Other water column properties measured by the various instruments and stored as attributes include chlorophyll, dissolved oxygen, salinity, depth, and pressure. The case study selected temperature as the variable, or field of values, to interpolate in the 3D environment. The main question to answer is "Where are 8°C temperature values historically found in the water column?"

One of the major problems with using a 3D interpolation engine is searching for the neighboring points before applying the 3D interpolation algorithm. An approach that can help speed up the search of neighboring points is to perform a 3D tessellation and create relationships between neighboring points for interpolation. Voronoï tessellation is an algorithm that divides space based on the influence zone of each point in space and is a good method to work within the interpolation of multidimensional datasets (e.g., Gold 1991, 2000; Pilouk 1996). In 2D, Voronoï neighbors form a triangulation network, while in 3D they form a tetrahedral network. Both networks are the simplest geometric primitives in 2D and 3D, respectively (figure 8.3).

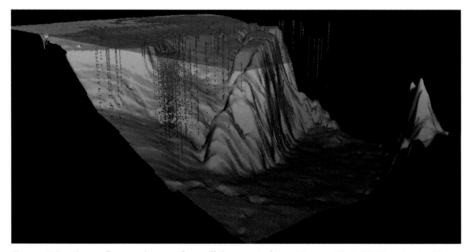

Figure 8.2 The seafloor and sea surface off the coast of San Diego, with CalCOFI water bottle data, where vertical casts are colored in reds, yellows, and greens for warmer near-surface temperatures, and in shades of blue for colder, deep-water temperatures.

Courtesy of NOAA and the California Cooperative Oceanic Fisheries Investigation CalCOFI.

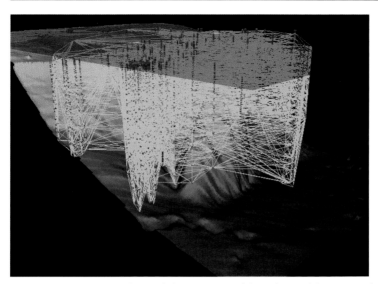

Figure 8.3   To better understand characteristics of the volume of the water column, the interpolation of known discrete point values is spanned in rays that store the interpolation results. The new values created are stored in this network of lines called a tetrahedral network. Similar to the TIN (triangulated irregular network), this model maximizes on the geometric merit of the triangle for interpreting the values of angles, known and unknown. Unlike the TIN, however, the tetrahedral network searches a neighborhood that includes multiple z-values, so it can be used to generate true 3D objects.

Courtesy of NOAA and the California Cooperative Oceanic Fisheries Investigation CalCOFI.

The 3D interpolation engine performs a fast 3D Voronoï tessellation using a raster approach, as described in Pilouk (1996). A Delauney tetrahedral network (TetNet) is formed to maintain relationships between neighboring points in 3D space to cut down time for searching for neighboring points. The TetNet facilitates quick interpolation into a 3D point set, a volume stack (3D rasters or voxels), and isosurfaces (figure 8.4). The tool currently uses only a linear interpolation algorithm for the sake of simplicity.

Triangles and tetrahedrals can be used as primary geometric structures for interpolation to create a continuous (or prediction) surface from sampled point values. Each vertex of these geometric shapes carries coordinates of the known measurement locations and values. If a point location has no measurement value within the interpolation unit, this tool will allow users to calculate the new attribute value in the same vicinity as the measurements. When users select the attribute values (as in this case with temperature) the tool can calculate the location associated with the given value and create isolines and isosurfaces (figure 8.5). This tool can work with point features stored in many of the data models, including Arc Marine. InstantaneousPoints are an example of a point type in Arc Marine that may store a z or depth value, as well as a biological or chemical parameter to be interpolated using this tool. However, oceanographic data is often sparse in one or two dimensions

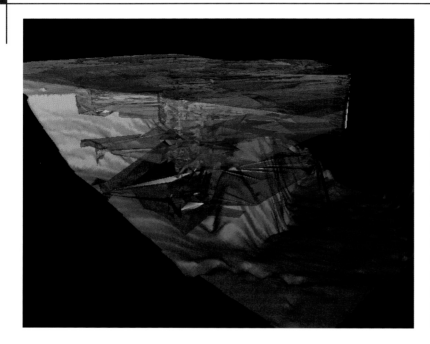

Figure 8.4 These facets of temperature zoning are isosurfaces created with the values stored in the tetrahedral network (TetNet). Each surface represents points of constant value (in this case, temperature in 3 ranges) within the volume space. These facets are stored as a multipatch object in the geodatabase.

Courtesy of NOAA and the California Cooperative Oceanic Fisheries Investigation CalCOFI.

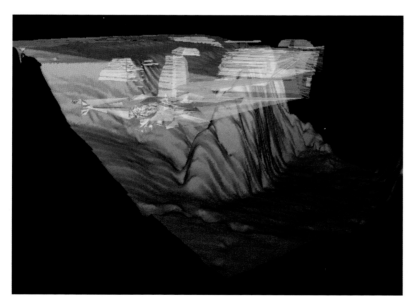

Figure 8.5 The resulting multipatch layer represents the cutoff of 8°C water in the water column. Some shark species like to feed in this range, and it is interesting to see the signature of upwellings that may correspond to underlying bathymetry.

Courtesy of NOAA and the California Cooperative Oceanic Fisheries Investigation CalCOFI.

compared to the third dimension (e.g., seafloor borehole data or vertical casts for salinity/temperature/density, where sampling is frequent in the vertical direction but sparse in the horizontal; Wright and Goodchild 1997). This longstanding issue continues to be a challenge for 3D interpolation algorithms.

NetCDF data

As mentioned earlier, the preparation and formatting of the data and its constructs for storage are important considerations in designing a data model and any accompanying tools. For marine applications, network Common Data Form (netCDF) is an important network developed by the University Corporation for Atmospheric Research (UCAR) as a machine-independent, binary format for exchanging scientific data, particularly for applications in climatology and meteorology. This format often is used to store data as an array, but netCDF is also a series of software libraries and input/output routines that facilitate data storage and documentation. The netCDF format is essentially multidimensional, so the goal is to effectively display and manipulate the variables in the array from within the GIS software itself. Examples of oceanographic data commonly stored in netCDF include sea surface temperature, current speed and direction, wave height, and wind speed. A variation on netCDF is also used as a common format for multibeam bathymetric and backscatter grids that represent the seafloor. Generic Mapping Tools (GMT; http://gmt.soest.hawaii.edu/) and MB-System (http://www.mbari.org/data/mbsystem/) are two of the most commonly used software packages worldwide for the processing, display, and cartographic output of these datasets. Both rely on netCDF libraries and produce output in a netCDF-style format, although the resulting grids do not have the netCDF climate and forecast (CF) metadata convention.

The CF convention is one of many netCDF conventions that provide a description of what each variable in a dataset represents spatially and temporally. The CF convention defines the overall metadata of a grid (e.g., see Unidata's descriptions at http://www.unidata.ucar.edu/software/netcdf/conventions.html). The Cooperative Ocean/Atmosphere Research Data Service (COARDS) convention was introduced in 1995, and CF was introduced in 2003 in order to extend and generalize COARDS. This makes it possible for a wide range of users to recognize and understand the array of numeric values that follow the header in a netCDF file. ArcGIS can display the datasets as a table, a set of points, and a raster, and resulting arrays can be animated based on a user-selected time frame. When the raster view is created from a netCDF file, the dataset remains in its native format and is rendered only for display—new datasets are not created. This is especially useful for physical oceanographic, bio-optical, or air-sea interaction applications, because much of the data derived from satellites or shipboard observations may be stored and shared in this original format. This extends the existing functionality to support time and multidimensional data.

The oceanographic and atmospheric communities have faced the longstanding challenge of using multidimensional array data in a GIS. With the addition of netCDF tools for ArcGIS, it is now much easier to display and analyze multidimensional marine data. The tools enable the direct read and write of netCDF (CF) directly into ArcGIS as input, or within a geoprocessing model to represent oceanographic processes such as tsunami wave propagation or air-sea interactions during a hurricane. In addition, netCDF is one format used for numerical modeling or simulation modeling that can be looped to represent patterns of parameters such as global temperature warming or seasonal rainfall (figure 8.6).

The animation tools can be used together to control the rendered output to display the results over a time span, based on specific user-defined variables. For example, a netCDF file may store sea surface temperature (SST) in an array of numeric values, where each grid cell holds one value of temperature. The same SST grid may look like figure 8.7 when viewed as a raster in ArcGlobe.

The animation of a netCDF layer is a way to capture the multidimensionality of datasets collected by satellites or ships (static or real-time). When bringing netCDF files into ArcGIS, one is essentially viewing a slice of the data, but the capability of viewing data in a 3D volume is most desirable, underscoring the importance of new tools such as the 3D interpolator. Viewing these slices or volumes together with socioeconomic datasets may inspire new ideas for analyses using many different data models. ArcGIS has improved the

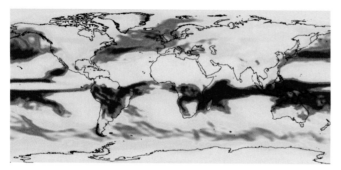

Figure 8.6   Display tools in ArcGIS can animate 10 years worth of rainfall data to show areas of heavy precipitation over a time span. Variables also can be isolated within that time span, such as "months of May rainfall." This type of dataset, similar to the "time duration" feature classes in Arc Marine, can be useful in monitoring change or in predictive models.

Courtesy of CCSM.

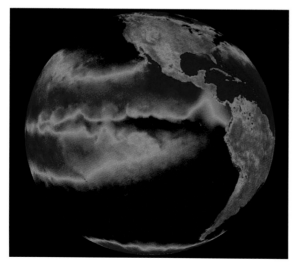

Figure 8.7   A collection of animated raster images represents changes in sea surface temperature (SST) during the 1997-1998, El Niño. During an El Niño-Southern Oscillation, Pacific trade winds and atmospheric pressure cells reverse, resulting in an eastward transport of anomalous warm water across the tropical Pacific (shown by the warm colors).

Courtesy of the NASA Physical Oceonography Distributed Active Archive Center (PO DAAC).

quality and control of animation sequences and the handling and rendering of dynamic content in applications such as ArcGlobe and related server-based viewers. On the horizon are the retrieval, storage, query, and serving of these datasets over the Internet.

Similarities to other ArcGIS data models

Collaboration with other industry and academic leads in ArcGIS model design efforts has provided useful insights regarding new ways to approach the many challenges that we face when implementing GIS using multidimensional datasets (Buckley et al. 2006).

3D objects in the Groundwater data model

The Groundwater data model focuses on multidimensional representation of groundwater in ArcGIS, normally including subsurface stratigraphy of sediment and rock layers, aquifers, geologic cross sections, and volumes. The model builds on the existing functionality of Arc Hydro for surface water (Maidment 2002), future development initiatives, and collaborations with other organizations. It enables the integration of surface water and groundwater data, while supporting the representation of site-specific groundwater data, regional groundwater systems, and the integration of groundwater simulation models with GIS (Strassberg 2005). Four of the primary features of the model are 3D points, 3D lines, vertical cross sections, and volumes (figure 8.8).

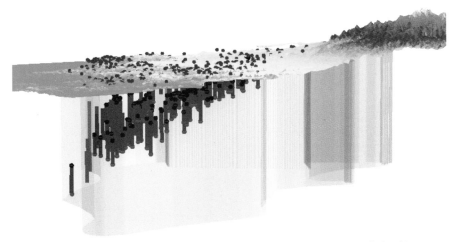

Figure 8.8 Some of the features in the Groundwater data model show the relationship between wells (blue points), bore points (purple and green points), and bore lines (vertical lines) representing rock stratigraphy or hydrostratigraphy.

Figure used by permission, G. Strassberg, University of Texas.

As with Arc Marine, the source dataset is most often a set of 3D points that store measurement values. In the case of the Groundwater data model, these are collected from boreholes and wells. Other features for Groundwater, such as stream depths or riverbeds, can be represented by soundings similar to the single or multibeam echosoundings used to capture depth information for the seafloor. The GIS stores these values as Z-aware points, also called PointZ. The use of 3D lines (PolylineZ) also represents the vertical classifications for the lithology of the well and can define subsurface units such as aquifers. Three-dimensional polygons make cross sections that connect the top and bottom of the 3D points, while the database can store the values of more complex geometry as a multipatch feature class. In ArcGIS, a multipatch is a type of geometry composed of 3D rings and triangles and may be used to represent geometric objects that occupy a 3D area or volume (such as spheres and cubes), or real-world objects such as buildings and trees (http://support. esri.com/knowledgebase/). The multipatch describes and stores volume objects in the Groundwater data model. The volume of this shape can be calculated and assigned as an attribute or label to the object. The aforementioned 3D interpolator tool can also be used to fill regions between horizontal stacks of points or lines. This brief overview is meant to show some of the touch points between the Groundwater data model and Arc Marine. For more information related specifically to Groundwater, please see Maidment (2002), Strassberg (2005) and the Groundwater link at http://support.esri.com/datamodels.

The Climate and Weather data model: Another approach to multidimensionality

The input of weather and climate data, using varying methods for measuring and storing time, has been a common interest between many data models, including Climate and Weather, Hydro, Groundwater, Agriculture, Transportation, and Biodiversity/Conservation. Remotely sensed data often includes land and sea surface parameters, biological distributions, atmospheric conditions at the earth's surface, and layers of information representing the air-sea or land-sea interface (figure 8.9). Satellite sensor readings that are collected in

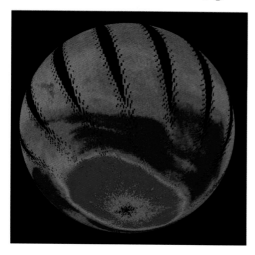

Figure 8.9 Global satellite ozone data with time attributes can be viewed and analyzed, such as this example from ArcGlobe, showing a significant hole in the ozone layer over Antarctica. The challenge is combining this data to effectively represent change over time.

Courtesy of the NASA Physical Oceanography Distributed Active Archive Center (PO DAAC).

swaths, or belts, of data can also be used to derive parameters just beneath the surface of the ocean. The way these variables are represented in the source dataset and stored in the data model can influence how the application tools work with them.

The application of GIS in climate change research aims to work with the integration of global climate model outputs, with many types of socioeconomic data from various sources (e.g., see the National Center for Atmospheric Research's GIS climate change scenarios at http://www.gis.ucar.edu). For the Climate and Weather data model, the values associated with time are an essential consideration in data analysis, query, display, and visualization. One way to accommodate this is to use the personal or enterprise geodatabase to store a time-stamp or time-series table that can associate point, line, or polygon features to a relationship class. The relationship connects the feature to the table storing the time attributes. Ultimately, new tools provided direct read of netCDF data to support spatiotemporal queries and analyses of the dynamic characteristics of satellite data formats. For more information on the Climate and Weather data model, please see the Atmospheric link at http://support.esri.com/datamodels and the Web site of the Atmospheric Special Interest Group at http:/www.gis.ucar.edu/sig/.

Conclusion

This chapter has touched on practical issues of multidimensional representation. Marine geographical data and patterns will almost always be complex, constantly changing with time, spatial resolution, and even sampling strategy. The emphasis has been on the computational and mechanical aspects of inputting, organizing, manipulating, and rendering this multidimensional data. This requires faster processing hardware, more sophisticated computer graphics, and oftentimes computer animation. These essentially fall in the realm of data visualization (geovisualization), primarily as a method of computing. However, MacEachren (1995) regards visualization primarily as an act of cognition, allowing scientists to "develop mental representations to identify patterns and to create or impose order." Thomas and Cook (2005) echo the emphasis on cognition. They recognize that, aside from being a set of tools, visualization can assist in human information processing, which aims to generate new insights and potential solutions to the problems being addressed. As mentioned earlier, esoteric research and development in the computing and cognitive aspects of multidimensional data handling and visualization will be ongoing in the academic, government, and private sectors. These issues are deemed important enough to warrant the attention and support of several federal agencies and of large research cooperatives such as the University Consortium for Geographic Information Science (UCGIS), the International Cartographic Association Commission on Geovisualization and Virtual Environments, and the San Diego Supercomputer Center's Geosciences Network (GEON). However, the most immediate impact likely will be felt in the data models and associated tools placed in the hands of average users. These approaches and tools need not be limited to one data model in a single application area. Readers are encouraged to leverage the ideas, tools, and

Web sites described in this chapter as they use Arc Marine and to stay abreast of related developments as the integration of multidimensional data into GIS continues to challenge related data models.

References

Buckley, A., M. Gahegan, and K. C. Clarke. 2004. Geographic visualization. In *A research agenda for geographic information science,* ed. R. B. McMaster and E. L. Usery, 313–34. Boca Raton, Fla.: CRC Press.

———. 2006. *UCGIS geographic visualization research priorities, revisited,* white paper, Alexandria, Va., University Consortium for Geographic Information Science, http://www.ucgis.org/priorities/research/2006research/chapter_11_update.pdf.

Fonseca, L., L. Mayer, and M. Paton. 2002. ArcView objects in the Fledermaus interactive 3D visualization system: An example from the STRATAFORM GIS. In *Undersea with GIS,* ed. D. J. Wright, 1–21. Redlands, Calif.: ESRI Press.

Gold, C. M. 1991. Problems with handling spatial data—the Voronoï approach. *Canadian Institute of Surveying and Mapping Journal* 45:65–80.

———. 2000. An algorithmic approach to a marine GIS. In *Marine and coastal geographical information systems,* ed. D. J. Wright and D. J. Bartlett, 37–52. London: Taylor & Francis.

Hobona, G., P. James, and D. Fairbairn. 2006. Multidimensional visualization of degrees of relevance of geographic data. *International Journal of Geographical Information Science* 20(5): 469–90.

MacEachren, A. M. 1955. *How maps work: Representation, visualization, and design.* New York: The Guilford Press.

Maidment, D. R., ed. 2002. *Arc Hydro: GIS for water resources.* Redlands, Calif.: ESRI Press.

Mayer, L. A. 2006. Frontiers in seafloor mapping and visualization. *Marine Geophysical Researches* 27:7–17.

Pilouk, M. 1996. *Integrated modelling for 3D GIS.* Ph.D. diss., Enschede, The Netherlands: International Institute for Aerospace Survey and Earth Sciences.

Raper, J. 2000. *Multidimensional geographic information science.* London: Taylor & Francis.

Strassberg, G. 2005. *A geographic data model for groundwater systems.* Ph.D. diss., Austin, Tex.: University of Texas.

Thomas, J. J., and K. A. Cook, ed. 2005. *Illuminating the path: The research and development agenda for visual analytics.* Washington, D.C.: National Visualization and Analytics Centers, U.S. Department of Homeland Security. http://nvac.pnl.gov.

Vance, T. C., S. Mesick, C. Moore, and D. Wright. 2006. GeoModeler—linking scientific models with a GIS for scenario testing and geovisualization, *Proceedings of Auto-Carto 2006.* Vancouver, Wash.: Cartography and Geographic Information Society.

Wright, D., and M. Goodchild. 1997. Data from the deep: Implications for the GIS community. *International Journal of Geographic Information Science* 11(6): 523–28.

Further reading

Chen, J., C. M. Li, Z. L. Li, and C. Gold. 2001. A Voronoï -based 9-intersection model for spatial relations. *International Journal of Geographical Information Science* 15(3): 201–20.

Gold, C., and A. Condal. 1995. A spatial data structure integrating GIS and simulation in the marine environment. *Marine Geodesy* 18:213–28.

Goldfinger, C., L. McNeill, and C. Hummon. 1997. Case study of GIS data integration and visualization in marine tectonics: The Cascadia Subduction Zone. *Marine Geodesy* 20:267–89.

Hamre, T. 1994. An object-oriented conceptual model for measured and derived data varying in 3D space and time. In *Advances in GIS Research, Proceedings of the 6th Symposium, Vol. 2.* London: Taylor & Francis, 868–81.

Hamre, T., K. Mughal, and A. Jacob. 1997. A 4D marine data model: Design and application in ice monitoring. *Marine Geodesy* 20:121–36.

Kucera, G. 1995. Object-oriented modeling of coastal environmental information. *Marine Geodesy* 18:183–96.

Langran, G. 1993. *Time in geographic information systems.* London: Taylor & Francis.

Li, R., L. Qian, and J. Blais. 1995. A hypergraph-based conceptual model for bathymetric and related data management. *Marine Geodesy* 18:173–82.

Li, Z., and C. Gold. 2004. Multi-dimensional geospatial technology for geosciences. *Computers & Geosciences* 30:321–23.

Macedo, M., D. Cook, and T. Brown. 2000. Visual data mining in atmospheric science data. *Data Mining and Knowledge Discovery* 4(1): 69–80.

Mason, D., M. O'Conaill, and S. Bell. 1994. Handling four-dimensional geo-references data in environmental GIS. *International Journal of Geographical Information Systems* 8(2):191–215.

Mchaffie, P. 2000. Surfaces: Tacit knowledge, formal language, and metaphor at the Harvard Lab for Computer Graphics and Spatial Analysis. *International Journal of Geographical Information Science* 14(8): 755–73.

Meaden, G. J. 2004. Challenges of using geographic information systems in aquatic environments. In *Geographic information systems in fisheries,* ed. W. L. Fisher and F. J. Rahel, 13–48. Bethesda, Md.: American Fisheries Society.

Miller, E. and Z. Kemp. 1997. Towards a 4D GIS: four-dimensional interpolation utilizing kriging. In *Innovations in GIS 4,* ed. Z. Kemp, 181–97. London: Taylor & Francis.

Mostafavi, M. A., and C. Gold. 2004. A global kinetic spatial data structure for a marine simulation. *International Journal of Geographical Information Science* 18(3): 211–27.

Nativi, S. 2004. Differences among the data models used by the geographic information systems and atmospheric science communities. *Proceedings of the 20th Conference on IIPS, AMS 2003,* 17.4.

Pilouk, M., and Y. Fine. 2006. Best practices for developing with ArcGlobe, *Proceedings of the ESRI Developer Summit 2006.* http://gis.esri.com/library/userconf/devsummit06/index.html.

Su Y. 2000. A user-friendly marine GIS for multi-dimensional visualization. In *Marine and coastal geographical information systems,* ed. D. J. Wright and D. J. Bartlett, 227–36. London: Taylor & Francis.

Yang, B., Q. Li, and W. Shi. 2005. Constructing multi-resolution triangulated irregular network model for visualization, *Computers & Geosciences* 31:77–86.

Yuan, M. 1999. Use of a three-domain representation to enhance GIS support for complex spatiotemporal queries. *Transactions in GIS* 3(2): 137–59.

———. 2001. Representing complex geographic phenomena with both object- and field-like properties. *Cartography and Geographic Information Science* 28(2): 83–96.

Epilogue

This book has provided a detailed presentation of the Arc Marine data model: its main objectives and intended uses, various aspects of its design, descriptions of the main features and objects, thematic groups and classes, and practical ways to implement the model with data. The previous chapters guide users through the implementation of marine GIS projects with Arc Marine and show them standard ways to describe data and develop GIS tools to consistently and effectively solve ocean and coastal problems. This epilogue closes the book with some views on what the future may hold for this and related ESRI-supported data models.

Basic GIS tasks involving the Internet include searching for appropriate data through spatial data clearinghouses, adding datasets to ArcCatalog for analysis, mapping from the Geography Network and endless other sources, and accessing metadata about datasets. Recent developments in technology include the ability to make maps and data available on the Internet via map servers and the addition of decision support tools to Web GIS sites. This can be done either by downloading an extension to the desktop or the more difficult coding of the analysis functions directly into Web GIS sites, to be used interactively. The Ocean Biogeographic Information System-Spatial Ecological Analysis of Megavertebrate Populations (OBIS-SEAMAP) described in chapter 4 is an excellent example of marine data acquisition. Interactive mapping is one of many key site features (examples may be found at http://marinecoastalgis.net). These are based on commercial solutions such as ArcIMS, or open source solutions such as Minnesota MapServer, PostGIS, and GRASS GIS.

With the recent explosion of Internet mapping sites and data clearinghouses on the Web, the relationship of data models to generic Web services and to project-specific Internet map servers such as OBIS-SEAMAP will certainly increase in importance, as will the emergence of capabilities for streaming data from these sites directly into the Arc Marine structure. Trends in this arena include serving more and more real-time data (often with automated sensors, sensor networks, and wireless technology), the continued popularity of open source, and the continued quest to add more analysis functions to Web GIS (going "beyond mapping"). The coupling of desktop applications or on the server with the Web (e.g., the ESRI ArcWeb, the Microsoft Web programming environment .NET, or the Sun J2EE) will become more commonplace. Another example is the ArcGIS Server that complements ArcGIS desktop by allowing GIS analysts to author maps, globes, and geoprocessing tasks on their desktops and publish them to ArcGIS Server using integrated tools (http://www.esri.com/software/arcgis/arcgisserver/).

Arc Marine will increase the interoperability of tools and data for marine applications by providing standardized data structures for Internet-based, Web-services processes (for a related review see Wright and Halpin 2005). Providing marine data as Web services using Open Geospatial Consortium protocols is increasingly popular. The technology for enabling Internet-based automation centers on the use of Extensible Markup Language (XML), which provides the tag-control encoding for data transfer. The Open Geospatial Consortium has issued spatially explicit specifications for image (Web map service, WMS), vector (Web feature service, WFS), and raster (Web coverage service, WCS) Web services. The request and response communications rely on XML encoding. More specifically, Geographic Markup Language (GML) handles vector representations.

The need for standardized data models also increases as more applications rely on standardized Web-services data to integrate this data into scientific workflows. Developers must anticipate the data structures clients will likely use. Initial development will likely include tools or scripts using the ArcGIS ModelBuilder workflow to harvest data directly from Web services to help offload computational processes through remote grid services.

With the recent rise of Google Earth and the ESRI ArcGIS Explorer as GIS visualization applications, developers have quickly adopted the simplified XML-based representation of spatial objects using Keyhole Markup Language (KML) (e.g., Pilouk and Fine 2006). The wrapping of Web services has more generically gained momentum with the implementation of Simple Object Access Protocol (SOAP), which enables a common set of programming interfaces to Web services. ArcGIS Server will also have a large impact on data and services that researchers will be able to share via the Web. ArcGIS Server combines mapping, visualization, geoprocessing, and data management in one product, while supporting customization using .NET and Java programming (including asynchronous JavaScript and XML, also known as AJAX), and Open Geospatial Consortium WMS, WFS, GML, and Standard Query Language application programming interfaces.

How are these various Internet protocols and Web services related to Arc Marine? The tools for data harvest and grid services can also take advantage of the most sensible relational database storage for the data, that is, the Arc Marine data model. The tools based on the harvested data may more automatically configure the mechanics of the local storage. For instance, one may specify into a tool the bounding box and species of interest, which is then harvested from an OBIS Web service. The tool parses the XML data response into the sensible Arc Marine geodatabase, allowing for subsequent processes to take advantage of the Arc Marine format.

Semantics and ontology will also become critical for marine Internet GIS applications. These applications are the key to successful discovery of data beyond just searching the metadata. Semantics are captured by associating formal terms and descriptions (e.g., "shoreline" versus "coastline") and making cross-disciplinary connections between them to attach well-defined meaning to data and to other Web resources. This greatly increases the quality of data retrieval or integration based on meaning instead of on mere keywords (Berners-Lee et al. 2001). Ontology is briefly defined as the formalization of concepts and terms used in a practice or discipline (for background see Gruber 1993; Mark et al. 2003). Ontologies can thus provide the semantic aspects of metadata, including lists of terms with definitions, more complex relationships between terms, rules governing those relationships, and potential values for each term. Closely related is the area of semantic interoperability and the semantic Web (Egenhofer 2002). Despite ontologies, words may still mean different things to different people within an interdisciplinary community. How does one, for example, search effectively through shared databases based on the words in the metadata (e.g., coastline versus shoreline, seabed versus seafloor, engineering versus ecological resilience, coastal wetland buffering versus GIS buffering).

In a hypothetical marine Internet GIS scenario, a keyword search for "shoreline" in a data portal may return hundreds of datasets, but a search for "coastline" will return none. Users and developers will need to incorporate innovative changes to metadata catalogs to more effectively search among the existing portal datasets (for an example in ocean and coastal management, see Eleveld et al. 2003). The language of data models may provide the key.

Data portals have been criticized as providing data descriptions only at the syntactic level (i.e., explicit, machine usable), making it difficult for users and providers to interpret or represent the applicable constraints of data, including the related inputs and outputs of analyses or decisions (e.g., Cabral et al. 2004). Compared to a syntactic means, a semantic approach provides higher quality and more relevant information for improved decision-making (Helly et al. 1999; Sheth 1999; Cabral et al. 2004). Semantics deal with meanings of terms that may not be machine usable at the outset. For instance, we know what the term "sea lion" means, but a computer may not initially "know" this and cannot infer additional meaning, such as a "sea lion" is a kind of "marine mammal" and automatically point a user to other datasets that might be related.

Equally important will be the development of multiple spatial and terminological ontologies to define meanings and formal descriptions (Egenhofer 2002; Goodchild 2003). One may think of an ontology at various levels, from a simple catalog (i.e., a list of terms), to a glossary (a definition of those terms), to a thesaurus (the terms and definitions, but with hierarchical relationships between terms and synonyms). All of these are ontologies. A more formal and desirable ontology would be a listing of terms with definitions, more complex relationships between the term, rules governing those relationships, and potential values for each term (in other words, a data model!). Building the necessary tools to define, verify, and deliver these ontologies is a significant research challenge. Researchers must also understand the gaps and inconsistencies in ontologies and handle changes in the material represented by ontologies in ways that go beyond simple versioning (e.g., Fonseca et al. 2002; Cushing et al. 2005). These approaches will be greatly informed by the feature class glossaries of data models (in this case, the feature, object, and relationship classes of Arc Marine and the Common Marine Data Types that they build on).

To implement an effective semantic Web resource, a dataset's ontology should include a vocabulary drawn from its metadata, ultimately revealing which datasets are interoperable. Again, the ArcGIS Marine data model and its Common Marine Data Types may be a natural conceptual framework for identifying important metadata elements unique to different marine datasets for future large distributed data archives and cyberinfrastructures. Ontologies can act as registration mechanisms for vocabularies and as a means of mapping vocabularies to each other using defined relations. Consider the possibility of using relations such as "shoreline same as coastline" or "SST same as sea surface temperature" or "seafloor same as seabed" to map vocabularies. If that were possible, the results could be stored in a collected ontology and used to translate between covocabularies and generate other inferences about the relationships between the different vocabularies and their terms. The benefits of this approach include the following:

- Better and more complete discovery and filtering of data
- Clearer and more precise and computable characterization of data
- Contextualization of information, so that it is provided in the right format, place, and language
- Semantic value, where human users and also computerized inference engines and harvesters can make better use of information, leading to the next item in the list
- Better display of search results, where terms can be substituted if they are equivalent
- Integration into additional tools for data portals, which will then immediately be working with more appropriate datasets

These exciting challenges and developments are being considered now in the context of large ocean observatories with scores of (1) cabled or moored platforms, (2) mobile autonomous systems, and (3) remote-sensing platforms (e.g., the Global Ocean Observing System, GOOS, http://www.ioc-goos.org/, and the Integrated Ocean Observing System, IOOS, http://www.ocean.us/ioos_system). Related efforts such as OBIS, Ocean Research Interactive Observatory Networks (ORION), and more recently the Marine Metadata Interoperability (MMI) project consider scores of critical issues and possible solutions concerning marine data management. Here again, the enterprise solution approach of ESRI-supported data models may make an important contribution. MMI bears especially close watch as it seeks to engage and inform the ocean science community in the creation of interoperable, metadata-centric data systems by (a) providing guidance and reference documentation on properly using and developing metadata, controlled vocabulary, and ontology solutions for the ocean science community; (b) encouraging community involvement in the development and evaluation of those documents; and (c) using test-bed activities (including Arc Marine) to demonstrate cross-platform, cross-disciplinary, interoperable distributed data systems (Bermudez et al. 2005; http://marinemetadata.org/).

While we have described Arc Marine mainly as an isolated resource in this book, another emerging trend is the linking and integrating of two or more data models, where a user combines feature classes from one model with feature classes of another. For example, one could envision the interleaving of Arc Marine with Arc Hydro to study processes from a coastal watershed to an estuary and out into the pelagic ocean. Arc Marine and the Climate and Weather data model might combine to look at air-sea interactions, tracking hurricanes and the like. Arc Marine and the IHO S-57 data model could work together in understanding scientific and resource management applications in the context of navigation issues.

Finally, data models will likely play a larger role in university and professional workshop instruction, but not as initially assumed. Just as there is now a distinction between learning GIS and learning with GIS (Thompson and Buttenfield 1997; Hall-Wallace et al. 2002), we will likely see the use of data models as tools for teaching not just GIS concepts but scientific concepts in a host of disciplines. For example, courses arising throughout the United States use Arc Hydro as a means for teaching students about water resources (water quality, availability, flooding, the natural environment, and management of water resources and surface and groundwater hydrology). Because Arc Marine has been as much about marine science as it has about GIS, some may find the book suitable as a supporting textbook for courses in marine resource management, marine geography, and marine remote sensing. At the other end of the spectrum, the ESRI-supported data models will always provide an effective avenue for teaching students about the advanced features of ArcGIS.

In this and other undertakings, a final note is that this book need not and should not stand alone. There are important resources on the Web (http://dusk.geo.orst.edu/djl/arcgis and the Marine link at http://support.esri.com/datamodels). These include several Arc Marine schemas from the case studies, geodatabases already populated with data from the case studies, the detailed Arc Marine poster, tools and scripts, animations, the Arc Marine tutorial, and various background documents and Microsoft PowerPoint files.

References

Bermudez, L., J. Graybeal, N. Galbraith, and D. J. Wright. 2005. Engaging a community towards marine cyberinfrastructure: Lessons learned from the Marine Metadata Interoperability Initiative. *Eos, Transactions of the American Geophysical Union* 86(52), Fall Meet. Suppl., Abstract IN44A–08.

Berners-Lee, T., J. Hendler, and O. Lassila. 2001. The semantic Web: A new form of Web content that is meaningful to computers will unleash a revolution of new possibilities. *Scientific American* 284:34–43.

Cabral, L., J. Domingue, E. Motta, T. Payne, and F. Hakimpour. 2004. Approaches to semantic Web services: An overview and comparisons. In *The semantic Web: Research and applications: First European Semantic Web Symposium, Lecture Notes in Computer Science,* ed. Bussler, C., J. Davies, and D. Fensel, vol. 3053, Sep. 2004, 225–39.

Cushing, J., T. Wilson, L. Delcambre, E. Hovy, et al. 2005. *Preliminary report of eco-informatics & decision making: Defining research objectives for digital government for ecology,* Workshop on Biodiversity and Ecosystem Informatics, NSF, NASA, USGS-NBII, Olympia, Wash., http://www.evergreen.edu/bdei/home.php.

Egenhofer, M. J. 2002. Toward the semantic geospatial Web. In *Proceedings of the Tenth ACM International Symposium on Advances in Geographic Information Systems,* McLean, Va.

Eleveld, M. A., W. B. H. Schrimpf, and A. G. Siegert. 2003. User requirements and information definition for a virtual coastal and marine data warehouse. *Ocean and Coastal Management* 46:487–505.

Fonseca, F. T., M. J. Egenhofer, P. Agouris, and G. Camara. 2002. Using ontologies for integrated geographic information systems. *Transactions in GIS* 6(3): 231–57.

Goodchild, M. F. 2003. The nature and value of geographic information. In *Foundations of geographic information science,* ed. M. Duckham, M. F. Goodchild, and M. F. Worboys, 19–32. New York: Taylor & Francis.

Gruber, T. R. 1993. A translation approach to portable ontologies. *Knowledge Acquisition* 5(2): 199–220.

Hall-Wallace, M. K., C. S. Walker, T. C. Wallace, and R. F. Butler. 2002. Geographic information systems help teach introductory earth science. *EOS, Transactions, American Geophysical Union* 83(31): 333, 339–40.

Helly, J., T. T. Elvins, D. Sutton, and D. Martinez. 1999. A method for interoperable digital libraries and data repositories. *Future Generation Computer Systems* 16:21–8.

Mark, D. M., M. Egenhofer, S. Hirtle, and B. Smith. 2003. *Ontological foundations for geographic information science,* UCGIS long-term research challenge white paper, Leesburg, Va., University Consortium for Geographic Information Science, http://www.ucgis.org.

Pilouk, M., and Y. Fine. 2006. Best practices for developing with ArcGlobe, *Proceedings of the ESRI Developer Summit 2006.* http://gis.esri.com/library/userconf/devsummit06/index.html.

Sheth, A. 1999. Changing focus on interoperability in information systems: From system, syntax, structure to semantics. In *Interoperating geographic information systems,* ed. M. F. Goodchild, M. J. Egenhofer, R. Fegeas, R., and C. A. Kottman, 5-30. New York: Kluwer.

Thompson, D., and B. Buttenfield. 1997. *Learning with GIS, learning about GIS.* UCGIS education priority paper. Washington, D.C.: University Consortium for Geographic Information Science, http://www.ucgis.org/priorities/education/priorities/learning.htm.

Wright, D. J., and P. N. Halpin. 2005. Spatial reasoning for Terra Incognita: Progress and grand challenges of marine GIS. In *Place matters: Geospatial tools for marine science, conservation and management in the Pacific Northwest,* ed. D. J. Wright and A. J. Scholz, 273-87. Corvallis, Ore.: Oregon State University Press.

About the authors

Dawn J. Wright is professor of geography and oceanography at Oregon State University and the director of the Davey Jones' Locker Seafloor Mapping/Marine GIS Laboratory. Her research interests include geographic information science, marine geography, tectonics of midocean ridges, and the processing and interpretation of high-resolution bathymetric, video, and underwater photographic images. She has completed oceanographic fieldwork in some of the most geologically active regions of the planet, including volcanoes under the Pacific, Atlantic, and Indian oceans. Wright serves on the editorial boards of the *International Journal of Geographical Information Science, Transactions in GIS,* and *Geospatial Solutions,* and is a member of the National Academy of Sciences' Committee on Geophysical and Environmental Data. Her other books include *Marine and Coastal Geographical Information Systems* (edited with D. Bartlett, Taylor & Francis, 2000), *Undersea with GIS* (ESRI Press, 2002), and *Place Matters: Geospatial Tools for Marine Science, Conservation, and Management in the Pacific Northwest* (edited with A. Scholz, Oregon State University Press, 2005). Wright holds a PhD in physical geography and marine geology from the University of California-Santa Barbara, an MS in oceanography from Texas A&M, and a BS in geology from Wheaton College in Illinois.

Michael J. Blongewicz is a senior GIS specialist at DHI Water & Environment, Inc., in Portland, Oregon, where he has been responsible for creating and developing GIS-based resources within DHI as they relate to data management and integration for hydrological and hydraulic modeling. His experience includes designing and developing decision-support systems, spatial databases, and analytical applications, and managing data conversion efforts. He has been responsible for the GIS aspects of a variety of projects throughout Europe and North America. Blongewicz contributed to the Arc Hydro data model and has been the technical lead for the design of the Arc Marine data model. He designed the extended version of those data models for the DHI implementation of the ESRI geodatabase. He holds a BA in geography from the University of Northern Arizona and a BA in art from the University of Northern Colorado.

Patrick N. Halpin is Gabel Associate Professor of the Practice of Marine Geospatial Ecology and director of the Geospatial Analysis Program at the Nicholas School of the Environment and Earth Sciences, Duke University. Halpin specializes in geospatial analysis for ecological and conservation applications in marine and terrestrial environments. He is a principle investigator for the Ocean Biogeographic Information System (OBIS-SEAMAP) program that provides geospatial data and analysis of marine mammals, sea turtles, and seabirds as well as numerous other marine GIS and marine spatial ecology programs. Halpin holds a PhD in environmental sciences from the University of Virginia and a MPA in international management and BA in international studies from George Mason University.

Joe Breman is data model program manager at ESRI and the marine and coastal community manager responsible for the ESRI marine Web site and the marine newsletter, "The Wave." He also serves as an oceanography instructor at the graduate level, scuba diving instructor, grant reviewer for the ESRI Conservation Program's (ECP) marine branch, and is on the advisory council to the board of directors for the Society for Conservation GIS (SCGIS). Other published works include *Marine Geography* (ESRI Press, 2002) and the marine geography section of *Conservation Geography: Case Studies in GIS, Computer Mapping, and Activism* (ESRI Press, 2001). Breman holds an MA in maritime civilizations from the University of Haifa, Israel, and a BA in anthropology from the University of California-Santa Cruz.

Image Credits

The editors gratefully acknowledge the copyrighted photo contributions of the following individuals and organizations:

Table of contents, foreword, preface, and acknowledgements pages courtesy Michelle Kinzel

Chapter introduction photos:
Chapter 1 courtesy Michelle Kinzel
Chapter 2 courtesy Michelle Kinzel
Chapter 3 courtesy Dawn Wright
Chapter 4 courtesy Michelle Kinzel
Chapter 5 courtesy Dawn Wright
Chapter 6 courtesy Michelle Kinzel
Chapter 7 courtesy Jennifer Smith
Chapter 8 courtesy Photodisc
Chapter 9 courtesy Michelle Kinzel

About the authors page courtesy Michelle Kinzel

Index